G000096233

Überpreneurs

ÜBERPRENEURS

How to Create Innovative Global Businesses and Transform Human Societies

PETER ANDREWS

FIONA WOOD

© Peter Andrews and Fiona Wood 2014

All rights reserved. No reproduction, copy or transmission of this publication may be made without written permission.

No portion of this publication may be reproduced, copied or transmitted save with written permission or in accordance with the provisions of the Copyright, Designs and Patents Act 1988, or under the terms of any licence permitting limited copying issued by the Copyright Licensing Agency, Saffron House, 6–10 Kirby Street, London EC1N 8TS.

Any person who does any unauthorized act in relation to this publication may be liable to criminal prosecution and civil claims for damages.

The authors have asserted their rights to be identified as the authors of this work in accordance with the Copyright, Designs and Patents Act 1988.

First published 2014 by PALGRAVE MACMILLAN

Palgrave Macmillan in the UK is an imprint of Macmillan Publishers Limited, registered in England, company number 785998, of Houndmills, Basingstoke, Hampshire RG21 6XS.

Palgrave Macmillan in the US is a division of St Martin's Press LLC, 175 Fifth Avenue, New York, NY 10010.

Palgrave Macmillan is the global academic imprint of the above companies and has companies and representatives throughout the world.

Palgrave® and Macmillan® are registered trademarks in the United States, the United Kingdom, Europe and other countries.

ISBN 978–1–137–37614–5

This book is printed on paper suitable for recycling and made from fully managed and sustained forest sources. Logging, pulping and manufacturing processes are expected to conform to the environmental regulations of the country of origin.

A catalogue record for this book is available from the British Library.

A catalog record for this book is available from the Library of Congress.

Typeset by MPS Limited, Chennai, India.

Überpreneur

Pronunciation: /ˈuːbəprəˈnəː/
(also über- /ˈyːbəprəˈnəː/)

An individual with an epic ambition to change the world, who …
… sees and seizes opportunities for change …
… senses the way forward …
… attracts the necessary resources …
… and pursues the dream …
… regardless of the odds.

CONTENTS

PREFACE

WE CAME TO THIS PROJECT from different backgrounds and via different paths.

Fiona taught public policy and resource management, researched funding mechanisms for science and innovation, and served as a consultant to governments in Europe, Asia and North America. Along the way, she became increasingly interested in the nature of entrepreneurs.

Peter's research on drug design led him to found a series of biotechnology companies and research institutes in Australia, and then into the role of Queensland Chief Scientist, where he learnt both the pleasure and the pain of operating at the interface of research, business and government.

The meeting of our paths, and the genesis of this book, occurred in Tokyo in 2008, when we were both invited speakers at a symposium organised by Professor Takeda Shuzaburo of the Business University Forum of Japan.

The meeting was remarkable in that it brought together the leaders of major foundations, corporations, universities and governments, all intent on seeking innovative ways to tackle the global challenges of climate change, ageing populations, environmental sustainability, and the shift away from manufacturing industries to knowledge and information-based industries as sources of wealth creation.

We came away from that meeting with one clear conclusion and several questions.

Our conclusion was simple: none of these challenges can ever be adequately addressed by governments constrained to three- or four-year terms, by corporations answering to shareholders, by nongovernmental organisations rife with political agendas or even by philanthropic organisations hamstrung by competing ideologies. Addressing them effectively requires creativity and courage, passion and vision, speed and flexibility. These are not the characteristics of organisations accountable to stakeholders - be they electors, shareholders or donors. These are the attributes of people.

Ultimately, the ones tackling our global challenges most effectively are people: inspirational and inspired individuals driven by an epic ambition to change the world.

Our questions were more complex. Who are these individuals? Where do they come from? What motivates them? Do the ones building new industries share the same characteristics as those addressing our grand social and environmental challenges? Are they made or born?

Seeking the answers to these questions has preoccupied us, initially superficially, and then intensely, for the past five years.

ਇਇਇ

Our first thought was to seek to interview individuals who had clearly changed the world. We compiled lists of the world's most inspirational and entrepreneurial people, using sources such as *Forbes*, Ernst and Young Entrepreneurs of the Year, TED lectures and *Time Magazine*, as well as the Web sites of foundations such as Schwab, Skoll, Kauffman and Ashoka.

Distilling the best and brightest from those lists, we finished up with just over 100 names, more than half of which came from North America.

It was then that we realised we had a problem. We were well on our way to producing yet another collection of US-oriented mini-biographies,

when what we really wanted was a book focused on the grand challenges
of our times and on the people addressing them, wherever they might be.

So we started at the other end. We chose 14 of the challenges that seemed
to us to be among the biggest issues now facing mankind, and accessed
the immense array of information publicly available on the Internet and
elsewhere to explore both the dimensions of the problems and the nature
of the individuals addressing them. Some of the challenges we chose were
economic, some technological, some personal and some societal. All
of them, to our delight, are being successfully tackled by extraordinary
individuals. And, furthermore, as we delved into their characters and
achievements, we found answers to all of our questions.

We look forward to sharing them with you.

Peter Andrews and Fiona Wood

ACKNOWLEDGEMENTS

WE WISH TO ACKNOWLEDGE OUR debt to the authors and journalists whose interviews with members of our übercast have provided the sources of much of the biographical information and all of the quotations collected in this book. A list of these key sources is provided at the end of each chapter, and we recommend them as a starting point for anyone interested in further exploring the lives and work of our überpreneurs.

We are also grateful to the Publications Section of the United Nations, New York, for its kind permission to use the opening quote to Part IV: Better World, and to The University of New England for the use of its facilities by Fiona during the writing of the book.

Finally, we would like to extend our gratitude to our families, friends and colleagues for their encouragement, advice and support, and to the 36 members of our übercast for their inspirational example.

Chapter 1

ÜBERPRENEURS. OVERTAKERS!

THE FIRST 14 YEARS OF the 21st century have been steeped in doom and gloom.

Everyone is talking about the huge and insoluble problems facing mankind.

How will we feed 9 billion people? Tackle climate change? Rein in obesity? Overcome economic crises? Eliminate AIDS? Build more inclusive societies?

But who will provide the solutions?

In this book we introduce you to 36 extraordinary individuals who are addressing and resolving all of these issues. They come from all continents and 18 nations. They come from all walks of life, and they operate in all spheres of human endeavour.

We call them überpreneurs.

ଝଝଝ

Why überpreneurs? Why not just "entrepreneurs"?

Simply put, despite the armies of academics who have devoted their careers to the study of entrepreneurship, there is still no consensus as to who these entrepreneurs really are, or what they actually do.

Are they the old immigrant couple running the corner grocery store?
The snake-oil salesman flogging "get rich quick" schemes? The retailer
who franchises her business model into a global cosmetics industry? The
executives who drive the development of products that transform their
companies into multinational enterprises? Or the young guy who makes
billions of dollars overnight floating his Internet company on the stock
exchange?

Yes, on all counts.

The literal translation of the original French word "entrepreneur"
is someone who *undertakes* something, most commonly a business
endeavour. In the 18th century, it referred to an individual who *undertook*
the risk of buying at certain prices and selling at uncertain prices. More
recently, entrepreneurs have been defined as business innovators who
recognise opportunities to introduce new products or services, and who
undertake to assemble the necessary resources, and take the necessary
risks, to exploit those opportunities.

In short, it's all about undertakers. Deathly boring stuff.

We are not interested in undertakers. We want to go way beyond that. We
want to get to grips with the people who are addressing and meeting the
grand economic, social and environmental challenges of our times.

The people upending our world.

Überpreneurs. Overtakers!

ଧଧଧ

The 36 überpreneurs who populate this book are transforming all our lives.

Nine of them are business leaders who have redirected the energies
of entire industries in the West, and built brand new industries in the
developing world.

Nine more are visionaries who are driving the discovery and
implementation of stunning new developments in biotechnology, clean
energy, and information and communications technologies.

Another nine are bond-builders who have brought renewed happiness to billions of individuals whose social networks have been disrupted by the anonymity of life in modern megacities.

And the final nine are change-makers who have begun the Herculean task of bridging the gap between the haves and have-nots of the developed and developing worlds.

ನ‍ನ‍ನ

How do they do it? What makes them tick? Are they all different, or are there vital shared characteristics that give them the unique ability to create innovative global enterprises and transform human societies?

We think there are. As we explored the lives and achievements of our übercast we found remarkable consistencies in their motives, their characteristics, their tactics and their achievements.

First, there's the driving force. All of them are driven by an epic ambition to change the world. All of them have seen and seized opportunities for change, sensed the way forward, garnered the necessary resources, and pursued their dreams, regardless of the odds. All of them, in the late Steve Jobs' words, "push the human race forward".

Second, they all - irrespective of the nature of their enterprises, or their personal or cultural backgrounds - share a set of definitive characteristics. They are all:

- *opportunistic* and *visionary*, constantly on the lookout for new ideas and intuitively grasping their potential implications, seeing and seizing opportunities for change;
- *innovative*, yet *pragmatic*, willing and able to jump cultural, organisational and geographic boundaries as they sense their way toward novel but practical solutions;
- *persuasive* and *empowering*, offering irresistible investment propositions and attracting talented and loyal followers as they garner the resources to pursue their goals;

- *focussed* and *confident*, indomitable spirits who assume total control
  and drive full steam ahead toward the realisation of their dreams; and
- *resilient* and *courageous*, taking bold but calculated risks, learning
  from their mistakes, and thriving on change and uncertainty as they
  upend your world, regardless of the odds.

And third, there are the outcomes. All of them have created massive new capital, be it financial or technological, social or spiritual. All of them have transformed the condition of mankind - for the better.

In each of the following 14 chapters, we describe one of the grand economic, technological, personal or societal challenges facing mankind, and the innovative ways in which it is being tackled, successfully, by two or three individuals. And, at the end of each chapter, we provide tabular overviews demonstrating that, despite the massive diversity of their ambitions and achievements, all 36 of these men and women are indeed driven by the same powerful forces and share the same key attributes.

ପ୍ରପ୍ରପ୍ର

So, where do they come from?

That's the perennial question asked by governments who want to build smarter economies, businesses who want to capture the economic, social and environmental benefits of new technologies, philanthropists who want a fairer and more prosperous society, and ambitious young students - and their parents - who just want to know what it takes to change the world.

In the last chapter of this book we explore the lessons learnt from the lives and achievements of these 36 extraordinary individuals. We analyse their vital characteristics and assess the extent to which they are made or born. To the extent that they are made, we review the impact of government policies, parental supervision and training programs on the quality and quantity of their creation. And to the extent that they are born, we explore how best we can identify and nurture their talents.

Part I

BIG BUSINESS

THE GLOBAL FINANCIAL CRISIS OF 2008 revealed not just the inherent fragility of Western financial systems, but also the accelerating movement of economic power away from the West toward the rapidly expanding Asian economies, with their burgeoning middle classes and growing aspirations.

Already burdened with unprecedented levels of household and government debt, Western nations were faced with massive losses of manufacturing jobs and associated unemployment. And, to make matters worse, the stream of immigrants skilled in science, technology, engineering and mathematics, a key driver of postwar Western innovation, had begun to dry up as more technically demanding jobs became available in the developing world.

And there, among the developing economies, new issues arose as emerging industries sought to meet rising demand for quality goods and services, against a backdrop of scarcer and more expensive natural resources and a backlash of mounting environmental concerns.

ଓଓଓ

Who can help us to meet these daunting economic challenges?

By far the most likely candidates were first identified and celebrated just over a century ago by the brilliant and colourful Austrian economist Joseph Schumpeter. Schumpeter called them "high-level entrepreneurs", and described them as "the primary agents of economic development and change", who employ innovative products, processes, markets, sources of supply and organisational structures to drive the "creative destruction" of the status quo, and thus lead us to a better, more prosperous, world.

Although not always "better", of course, as pointed out by another influential 20th-century economist, William Baumol, who astutely separated Schumpeter's high-level entrepreneurs into three distinct categories:

- *productive* entrepreneurs, who apply their entrepreneurial talents to activities that produce valuable goods and services. Think Thomas Edison or Eiji Toyoda, founder of Toyota Motor Corporation;
- *unproductive* entrepreneurs, whose sometimes equally formidable entrepreneurial skills are applied to activities that simply move the deck chairs, such as litigation, company takeovers and arbitrage, without producing additional value. Think Bernie Ebbers or Alan Bond; and
- *destructive* entrepreneurs, whose activities are seriously detrimental to our communal well-being. Think Mafia chiefs and Colombian drug lords.

ଔଔଔ

In the next three chapters we introduce nine of Schumpeter and Baumol's productive entrepreneurs, business überpreneurs whose "creative destruction" of stagnating industries and stalled economies sheds light on the ways in which our current economic woes might be met.

Three of them, Ingvar Kamprad, Chuck Feeney and Amancio Ortega, helped drive the Western world's economic recovery in the aftermath of the Great Depression and the Second World War. They changed the world's notion of luxury, putting products that had once been solely the province of the rich into the hands of rapidly expanding middle classes.

And, along the way, they developed the biggest furniture, liquor and fashion chains in the world.

In similar vein, Kiran Mazumdar-Shaw, Liu Yonghao and Mo Ibrahim led the emergence of new manufacturing and service economies in India, China and Africa during the 1980s. By introducing innovative technologies and practices to industries and sectors already comfortably established in the West, they created pharmaceutical, agricultural and telecommunication enterprises that are transforming the developing world.

And then, back in the West, came the standard bearers of vast new empires: Richard Branson, Jeff Bezos and Elon Musk. Their creative destruction of substantial chunks of the traditional airline, bookselling and finance industries has prepared them well as they race to be the first to create the ultimate new industry: space travel.

KEY SOURCES[1]

William J. Baumol, "Entrepreneurship: Productive, Unproductive, and Destructive", *Journal of Political Economy*, Vol. 98, 1990.

Joseph Schumpeter, *The Theory of Economic Development*, Oxford University Press, 1934 (original German edition: *Theorie der Wirtschaftlichen Entwicklung*, Dunker and Humblot, 1912).

---

[1] In keeping with our goal of making this book factual and authoritative as well as entertaining, we have not included an exhaustive list of all the material consulted. Rather, a short list of the most useful references, including all of those from which quotes have been taken, is provided at the end of each chapter.

Chapter 2

SOFAS, SPIRITS AND SKIRTS

IN 1926, ECONOMIST GEORGE TAYLOR came up with a delightfully simple indicator for the health of the economy: the higher the hemline, the higher the stock market. And, at least for the next 50 years or so, he was pretty much on the money. In the early 1930s, in the depths of the Great Depression, hemlines plummeted to ankle length, rising slowly toward knee-level during the Second World War, before soaring to the dizzy heights of the miniskirt in the mid-1960s.

But the booms in employment levels, birth rates and consumer demand that characterised the postwar recovery of Western economies were far from uniform.

At the head of the pack was Sweden. Neutrality during both world wars meant its industrial infrastructure was still intact. And substantial devaluations of the krona strengthened export markets in the depths of the Great Depression and the aftermath of the Second World War. The "Swedish Model", introduced by the newly elected Social Democratic Party in 1936, further accelerated growth with its powerful combination of industrial privatisation and the notion of a classless society. By 1970, Sweden's GDP was the third highest in the world.

In the United States, the Great Depression hit much harder, with unemployment rising to 25% in 1933, and as many as one-third of the population lacking adequate food, clothing and housing. The drafting of 12 million American men, and the temporary employment of 6 million American women in armaments factories, boosted recovery during the Second World War, but the real economic growth came after the war. The Golden Age of Capitalism, driven by rapid industrialisation and wider access to tertiary education, lasted for 25 years.

Spain was the last to recover - about a decade later than other EU countries. Handicapped during the Great Depression by ineffectual government and the 1936 - 1939 Civil War, the policy of national self-sufficiency (the Spanish Autarchy) introduced by General Franco in 1939 led to ongoing and severe economic depression for the next two decades. By the early 1950s, Spanish GDP per capita was less than half of the Western European average. It was not until 1959, when the economy was opened up to foreign investment, that the Spanish Miracle emerged, with economic growth rates second only to those of Japan for the next 15 years.

So, by 1951, when *New York Post* columnist Sylvia Porter famously referred to the US postwar baby boom as "the biggest, boomiest boom ever known in history", Sweden's baby boom had already been running for ten years, while Spain's was still to come. But there was one critical change that they all had in common: the high employment levels and increased salaries that drove their burgeoning economies also kindled the aspiration that well-designed furnishings, quality clothing and fine spirits should no longer be the province of the rich alone.

And pouring fuel on that fire were three men who knew the hardships of the Depression years firsthand: Ingvar Kamprad would make his mark by producing low-cost high-quality furniture for a new generation of Swedish homemakers; Chuck Feeney catered for the voracious appetites of first Americans and later the Japanese for luxury goods; and Amancio Ortega provided high fashion at affordable prices for the newly emerging Spanish middle class.

They founded the largest furniture, liquor and fashion retailers of all time: IKEA, Duty Free Shoppers Group and Zara.

INGVAR KAMPRAD

There are three things you need to know about shopping at IKEA.

First, go with the flow. Any attempt to find a shortcut to the section that sells the gizmo that you came to buy will result in dismal failure. Follow the prescribed "natural" path and resign yourself to buying a selection of nicely designed and competitively priced items that you didn't know you wanted and may never use.

Second, reward yourself with a delicious lunch of Swedish meatballs, potatoes and lingonberry jam.

And third, reward the kids with an hour in the free crèche, where they can leap around the ball pit and watch movies to their hearts' content, while you get lost looking for that shortcut.

Like many things at IKEA, the crèche has a charming Swedish name: Småland. Literally, it means "small land". Symbolically, but hardly metaphorically, it's named after Småland, the harsh and unyielding southern province of Sweden where both Ingvar Kamprad and IKEA were born.

As the IKEA catalogue puts it: "Because thin soils can't be farmed in the same way as a fertile field, Smålanders have always had to work harder, adapt their ideas and do things differently".

Ingvar Kamprad is the prototypical example.

ᛒᛒᛒ

Kamprad's grandfather emigrated from Germany to Småland with his wife and three children in 1894, and established a farm near the village of Agunnaryd. Three years later, faced with a hefty mortgage and a scarcely viable farm, he took his own life, leaving Kamprad's grandmother to resurrect the business. She must have been a formidable woman, for she not only managed to bring the farm to profitability while raising her young family, but also, according to Kamprad, led him down the path toward his youthful flirtation with extremist right-wing politics.

ᛒᛒᛒ

Ingvar Kamprad was born in the village of Pjätteryd, near Agunnaryd, on March 20, 1926. It's not clear when he first developed his voracious work ethic - his grandmother once again no doubt played a role - but by the time he was ten years old he was already running a business buying matches wholesale in Stockholm and reselling them to neighbours in the village at a tidy profit.

Then, in 1943, when he was just 17 years old, Kamprad went into business in earnest. Impressed by his academic performance in his final year at school, his father had given him a small cash reward to use however he wished. Unlike most boys of his age, then and now, Kamprad chose not to put the money toward a car, but invested it instead in setting up a business which he named IKEA: the combination of his own initials with those of the family farm (Elmtaryd) and the village (Agunnaryd) where he grew up. Using his bicycle as a mobile convenience store, he peddled Christmas cards and other small luxury items that thrifty Smålanders could not previously afford. And his timing was perfect: Sweden's economy, insulated by its neutral stance from the rigours of the war, was beginning to boom.

Over the next few years Kamprad expanded his range of products, developing a mail-order business capitalising on the spare space available in the local milkman's delivery van, and in 1947 he began to include furniture among his product lines. This proved so successful that by 1951 Kamprad made the decision to focus solely on furniture, and in 1953 he opened his first showroom, offering his customers the opportunity to buy quality locally made furniture at prices below those of his competitors. But the Swedish National Association of Furniture Dealers was not amused. Its members responded by encouraging their suppliers to boycott IKEA, and Kamprad was forced to begin sourcing materials, often from outside Sweden, and manufacturing himself.

The success of this operation was vastly enhanced by the creative inspiration of one of IKEA's draughtsmen, Gillis Lundgren, who realised that removing the legs from a table that he was delivering not only enabled him to fit it into his car, but also provided the basis for what came to be known as flat-pack furniture. In a single stroke, IKEA was able to reduce shipping costs, minimise transport damage, increase store capacity and, most impressively of all, transfer the task of assembling furniture from the company to its customers. Kamprad called it "commercial dynamite".

The flat-pack innovation, combined with unstinting commitment to quality design and affordable prices, led to phenomenal growth. In 1963 Kamprad opened the first IKEA store in Stockholm, followed by others across Scandinavia in the 1960s, Europe and the Far East in the 1970s, and the United Kingdom and the United States in the 1980s.

By 2012, there were over 150,000 employees and more than 300 stores throughout the developed world. Total sales turnover reached €27.5 billion, driven by 200 million catalogues in 20 different languages and more than 1 billion visits to IKEA websites.

And throughout that remarkable expansion, Kamprad's business model remained exactly the same. In typically blunt language, he summarises the philosophy behind the company with the comment:

> The temples of design in places like Milan or God knows where overflow with beautiful, original furniture that costs extortionate amounts of money. The vast majority of people don't have six figure amounts in the bank and don't live in enormous apartments ... it is for just such people that I created Ikea. For everybody who wants a comfortable house in which to live well. A need that crosses all countries, races and religions.

The execution of the philosophy is equally straightforward.

At the heart of the business is a team of designers, based in Småland, tasked with creating designs for top-quality furniture suitable for low-cost manufacturing from local timber and other raw materials in multiple locations, often in developing nations, around the world. The whole operation is conducted on such a huge scale that IKEA is now the world's third-largest consumer of timber.

Transferred to massive warehouses outside city centres in more than 40 countries, the entire range of furniture is displayed in adjacent showrooms, through which customers are guided on a long "natural walk" to lead them past items that they might be tempted to purchase.

As former (albeit disenchanted) IKEA executive Johan Stenebo observes: "Once you are inside IKEA, it's as if you have been grabbed by the hand and guided through the store to make you buy as much as possible. It's called mechanical selling - selling without a salesperson".

And to aid those, like Kamprad, who suffer from dyslexia, individual items have not just the standard Stock Keeping Unit codes but also their own highly evocative names: bathroom furnishings are named after Swedish lakes; bookcases after occupations. By the end of the long walk, the average customer has spent between $50 and $100 on items ranging in price from a few cents to thousands of dollars.

And then, in keeping with IKEA's cult-like commitment to hard work and frugality, they collect their flat-packs from the warehouse, the kids from Småland, and head home to assemble the furniture.

ଝଝଝ

But IKEA's cult of frugality doesn't stop there. In tune with Kamprad's view that "waste of resources is a mortal sin", the company was an early advocate of the principles of Corporate Social Responsibility. In particular, the Natural Step Framework, a widely adopted sustainable development strategy pioneered by fellow Swede Karl-Henrik Robèrt in the late 1980s, has played a key role in IKEA's environmental policy since its initial implementation in 1990.

But, despite his social and environmental scruples, controversy has never been far from the IKEA founder - be it criticisms of the company's obscure ownership by a low-tax not-for-profit based outside Sweden, which Kamprad defended as the only way to secure true financial independence for the company, or his unrepentant admiration for the one-time leader of the extreme right-wing New Swedish Movement, Per Engdahl.

Recalling the many mistakes he had made during his life, and particularly his involvement with extreme right-wing politics, he wrote a letter to IKEA employees in the mid-1990s, saying: "You have been young yourself, and perhaps you find something in your youth you now, so long afterward, think was ridiculous and stupid". The reply, sent in a letter of support from several hundred IKEA employees, says a great deal for both Kamprad's philosophy and the IKEA family cult that it has spawned. They wrote: "Ingvar, we are here whenever you need us. The IKEA family".

For Kamprad it is indeed all about family. Through his books as well as his frequent informal appearances throughout the IKEA empire, he has never ceased schooling his co-workers in the IKEA family in the virtues of Småland frugality and self-sufficiency. And his own famous frugality extends to driving a 15-year-old car, haggling over the price of vegetables in the local market, and buying all of his furniture from IKEA: "Why would I buy anything my customers could not afford"?

CHUCK FEENEY

When Chuck Feeney first set foot on the Ithaca campus of Cornell University's School of Hotel Administration in September 1952, he must have found the environment a fascinating mix of the foreign and the familiar.

Foreign, because unlike the vast majority of the Ivy League university's well-heeled students, Chuck came from a poor Irish-American family. He entered Cornell on a GI scholarship at the age of 21 after graduating from the local Catholic high school in his hometown of Elizabeth, New Jersey, and serving for four years as a volunteer in the American occupying force in Japan, including the first two years of the Korean War.

Familiar, because the School of Hotel Administration was a breeding ground for entrepreneurs, and Chuck's entrepreneurial talents were already clearly evident. As a schoolboy, he always had one or more enterprises on the go, often hiring his schoolmates to do the grunt work as he drummed up business selling beach umbrellas, caddying at the local golf links, or shovelling snow.

At Cornell, Chuck soon combined the foreign with the familiar. Observing the lack of local fast-food outlets capable of supplying wealthy Cornell students with midnight snacks, he set up a sandwich business, making and delivering up to a 100 sandwiches a night to his fellow students. It was the first example of a talent that would make

Chuck and his future partners super-rich: the ability to identify looming demographic gaps between supply and demand.

ະະະ

Graduating from Cornell in 1956, Feeney decided to see the world. With four months of his GI scholarship still to run, he spent the winter in the French Alps, earning a master's degree in political science from the University of Grenoble before moving south to seek new business opportunities.

They weren't slow coming. Within weeks he was running a summer camp for the children of US naval officers based at Villefranche-sur-Mer, and by the end of summer he was pioneering the business that would occupy him for the next 40 years: duty-free shopping.

With fellow Cornell graduate Bob Miller, readily lured away from his desk job at the Ritz Hotel in Barcelona, Feeney sold liquor and cars to US servicemen returning home from the Mediterranean, established a one-stop shop in Paris that offered American tourists the opportunity to purchase luxury goods from anywhere throughout Europe, and finally set up a chain of stores selling duty-free spirits to any American civilian willing and able to take a day trip across the border into Canada.

It was a lucrative business, made more so by the fact that there was never any need to invest capital in stock. They simply collected deposits, arranged for delivery from the country of origin to the customer's home in the United States, and banked the cheques. By 1964 they had 200 employees in 27 countries.

Then, in 1965, came a double whammy. First, inspired by their success, fierce competition began to emerge. Second, US President Lyndon Johnston, under pressure from US retailers, introduced savage reductions in US duty-free liquor allowances, bringing their business to the verge of bankruptcy.

But Feeney and Miller were not that easily beaten. They reshaped the business, now named Duty Free Shoppers (DFS), eliminated car sales and other loss-making operations, and focused their attention on the duty-free concessions they had acquired in Hawaii and Hong Kong. And their timing was perfect.

The 1964 Tokyo Olympics had not only opened Japan to the eyes of the rest of the world, but also the reverse. Encouraged by the lifting of restrictions on foreign travel that had been in place since the Second World War, millions of middle-class Japanese were raring to go. And Chuck Feeney, fluent in Japanese from his time in the air force, was waiting for them. Realising that most of the Japanese tourists visiting Hawaii would come in groups led by professional tour guides, and that all of them would be obliged by the culture of *omiyage* to buy gifts for family and colleagues at home, Feeney made the move that would form the basis for the remarkable subsequent growth of DFS: he offered Japanese tour guides and their parent travel agencies a flat fee for every customer they brought to his store.

The business grew exponentially. In 1968, Duty Free Shoppers bid $1 million for the duty-free concession they had first acquired three years earlier for $78,000. In 1971, the concession was renewed with a bid of $69 million, and, on February 5, 1988, DFS made the highest bid ever received for a duty-free concession: $1.15 billion for the next five years. During that period, the Japanese travel market expanded by 19% per year, and the profits to Feeney and his partners from the Honolulu business grew to hundreds of millions of dollars per annum.

But despite the success of the Honolulu operation, Feeney could see that the expanding Japanese tourism market would soon be seeking additional destinations, and he set out to be one step ahead.

In 1969, DFS acquired a duty-free concession in Anchorage, Alaska, on the polar route from Japan to Europe, and in 1971 they moved into the duty-free business in Guam, just four hours from Tokyo. In 1975, in a striking coup, they rebuilt the airport in the US-administered trust territory of Saipan, a delightful tropical island 200 km north of Guam, in return for tax-free rights to all duty-free activities for the next 20 years! Japanese tourists, it seemed, followed wherever he led.

But Feeney's knack for picking changing demographics went one stage further. In the early 1990s, observing that the tourists arriving in Hawaii from Japan were younger, less affluent and less inclined to buy expensive presents for their friends and colleagues back home, he decided it was time to get out. And in 1996 he sold his entire 38.5% stake to the French retail conglomerate Louis Vuitton Moët Hennessy for $1.6 billion, valuing DFS overall at $4.2 billion. Less than ten years later, plummeting sales had reduced the value of the company to an estimated $1 billion.

In farewell "thank you" letters to 2,400 long-term employees, Feeney underscored his appreciation of their loyalty and commitment with cheques totalling $26 million.

ଛଛଛ

Feeney himself has never had any interest in money, at least for its own sake. He travels at the back of the plane in T-shirt and jeans and lives with his wife in an apartment block that he built for homeless families in San Francisco. But, throughout his life, he has maintained an almost obsessive addiction to paying minimal or no tax, claiming that he could spend the money much more effectively than any government. And that is exactly what he set out to prove in his next überpreneurial endeavour.

When Feeney sold his share of DFS in 1996, only a handful of his family and friends, and none of his partners, were aware that he had actually transferred his DFS shares and most of his other assets to his charitable foundation, Atlantic Philanthropies, over ten years earlier. Apart from a small fraction of his wealth set aside to provide for his family, he had long since decided to use his fortune to change the world. And he has.

By the end of 2010, Atlantic Philanthropies had made grants totalling more than $5.4 billion. Initially, the focus was on Cornell and other US universities, but in the mid-1980s Feeney began to explore opportunities in Ireland. Always willing to help the underdog, he had a strong sentimental attachment to the land of his forebears, and a firm belief that Irish Americans should be doing more to help rebuild its flagging economy.

Feeney did that with a vengeance. All up, the foundation invested close to a billion dollars in research and education facilities in seven Irish universities, and Feeney himself followed up with funding for moderate elements within both Sinn Fein and the Ulster Defence Association. The latter donations, which fell outside the mandate of Atlantic Philanthropies and therefore had to be made by Feeney personally, are said to have played a key role in the cessation of hostilities in Northern Ireland.

Likewise in Vietnam. As Feeney told his biographer, Conor O'Clery: "We owe it to the Vietnamese after the way we treated them". Working with the East meets West Foundation, Atlantic invested heavily in public health and education in Vietnam. At the same time, investments in medical research in the United States and Australia, all of them leveraged with equal or greater contributions from governments, were themselves used to further leverage the foundation's work in Vietnam.

ଝଝଝ

In 2011, in his 80th year, Chuck Feeney was back on the road in the United States and Australia, encouraging high-net-worth individuals and families to join him in The Giving Pledge, an international group led by Warren Buffett and Bill Gates. At a dinner attended by Feeney in Tucson, Arizona, in May 2011, Buffett praised Feeney as the spiritual leader of the group, all of whose members have pledged to give away the majority of their fortunes while still alive. Feeney, said Buffet, "wants his last check to bounce".

AMANCIO ORTEGA

When Kate Middleton and Prince William stepped out of Buckingham Palace on the day after their wedding in April 2011, Kate was wearing a simple blue dress that she had bought a few days earlier for £49.99 at a high-street store named Zara.

But the newly titled Duchess of Cambridge was far from alone among fashion-conscious young women shopping at Zara. The label can be found in stores in 400 cities across 5 continents.

Overall, Zara's parent company, Inditex, has more than 5,000 stores in 84 countries and employs over 100,000 staff. But of the eight brands within the Inditex empire, it is Zara that accounts for the lion's share of the business.

ଝଝଝ

Amancio Ortega Gaona, the mastermind behind Inditex, was
born in the province of León in the north of Spain in 1936, and moved with
his family to the Galician port town of A Coruña when he was just eight
years old. His parents, like many during General Franco's 20-year reign,
struggled to make ends meet. Nonetheless, as Ortega recalls, they instilled in
him a strong work ethic, telling him: "Don't ever complicate things. Work,
and work with passion". His first job, at the age of 13, was as a delivery boy
for an A Coruña shirtmaker, where he learnt firsthand of the benefits of
delivering merchandise directly from the manufacturer to the customer.

Over the following decade Ortega worked in all facets of the clothing
business, rising eventually to the position of store manager. In the process,
he drew a simple and far-reaching conclusion: the world of fashion revolved
around supplying very wealthy women with very expensive clothes.

Amancio Ortega resolved to change all that. He and his first wife, Rosalia
Mera, set out to produce well-designed, fashionable clothing at prices the
woman in the street could afford.

They began in 1963, initially using cheap fabrics to make and market
fashionable high-quality bathrobes and lingerie from their home, and later,
in response to growing demand from wholesalers, establishing a dedicated
garment-making factory, Confecciones Goa (Ortega's initials in reverse).
But, as always in the fickle world of fashion, demand fluctuated, and
when an international wholesaler defaulted on a major order, the Ortegas
were left with a massive supply of lingerie and little choice but to sell it
themselves. They opened a shop in downtown A Coruña, and called it Zara.

It was an interesting choice of name, with an interesting history. Initially
planning to call their new store Zorba, they had already invested their
hard-earned capital in expensive neon lettering when they were prevented
from using the name by the existence of a Greek restaurant operating
under the same business name nearby. Never ones to waste cloth, they cut
their losses, discarding *o* and *b* and purchasing another *a*.

But there was no skimping on location. Like all of its successors, the first
Zara shop was strategically placed on the best site in the best street in

town, relying on word of mouth, and carefully designed shop window displays, rather than advertising, which Ortega saw as a "pointless distraction". And it seems he was right. Between 1975 and 1990, he opened 100 strategically located Spanish stores controlled by a single vertically integrated holding company, Inditex. He was ready to take on the world.

So what was the basis for Ortega's success in the cut-throat world of fashion?

First, he listens. In the words of his long-term lieutenant, José María Castellano, "Ortega listens to everybody, and soaks it all up like a sponge". He listens to his young designers and he listens to the people who are in touch with the customers. And "his ability to synthesize the most complex ideas as though they were really simple is an extraordinary quality".

Second, Inditex maintains total, yet innovative, control of the entire process from sourcing fabrics, through design and manufacturing to distribution and sale: all the way from "loom to shop floor". And from the start, the company has focussed on local production in Spain and Portugal, arguing that the higher labour costs, relative to those in the developing world, are more than counterbalanced by increased flexibility and the ability to rapidly adjust supply to meet demand.

Third, and most important of all, Ortega offers "fast fashion". As *The Economist* quotes him as saying: "Flogging fashion is like selling fish. Fresh fish, like a freshly cut jacket in the latest colour, sells quickly and at a high price. Yesterday's catch must be discounted and may not sell at all". In stark contrast to the fashion industry at large, new designs appear in Ortega's stores twice per week, with store decorations and half of all stock being turned over at least once a fortnight. There is no "just looking" at Zara - if you don't buy it now, you'll be too late.

How do they do it?

On the one hand, it's all about market intelligence. The buzzword used by business strategists is "shared situation awareness", a key tool for decision-makers operating in complex and dynamic systems such as air traffic control or, at a more personal level, driving a car. At Inditex, this translates into market intelligence that is shared between commercial managers, clothing designers and store managers on a daily or even hourly basis, with all of it being integrated and analysed in "The Cube", the high-technology heart of Ortega's empire in A Coruña.

And on the other hand, it's all about using it. By co-locating key design and marketing staff in huge open-plan areas, the company can design, produce and assess prototype garments within a few hours of receiving vital sales information. Small runs of selected garments are then manufactured and distributed to representative stores, where the customers' interest or lack thereof determines the next step. If they're not interested, the products are withdrawn, at minimal cost to the firm. If they buy the garment, large quantities of fresh stock are manufactured and delivered to stores within days.

Which is why Zara stores around the globe were all stocked up and ready to go when Kate stepped out of Buckingham Palace in her little blue dress.

ଓଓଓ

Inditex went public in 2001, with Amancio Ortega retaining 59% of the stock, then valued at $6.6 billion dollars. His co-founder and former wife, Rosalia Mera, who held 7%, also became an overnight billionaire.

But Amancio Ortega showed no sign of stopping. After celebrating the float with lunch in the company canteen, he went back to his daily routine, working "like a donkey" with the designers and commercial managers at the nerve centre of his business. Ten years and 4,000 stores later, on June 30, 2011, he stepped down as chairman. He still lives, happily and very privately, with his second wife, Flora Pérez, in a nondescript apartment block in A Coruña. As he told Covadonga O'Shea, an old friend and the only journalist who he has ever allowed to interview him: "I want only my family, friends and colleagues to recognise me in the street".

CREATING MARKETS, BUILDING ECONOMIES

Apart from their obvious frugality and reclusiveness, what do Ortega, Kamprad and Feeney have in common?

More than anything else, all three of them have focussed single-mindedly on business models that they themselves created in their mid-20s, and that remained essentially unchanged throughout their careers. Each of them built their businesses from scratch on the foundation of their own cash flows. And each of their business models clearly addressed the same demographic opportunity: providing middle-class consumers with high-quality products at affordable prices. Kamprad referred to his business as democratising design; Ortega talked of democratising fashion.

With over 200,000 employees and hundreds of millions of customers, they captured and accelerated the massive demographic changes following the Second World War, creating not just new industries but entire new markets, and helping drive decades of economic growth throughout the Western world.

KEY SOURCES

INGVAR KAMPRAD

Oliver Burkeman, "The miracle of Älmhult", *The Guardian*, June 17, 2004.

Lauren Collins, "House perfect", *The New Yorker*, October 3, 2011.

Bob de Wit and Ron Meyer, *Strategy synthesis: Resolving strategy paradoxes to create competitive advantage*, Cengage Learning EMEA, 2010.

Jonas Fredén, "Ingvar Kamprad - King of IKEA", *The Swedish Institute*, March 2, 2011.

Ingvar Kamprad, *The testament of a furniture dealer. A Little IKEA Dictionary*, Inter IKEA Systems B.V., 2007.

Ulf Mårtensson, "IKEA's Ingvar Kamprad", *Nordic Reach*, November, 2007.

Johan Stenebo, "Ikea's flat-pack Fuhrer: Furniture chain founder is branded a tight-fisted former neo-Nazi in new book", *Daily Mail*, October 9, 2010.

Simon Tierney, "Lost in Ikea - the last great challenge for mankind", *The Irish Times*, May 14, 2012.

CHUCK FEENEY

"DFS 50: The journey continues", Anniversary Supplement. *The Moodie Report*, November 1, 2010.

Cathy Hayes, "Irish billionaire inspires Warren Buffet, Bill Gates to give it all away", *Irish Central*, May 10, 2011.

Conor O'Clery, *The Billionaire who wasn't: How Chuck Feeney secretly made and gave away a Fortune*, Public Affairs, New York, 2007.

"The secretive do-gooder", *The Economist*, October 4, 2007.

AMANCIO ORTEGA

Deborah Arthurs, "Kate is every inch the people's princess as she steps out in High Street frock for first day as a Royal", *Daily Mail*, May 2, 2011.

Leslie Crawford, "A brand tailored for fast-fashion", *Financial Times*, December 28, 2005.

"Inditex. Fashion forward", *The Economist*, March 24, 2012.

Covadonga O'Shea, *This is Amancio Ortega, the Man that created Zara*, Sphere Books, 2008.

Luke Stegemann, "Style legacy", *The Adelaide Review*, October 2011.

Donald Sull and Stefano Turconi, "Fast fashion lessons", *Business Strategy Review*, Summer 2008.

An individual with an epic ambition to change the world, who ...	Ingvar Kamprad	Chuck Feeney	Amancio Ortega Gaona
	Born: 1926, Pjätteryd, Sweden Education: Local high school Organisation: IKEA	Born: 1931, Elizabeth, New Jersey, USA Education: BSc (Hotel Admin), Cornell Organisation: Duty Free Shoppers Group	Born: 1936, Busdongo de Arbas, León, Spain Education: Elementary school Organisation: Zara
.. sees and seizes opportunities for change ..			
Opportunistic: aggressively seeks and adopts new ideas	Saw the growth in consumer demand in his local community for previously unaffordable goods ...	Observing the post-war demand among US sailors in the Mediterranean for duty-free goods ...	During his early years as a gofer, and eventually store manager, in the fashion business in A Coruña, Ortega saw that access to high-quality clothes was the privilege of the rich ...
& Visionary: intuitively grasps the big picture and how it might evolve	... and recognised the potential for a business providing high-quality well-designed furniture at a price that people on small incomes could afford.	... he foresaw the opportunity to provide similar services for tourists from the increasingly affluent middle classes of the United States and Japan.	... but the aspiration of the growing numbers of Spaniards who were no longer poor.
.. senses the way forward ..			
Innovative: thinks creatively, ignores boundaries, disrupts the status quo	He offered his customers stylish designs and quality materials in easily transportable flat-packs ...	He and his partners set up a mail-order business that enabled US citizens to drive across the border into Canada and pre-order five bottles of duty-free liquor for every person in the car, including children, for subsequent home delivery by their European suppliers.	He made it his mission to democratise fashion through vertical integration, designing and manufacturing high-fashion garments using less expensive materials and taking them directly from manufacturer to consumer.
but Pragmatic: recognises constraints, devises practical solutions, creates value	... and provided them with simple tools and instructions on how to build the furniture themselves!	But when US President Johnson slashed the duty-free allowance to one bottle per adult, Feeney saw the writing on the wall. He moved to Hawaii, ...	"I do not want our stores to be full of luxury items, things that have nothing to do with who we are, essentially, as human beings. Our strength is appealing to a real public, to real women. We don't sell dreams".

.. attracts the necessary resources ..			
Persuasive: articulate and convincing communicator, consummate networker	IKEA is a cult, and Kamprad is its leader. His homespun design philosophy is simple: "It must reflect an easier, more natural and unconstrained way of life".	... where his ability to chatter happily to customers and tour group leaders in Japanese ...	Shunning expensive advertising, Ortega relied on his chic window displays located in upmarket fashion locations to do the talking, ...
& Empowering: attracts talent, inspires loyalty, rewards excellence	And so is his view of human resources: "I have a very good sense of who will fit in to the IKEA family. The person, the individual, is the most important aspect of what we do, everything else can be solved".	... earned him their loyalty even after DFS lost its 1981 bid for the Honolulu duty-free concession. Their support, and that of his employees, prevented the competition from penetrating the market.	... while providing thousands of unemployed Spanish women with the opportunity to supplement family incomes by working at home.
.. and pursues the dream ..			
Focussed: passionate and highly energetic perfectionist, totally committed to an overriding vision	"Nobody can guarantee a company or a concept an eternal life, but no one can accuse me for not having tried".	Seeking new destinations for Japanese tourists wishing to make duty-free shopping trips closer to home, Feeney identified the US trust territory of Saipan in the Northern Mariana Islands ...	"Right from the start, I always wanted to invent something different from what was in the market".
& Confident: driven by unconditional self-belief, assumes absolute authority and accountability	"Any designer can design a desk that will cost 5,000 kronor. But only the most highly skilled can design a good, functional desk that will cost 100 kronor".	... and agreed to finance the construction of an airport in return for a twenty-year duty-free concession on the island.	And to drive the message home, he opened his first Zara outlet right across the street from A Coruña's trendiest fashion boutiques.
regardless of the odds ..			
Resilient: flexible, thrives on change and uncertainty, learns from mistakes	"Design requires innovation ... innovation demands risk ... risk-takers make mistakes".	In 1988, DFS bid $1.15 billion for the Honolulu concession, which turned out to be three-quarters of a billion more than the next best bid, ...	With Inditex expanding around the globe, Ortega hired computer buff Jose Maria Castellano to take care of running the business. ...
& Courageous: bold, intelligent risk-taker, undaunted by criticism, determined to succeed	"I have made many mistakes".	... but that, said Feeney, was still better than the alternative: "The worst thing to do was lose".	... while he explored fresh demographic sectors, including new markets in India, China and Japan.

Chapter 3

BUILDING HOPE AND PRIDE

THE ASCENT OF REVOLUTIONARY LEADERS in China, India and Egypt in the middle of the 20th century was expected to herald a new age of prosperity, but the reality was somewhat different.

In India, Jawaharlal Nehru came to power with a vision for centrally planned economic development modelled on that of the Soviet Union. His draconian Licence Raj, which required as many as 80 government departments to approve the establishment of a new business, stifled economic growth from 1947 until the assassination of his daughter, Indira Gandhi, in 1984.

In China, Chairman Mao's grand plan for a socialist state built on the twin pillars of agriculture and industry, including the reorganisation of farms into communes, the abolition of private ownership and the forced relocation of peasants from farms to factories, slowed the nation to a halt between 1949 and 1976.

And in Egypt, then including Sudan, Gamal Nasser's command economy, suffocated by its inefficient and ubiquitous public sector, closed the nation for business from 1952 to 1970.

Then, after decades of pain, more liberal leaders emerged. In Egypt, Anwar Sadat introduced the *Infitah*, opening the door to both domestic and foreign investment in Egypt's private sector; in China, Deng Xiaoping, newly reappointed Vice-Premier, spelt out his *gaige kaifang* (Reform and Opening Policy) for economically focused development; and in India, Narasimha Rao tore up the rule books for the Licence Raj.

Slowly, hesitantly at first, nascent überpreneurs began to appear, and then to prosper. By the end of the century, Liu Yonghao - dirt-poor at the time of the Cultural Revolution - was one of the richest men in the world. Kiran Mazumdar-Shaw - rebuffed in her early attempts to do business during the reign of Indira Gandhi - owned the biggest biotech company in India. And Mo Ibrahim, a student at Egypt's Alexandria University in the last days of Gamal Nasser, was on the cusp of creating the largest mobile phone network in Africa.

Each of them built massive businesses and equally massive fortunes. But, more importantly, each of them helped pioneer the rebuilding of their nations.

MO IBRAHIM

Mo Ibrahim was ahead of the mobile phone game right from the start. Born on May 3, 1946, his birth preceded the world's first mobile phone call by just six weeks.

That call was made from a car in St Louis, Missouri, on June 17, 1946, using a mobile phone that weighed in at just over 35 kg. Within a year, AT&T had introduced a mobile telephone service in St Louis and other US cities, offering a select group of wealthy individuals the opportunity to make operator-connected push-to-speak calls from their cars.

But progress was slow. Twenty years later, by which time Mo Ibrahim was at university, restrictions on the number of radio channels still meant that only 12 of the 2,000 New Yorkers with mobile car-phones could be connected at any one time.

It was not until 1979, when NTT in Japan introduced the first commercial cellular phone network using smaller base stations in separate land areas (cells) to allow multiple use of the same radio frequencies, that larger numbers of users could simultaneously access the service, and even then usage was largely limited by phone size and weight to customers in cars.

Finally, in 1983, commercial networks in the United States began to introduce handheld phones, and the rush was on. Despite the fact that they still weighed half a kilogram, cost $4,000 each, and required a 10-hour recharge for every 30 minutes of talk time, the demand for handhelds was prodigious.

Around the world, telecommunication companies scrambled to join the race, with British Telecom being no exception. And to lead their team, they hired Mo Ibrahim, appointing him technical director of Cellnet, with responsibility for taking mobile phones out of cars and into the hands of their customers.

So, how did a young engineer from the Sudan finish up in a job like that?

ଧ୧ଧ

In 1946, when Mo Ibrahim was born in northern Sudan, in the largely Muslim region known as Nubia, Sudan was still under the joint administration of Britain and Egypt. But revolution was in the air, and by the time Mo was ten years old Gamal Nasser had seized control as Prime Minister and then President of Egypt, and Sudan, having sought and gained independence, was on the brink of its first civil war.

Mo's parents were not well off, but they were determined that he and his four siblings should receive a good education. They moved to Alexandria, in Egypt, where Mo excelled in mathematics and science at his Nubian school before going on to study engineering at Alexandria University.

Ibrahim was a typical university student of the late 1960s, joining in demonstrations against the arrests of Congolese freedom fighter Patrice Lumumba and Kenyan president Jomo Kenyatta. But he was also vastly ambitious, both for himself and for his people: first, he wanted to put an end to Africa's dependence on other countries by using his engineering skills to build the roads, bridges and other infrastructure needed to make the continent self-reliant; second, he wanted to win a Nobel Prize in physics.

Sudan was still in turmoil when Mo Ibrahim completed his degree and returned to work for Sudan Telecom in Khartoum. But his job exposed him to regular contacts with foreign experts as well as opportunities for overseas travel, and in 1974 he was awarded a British Council/Sudanese government scholarship to undertake a master's degree in engineering at Bradford University, followed by a PhD in mobile telecommunications at Birmingham University.

The subject of his PhD thesis was "Signal strength prediction for mobile radio communication in built-up areas". Suddenly, Mo Ibrahim was a world expert on the core issue confronting planners of cellular phone networks around the globe.

ଔଔଔ

British Telecom's choice of Mo Ibrahim as a technical director with Cellnet proved to be a wise one: by 1985, he and his team of engineers had built the world's first mobile phone network specifically designed for handheld phones. But Mo was far from happy. British Telecom (BT), in his view, had vastly underestimated both the potential of the mobile phone market and the resources required for the project. Asked later what he had learnt from his years at BT, Mo replied: "I learnt what not to do".

In 1989, he bit the bullet, leaving BT to establish Mobile Systems International, a consulting company that he kicked off with $50,000, operating from the dining room of his London home.

It was a sellers' market. Around the globe, opportunistic buyers were acquiring licences to create mobile phone networks, but few had any idea of how to design and build them. Mo did. He developed proprietary software that facilitated the design of inexpensive and effective handheld phone networks, combining minimum hardware requirements with maximum interference-free coverage, and the customers flocked to his door. As he told Moky Makura, author of "*Africa's Greatest Entrepreneurs*": "There is no major country where we have not at least designed one network. It was great. I mean it was just like selling hot cakes!"

Without shareholders, and having never written a business plan, Ibrahim's business model was straightforward. As demand grew, he simply recruited more and more skilled staff, initially from BT ("almost every single person wanted to leave BT with me"), all of whom he offered equity in the company. And it was a cash business, making money from day one. Within ten years, MSI employed over 800 staff, almost all of them engineers, in markets throughout Europe, Asia and the Americas.

But not in Africa. Despite the lack of competition from landline services run by existing telecommunication companies, none of the big operators wanted to go there, and mobile network licences were going begging. For Mo Ibrahim, it was too good an opportunity to miss. Here was the chance to become a network operator in his own right, while simultaneously achieving his boyhood dream of transforming Africa.

In 2000, he sold the consulting arm of his business for a little under a billion dollars, and began to invest in Africa.

ଷଷଷ

But despite huge demand and favourable terms, acquiring and building new networks was an expensive business. To gain and retain a competitive position, Ibrahim needed money, lots of it, and the major banks weren't interested. Africa, with its notoriety for dictators and civil unrest, was seen as too risky.

Again, his solution was simple. Putting in place a board of experienced and ethical individuals drawn from Africa and Europe, he went to the markets with a story that emphasised not only the enormous potential of mobile phone technology to stimulate new economic growth in Africa, but also his personal commitment to building the business without resort to bribery. "Nobody in the company", he said, "could spend more than $30,000 without the signatures of the entire board".

Those arguments, together with Ibrahim's track record, struck a chord with both venture capitalists and international aid agencies. Over the next five years, they invested hundreds of millions in Ibrahim's company, now renamed Celtel, as it expanded to around 8,000 staff serving 20 million mobile phone owners in 15 countries.

Celtel's growth rate was phenomenal. But even more important, from Mo Ibrahim's perspective, were the ancillary benefits to Africa. Thousands of small businesspeople were making their living selling Celtel scratch cards, and mobile banking and telecommunication had revolutionised business opportunities in rural and urban communities. According to Ibrahim, mobile phone technology was contributing as much as 1% per annum to GDP growth across Africa.

So, where next? Mo Ibrahim reckoned the time had come to go public, but eager buyers were circling and his investors were looking forward to their returns. In 2005, Celtel was sold to a Kuwaiti company for $3.4 billion, and Mo Ibrahim was set for his next move.

ย็ย็ย็

After making one or two billion dollars having fun, what should a self-styled "reluctant entrepreneur" do next? For Ibrahim, it was a no-brainer. Throughout his years building Celtel, he had been frustrated by the difficulties of doing business in Africa. "After fifty years of independence", he said, "we have a catastrophic failure of leadership and governance: too many dictators, too many megalomaniacs, too many thieves".

Using his profits from Celtel he established the Mo Ibrahim Foundation, and put in place two extraordinary initiatives.

First, he established the Ibrahim Index of African Governance, which provides an annual ranking of 53 African nations according to their performance in safety and rule of law; participation and human rights; sustainable economic opportunity; and human development. The rankings are produced by a dedicated research team, reporting to an independent board that includes the likes of Mary Robinson, ex-president

of Ireland and former UN High Commissioner for Human Rights. It
is intended to not only name and shame those governments that are
behaving badly, but also recognise the achievements of those that are
doing well. And it works. According to USAID administrator Rajiv Shah,
the index has a huge impact on how he invests his $6.5 billion African aid
budget.

Second, he established the Mo Ibrahim Prize for Achievement in
African Leadership, awarded to a former African leader selected by an
independent prize committee that considers not only the performance
of the country during their time in office, but also their willingness to
relinquish power peacefully and democratically at the end of their term. It
is the world's largest prize, totalling $500,000 per annum for ten years and
then $200,000 per annum for life, and is unashamedly designed to attract
the undivided attention of Africa, if not the world. Since 2007, it has been
awarded in three out of six years, to former presidents Joaquim Chissano
of Mozambique, Festus Mogae of Botswana, and, most recently, Pedro
Verona Rodrigues Pires of Cape Verde.

And what of the other three years? Does the failure of the selection
committee to identify suitable recipients suggest that the prize is failing
to achieve its goals? Not at all, says Ibrahim. What if I were to "go back
to my prize committee and recommend that the prize be offered to the
European leader who came to office in the last ten years and transformed
his or her country. Can you please give me a name"?

ଧଧଧ

Between 1998 and 2011 the number of mobile phones in Africa increased
from 4 million to 400 million. Their ubiquity has transformed African
business and African society, and is en route to transforming the
governance of African nations.

And Mo Ibrahim is en route to achieving his goal: using his engineering
skills - both technical and social - to help make Africa self-reliant. The
Nobel Prize can wait.

LIU YONGHAO

The period from 1958 to 1976 was a complete write-off for the People's Republic of China. Starting with Chairman Mao's disastrous Great Leap Forward and the resulting famines from 1959 to 1962, degenerating further during the Cultural Revolution from 1966 to 1971, and culminating in the arrest of Deng Xiaoping following the death of Premier Zhou Enlai in 1976, China's economy was effectively brought to a standstill. Worse still, an entire generation of young Chinese was denied an education: university entrance exams, cancelled in 1966, were not restored until 1977.

For Liu Yonghao, who was just seven years old at the time of the Great Leap Forward, and his three older brothers in rural Sichuan, the Cultural Revolution meant not only the anathema of coming from a well-educated and once-wealthy family, but also the shame of seeing their father - the director of the county agricultural bureau - sent to a re-education camp, and their mother - a school teacher - denounced. Hard-pressed to feed the family, his parents had already given the third brother, Liu Yongmei, up for adoption by a local farmer, who renamed him Chen Yuxin.

Despite these setbacks, the Liu boys battled on. All four brothers ultimately graduated from technical vocational colleges, and were assigned to jobs in government factories and institutions. In the eyes of rural China, the Liu brothers had it made: after all, this was the time of the Iron Rice Bowl, and individuals with government jobs were entitled to sinecures for life.

But the Iron Rice Bowl wasn't enough for the Liu brothers. Becoming aware of Vice-Premier Deng Xiaoping's December 1978 speech in favour of market-oriented reforms, they hatched a plan to open an electronics business. Unhappily, their enthusiasm was a touch premature. In 1978, just 0.01% of China's population was engaged in the private sector, and Deng's economic liberalism was yet to penetrate rural Sichuan. The local party secretary rejected their application to start a business out-of-hand: "What? Following the capitalist path? No way!"

But Deng's reforms soon began to take hold, and four years later the Liu brothers came up with another scheme. What if they were to focus on agriculture, and couch their plans in terms of the government's newly introduced policy of replacing the failed commune system with specialist farms, where tenant farmers could keep or sell surplus produce after paying a share to the state?

This time their application was successful. Just two hurdles remained: capital and labour.

Unable to borrow money for a private business, they pooled all their resources, raising ¥1000 (about $150) from the sale of their bicycles, watches and other possessions. Labour was another matter: there was no way that they would all get permission to resign from their government jobs. So they decided to step down one by one, starting with Chen Yuxin, the only brother with farming experience, who stunned his colleagues and neighbours by seeking, and ultimately receiving, approval to join the private workforce.

In 1982, the Liu brothers established a quail breeding business in the impoverished village of Gujia, northeast of Chengdu, and brought their collective talents in computing, agriculture and engineering to bear on building an industry. It was an intensely competitive space, with very low margins, but the combination of advanced breeding programs, high-quality feed and computerised farm management introduced by the Liu's soon enabled them to dominate a rapidly expanding market. By 1988, they were producing millions of quail eggs per day and had accumulated family assets of over ¥100 million. In the space of six short years, the Liu brothers were millionaires.

So, where to next? The short answer was more food.

Dramatic increases in living standards throughout the 1980's had led to increased demand for meat, and Chinese farmers were failing to keep up. Recognising their opportunity, the Liu brothers moved into the animal feed business, beginning with a village by village campaign to convince farmers that their productivity would escalate if they provided their livestock with regular high-quality feed.

Initially, the business boomed, but not everything went their way. The brutal aftermath of the 1989 Tiananmen Square protests had slowed the pace of economic growth, reinforced government control over the private sector, and soured public opinion of entrepreneurial activity. According to Liu Yonghao, "The officials and journalists who had often been coming to our factory stopped. We didn't know why. Some people advised us to quit, saying we had to choose between the capitalist and socialist paths, or we might have big problems".

Once again, it was Deng Xiaoping who came to their rescue, using his 1992 "South Touring Talk" to clarify his view that economic growth should come before any argument about the relative merits of capitalism or socialism. By the mid-1990's, in a stunning repeat of their success in the quail industry, the Liu company - now named the Hope Group - had 100 feed plants and 30,000 sales outlets scattered across China. The Liu boys were making billions of yuan per annum. As Deng Xiaoping put it: "Poverty is not socialism. To be rich is glorious".

ଷଷଷ

Throughout their transition from poverty to riches, the brothers had avoided the issue of allocating value to their individual contributions. The eldest brother, Liu Yongyan, had come up with the idea of the quail business, and had poured his own limited financial resources into making it happen. The second and third brothers, Liu Yongxing and Chen Yuxin, had taken the risk of leaving their secure government jobs to build the business. And Liu Yonghao, long recognised as the public relations talent of the family, had earned respect for their activities through his membership of the Chinese People's Political Consultative Conference as a representative of private enterprise.

But now the time had come to use their collective wealth to pursue their own hopes and dreams. They agreed to split their assets, and China for that matter, four ways, and began to seriously expand their businesses.

The oldest brother, Liu Yongyan, took the northern arm, Continental Hope Group, and focused his attention on high-technology manufacturing; Liu Yongxing, the second brother, selected East Hope Group, and diversified into aluminium and energy; the third brother, Chen Yuxin, expanded West Hope Group with new companies based on animal health products and tourism; and Liu Yonghao, the fourth brother, built the southern arm - soon renamed New Hope Group - into one of the largest suppliers of meat, eggs and dairy products in China.

That was just for a start. Liu Yonghao had two more strings to his bow.

First, he wanted to build a truly integrated agricultural company, one that not only spanned the supply chain from feedstock to farm, and from food processing to market, but also linked agriculture to the capital required to drive the industry.

To that end, in 1996, New Hope Group became the sponsor and largest shareholder of China's first private bank, the China Minsheng Banking Company Ltd, with Liu Yonghao as Vice-Chairman. And in 1998, New Hope Group was listed on the Shenzhen Securities Exchange, raising ¥250 million and expanding its investments across what Liu Yonghao describes as "the four wheels driving the business": agribusiness and food, chemical industry and resources, real estate and infrastructure, finance and investment. By 2012, the company had more than 400 subsidiaries, 80,000 employees, and a market capitalisation of ¥30 billion.

Second, he wanted to play a leading role in improving the lot of China's peasant farmers.

Using his positions on the Chinese People's Political Consultative Conference and the All-China Federation of Industry and Commerce as a base, Liu Yonghau and nine other private entrepreneurs began by initiating the Guangcai (Brilliant Cause) Program, a nongovernmental aid program that facilitates investment from the private sector into sustainable development projects in less developed areas of China. Since 1994, the program has invested over ¥100 billion, providing training for 4 million people and helping another 5 million find jobs.

But that's small beer for China, with hundreds of millions of peasant farmers seeking work in cities to supplement their incomes. In Liu's view, increasing peasant income across the board will require a total overhaul of the scale and efficiency of farming operations. To that end, New Hope has "helped set up more than 100 agricultural co-operatives to help peasant farmers expand the scale of their farms from family plots to large industrialised tracts, and 16 underwriting companies that assist peasant farmers in obtaining loans to expand production". And in 2010 he established the New Hope Financial Company "to promote the development of our agricultural sector through combining capital and industry".

Where next for Liu Yonghau?

Somewhat modestly, he says that he is trying "to learn more about China's macro economy to develop a more sophisticated way of thinking", and to gain sufficient international experience "to build his company into a world-class feed producer and agribusiness operator within the next five years".

KIRAN MAZUMDAR-SHAW

Business in India in 1978 was no picnic for anyone, let alone a young woman attempting to establish a brand-new company in a then unknown industry.

First, there was Licence Raj, a nightmare of red tape established by Jawaharlal Nehru to implement his belief that economic development should be driven by government planning rather than free market supply and demand. Approval by multiple government agencies was required just to establish a manufacturing business, and both the quantity and the price of the goods produced were subject to government control.

Second, there was gender. Despite the example of women like Indira Gandhi, who was groomed for the role of prime minister by her father, businesswomen were regarded as high risk. Banks wouldn't lend them

money, men wouldn't work for them, and the bureaucracy was controlled
by the established male hierarchy of religion and caste.

ଔଔଔ

Under the circumstances, it should have come as no surprise that
25-year-old Kiran Mazumdar was in two minds when approached by Irish
bioentrepreneur Leslie Auchincloss with a proposition to establish a joint
venture producing industrial enzymes, from papaya and other raw materials
native to India, for use in brewing and food processing.

On the one hand, she knew the science, having completed both an
honours degree in zoology at Bangalore University and a Graduate
Diploma in Malting and Brewing at the Ballarat Institute of Advanced
Education in Australia. As her father, India's foremost master brewer,
put it: "Brewing is an applied science - it's got fermentation, it's about
microbiology, it's about genetics, it's about anything you want".

On the other hand, she had personal experience of Indian industry's
gender bias. After taking top place as the only female in her brewing
diploma, and following up with a brewing traineeship at Australia's
leading beer producer, Carlton and United Breweries, she had returned
to India to find that no one was interested in hiring a woman as a master
brewer.

But then, as she would do on many more occasions throughout her career,
Mazumdar paid heed to her own advice: "Listen to the little drummer
in you who keeps saying: break free, become large, build something
memorable". She formed a 70:30 joint venture with Auchincloss, and set
about building India's first ever biotechnology business, in a rented garage
in Bangalore, with Rs.10,000 (about $1200) and two employees.

ଔଔଔ

Despite threats of physical violence from rabid unionists and chronic
failures of key infrastructure, including clean water and stable power
supplies, Mazumdar built the business rapidly, exporting her first

enzymes to the United States and Europe within a year of establishing the company. By 1983 her business had grown sufficiently to acquire a 20-acre site outside Bangalore, borrow $250,000 to build a new solid substrate fermentation plant, and begin investing in R&D in novel enzyme technology.

But back in Ireland, Leslie Auchincloss had decided to retire, and in 1989 he sold his business, including his 30% stake in Biocon India, to Unilever.

Unilever's business was specialty chemicals, a good fit with enzymes, but the little drummer was back at work in Mazumdar's head. She looked at the extraordinary growth in India's contract IT business, powered by the reforms introduced by then finance minister Manmohan Singh, and thought "why shouldn't I do the same thing in biotechnology?" And in 1994, she did just that, establishing a new company, Syngene International, to provide cost-effective research and development for the international biotechnology and pharmaceutical industries.

From brewing to enzyme manufacturing, and from enzymes to contract R&D for the biotech industry, for Kiran Mazumdar and her little drummer the next move was obvious. It was time to set up a biopharmaceutical company in her own right. But her minority shareholder, Unilever, simply wasn't interested.

And then, in the mid-1990s, three transformational events occurred.

First, Biocon developed and patented a new solid substrate bioreactor that facilitated the cultivation and extraction of microorganisms used in the production of both industrial enzymes and biopharmaceuticals. The Plafractor, as it was known, was so successful that the company's business trebled in the course of a year.

Second, in a further demonstration of her ability to form alliances with the West, she accepted another proposal, this time from a Scot, who offered her his hand in marriage. Delighted by her acceptance, John Shaw left his textile business behind in the Netherlands to join Mazumdar, now Mazumdar-Shaw, and help build Biocon in India.

And, third, Unilever sold its specialty chemicals business, including its share in Biocon, to ICI, who were obliged under the articles of association of Biocon India to offer preemptive rights to existing shareholders.

The stars were all aligned. John Shaw put up the cash, and the newly family-owned company moved definitively into the business of biopharmaceuticals.

ฺ฿฿฿

Biocon's foray into biopharmaceuticals began with generic lovastatin, a high-value cholesterol-lowering agent whose patent expired in 2001, but soon extended to include a variety of other statins, hormones and monoclonal antibodies, including an innovative technology for the production of recombinant human insulin in yeast. Most of these products have been partnered with international pharmaceutical companies, and in 2012 Biocon announced an option agreement with Bristol-Myers Squibb to market Biocon's prospective oral insulin product - the Holy Grail of biopharmaceuticals. As Kiran Mazumdar-Shaw put it: "I would love to see one of our novel drugs make it big with the 'Made in India' label. Oral insulin is Biocon's big bet".

In 2004, Biocon listed on the Bombay Stock Exchange, becoming only the second Indian company to achieve a market capitalisation of over $1 billion on its first day. And in 2007, the company sold its enzymes business to Denmark's Novozymes, thus completing its transformation from an enzyme business to a fully integrated biopharmaceutical company. With around 5,000 employees, most of whom are university graduates, Biocon is now India's largest biotech company. Targeting chronic diseases where medical needs are as yet largely unmet, it has introduced two novel biological agents. The first, for head and neck cancer, was introduced in 2006, while the second, a monoclonal antibody for the treatment of the autoimmune disease psoriasis, received regulatory approval in India in 2013.

To paraphrase Kiran Mazumdar-Shaw, it's a piece of the new India, making Indians proud.

ଓଓଓ

But the little drummer is also hard at work on another front: "I am very concerned about the fact that India as a country does not have a national health system", says Mazumdar-Shaw, "and I am determined to try and influence the government to really build one".

Meanwhile, she's not holding her breath. Both personally and through the Biocon Foundation, Mazumdar-Shaw has committed substantial funds to establishing a series of initiatives aimed at providing affordable health services to the rural poor. They include the world's largest cancer hospital; grassroots health-monitoring networks linking small rural clinics to larger hospitals; and a micro-insurance program that has the potential to provide quality health care and medicines to millions of villagers for an annual fee of just $3/head.

As she told Anuradha Raghunathan of *Forbes Asia* in a recent interview: "Philanthropy is not charity; it is about social impact".

INNOVATION, BUILDING NATIONS

What made these three so successful? Of the many things they have in common, one stands out: innovation. All three have innovated constantly and at every level: in their business dealings, in their manufacturing processes, and in their impact on society.

All three came up with innovative ways to overcome hostile business environments: Kiran Mazumdar-Shaw got rid of antagonistic unionists by automating her production line; Liu Yonghao and his brothers recognised specialist agriculture as the only plausible starting point for a private company in post-Mao China; and Mo Ibrahim put in place board structures that made it impossible for his employees to offer bribes.

All three introduced new processes and products: Yonghao and his brothers computerised first their animal husbandry programs and then much of Chinese agriculture; Mo designed mobile phone networks that delivered the economic and social benefits of cellular phone technology to hundreds of millions of people in 15 nations across Africa; and Kiran found a new method for manufacturing human insulin and built it into India's largest biotechnology company.

And then they brought their innovative minds to bear on the problems of their societies: Mo Ibrahim created a prize to make African presidents honest; Kiran Mazumdar-Shaw designed an affordable national health service; and Liu Yonghao came up with an "Agriculture Lifting-off Plan" for China.

All three have seen the first two of their innovative ideas succeed and prosper, driving the development of manufacturing and service industries that are transforming the economies of their regions.

The outcomes of their social innovations, on the other hand, remain to be seen. Perhaps Kiran Mazumdar-Shaw speaks for all three when she says of her country: "It doesn't understand the economics of innovation - the whole innovation ecosystem isn't there".

But that's not to say that it won't be there soon, at least if these three have anything to do with it. All three of them are utterly committed to the future development of the lands of their birth: Kiran Mazumdar-Shaw says she is driven by a deep desire to "heal the old India by beating the West at its own game"; Mo Ibrahim describes himself as "an African boy who made good in Europe, but never forgot Africa"; and Liu Yonghao, conscious of the fact that China has 20% of the world's population but only 7% of its arable land, will not rest until he has completed the economic, social and technological transformation of Chinese agriculture.

KEY SOURCES

MO IBRAHIM

Ken Auletta, "The dictator index", *The New Yorker*, March 7, 2011.

Geraldine Bedell, "The man giving Africa a brighter future", *The Observer*, February 1, 2009.

Carrie Gracie, "Mo Ibrahim", *The Interview, BBC*, October 17, 2009.

Moky Makura, *Africa's Greatest Entrepreneurs*, Penguin Books, 2008.

William Wallis, "Lunch with the FT: Mo Ibrahim", *Financial Times*, February 15, 2008.

LIU YONGHAO
David Barboza, "Contradictions in China, and the rise of a billionaire family", *The New York Times*, January 1, 2009.

Hu Haiyan, "Fields of hope", *China Daily European Weekly*, March 11, 2011.

Mariko Hayashibara, "New hope for China's entrepreneurs", *Asian Business* (Hong Kong), June 1998.

"The 1980's: legend of wealth", *China Internet Information Center*, October 27, 2008.

KIRAN MAZUMDAR-SHAW
Subroto Bagchi, "Powerwoman Kiran Mazumdar-Shaw", *Forbes India*, September 5, 2009.

Ceylon-Ananda Blogspot, "Kiran Mazumdar-Shaw: Founder of Biocon, a biotech company and Asia's largest insulin maker", May 6, 2012.

Ariel Levy, "Drug test", *The New Yorker*, January 2, 2012.

Adi Narayan, "From brewing, an Indian biotech is born", *Bloomberg Businessweek*, February 24, 2011.

Anuradha Raghunathan, "Heroes of philanthropy: Kiran Mazumdar-Shaw's affordable health care legacy", *Forbes Asia*, June 10, 2013.

Kanika Singh, "In conversation with Kiran Mazumdar-Shaw", *Merinews*, February 20, 2009.

An individual with an epic ambition to change the world, who …	Mo Ibrahim	Liu Yonghao	Kiran Mazumdar-Shaw
	Born: 1946, Eshket, Northern Sudan; Education: BSc, Alexandria; MSc, Bradford; PhD, Birmingham; Organisation: Celtel	Born: 1951, Sichuan Province, China; Education: Sichuan Engineering Vocational Technology College; Organisation: New Hope Group	Born: 1953, Bangalore, India; Education: BSc (Hons), Bangalore; Grad Dip in Malting & Brewing, Ballarat Institute of Advanced Education; Organisation: Biocon
.. sees and seizes opportunities for change ..			
Opportunistic: aggressively seeks and adopts new ideas	Observing the lack of fixed-line telephone services in Africa …	Liu and his three brothers foresaw rising demands not only for high-protein foodstuffs, such as meat and eggs, but also for high-quality feed grains for China's pigs and poultry.	Offered the opportunity to partner an Irish biotechnology company, she initially applied her brewing skills to the production of enzymes for industrial applications …..
& Visionary: intuitively grasps the big picture and how it might evolve	… he realised that low-cost cellular phone technology could transform Africa's society and economy, creating new jobs and infrastructure …	"The market was huge and there was hardly any competition. We just happened to be 16 years ahead of anyone else".	… but soon realised that there was a much larger opportunity, for her business and for India, in applying the same technology to the production of biopharmaceuticals.
.. senses the way forward ..			
Innovative: thinks creatively, ignores boundaries, disrupts the status quo	… by establishing rural networks and banking services in areas where they were previously non-existent, …	"If the national economy functions like a human body, state-owned enterprises serve as the skeleton, while non-public businesses are the blood and muscles".	She developed a new orally active formulation of human insulin …
but Pragmatic: recognises constraints, devises practical solutions, creates value	… in "the one place on earth where licences were available for free. Nobody wanted to go in".	"Both are vital to sustain life".	… and struck a licensing deal with Bristol-Myers Squibb to market her product around the globe.
.. attracts the necessary resources ..			
Persuasive: articulate and convincing communicator, consummate networker	Ibrahim's closest colleagues moved with him from British Telecom to his consultancy business, and from there to Celtel, …	In 1993 he joined the Chinese People's Political Consultative Conference as a representative of industry, gaining "lots of opportunities to communicate with outstanding entrepreneurs and experts", and used it as a forum to persuade his fellow entrepreneurs …	Newly married to fellow businessperson John Shaw, she said "Now, John. You've got a career in the textile industry. I've got a career in the biotech industry. One of us has got to give up our career, and it's not me".

& Empowering: attracts talent, inspires loyalty, rewards excellence	... and when Celtel was sold in 2005 his staff walked away with $500 million. One hundred of them, mostly African, became millionaires.	... to establish and fund the Guangcai Program, which aims to alleviate rural poverty by helping communities build new enterprises.	Success is about "getting ordinary people to do extraordinary things".

.. and pursues the dream ..

Focussed: passionate and highly energetic perfectionist, totally committed to an overriding vision	"My heroes as a young man were people like Einstein, Madame Curie. I never had a doubt that I wanted to do engineering".	By 2010, 12 years after listing on the Shenzhen Stock Exchange, Liu Yonghao's New Hope Group was the third-largest animal feed producer in the world, and one of China's largest producers of pork, milk and poultry. But he was ready for more.	"I am a very determined person who will rise to any challenge thrown my way. I have a deep sense of values and integrity and will not stand for dishonesty and injustice. A sense of purpose has been my underlying incentive".
& Confident: driven by unconditional self-belief, assumes absolute authority and accountability	And after 20 years at the forefront of mobile communications technology, "it was a no-brainer that the cellular route would be a great success in Africa".	Arguing the need to "combine capital with industry", he founded New Hope Financial Company with the aim of giving the New Hope Group "the largest market value among the domestic enterprises in the fields of agriculture and animal husbandry".	"Biocon is about doing things in a differentiated way - daring to be different so that you stand out. Biocon's byline - 'The difference lies in our DNA' - has enabled us to chart our own business destiny".

.. regardless of the odds ..

Resilient: flexible, thrives on change and uncertainty, learns from mistakes	"Africa has a lot of resources. You start to ask yourself: Why are we poor? Why aren't we doing better?" The answer is, "We are poor because we are mismanaging our resources, our economy, our people, our government". Ibrahim resolved to tackle the issue head on, and ...	"Private companies couldn't easily buy land or build factories. Enterprises in western China found it even harder to get loans".	"Succeeding against all odds has always given me a great high".
& Courageous: bold, intelligent risk-taker, undaunted by criticism, determined to succeed	... in 2006, he established the Mo Ibrahim Foundation, which aims to enhance the performance of African governments and their leaders by publishing an annual ranking of all 53 African nations on the basis of the transparency and efficacy of their governance.	To grow, the company built stocks of equipment and land by aggressive takeovers of uncompetitive state-owned factories.	When unionists burned her effigy she gave them severance pay and automated their jobs.

Chapter 4

SPACE INVASION

THROUGHOUT HISTORY THE OPENING UP of new geographic frontiers has followed similar lines: first come the explorers, then the conquerors, and next the entrepreneurs.

When Vasco da Gama sailed around the Cape of Good Hope to India in 1497 he opened the way first to the armadas of Portuguese, Spanish, British and Dutch vessels intent on building empire, and then to the merchant ships belonging to traders eager to exploit the wealth of gold and silver, tea and spices of the East.

And when US explorers opened up routes across the mid-West and the Rockies to California, the slaughter of the Indian population was soon followed by transcontinental railroads taking settlers West and bringing back timber, cattle and gold.

And space is no different.

Driven by the Cold War, Russia launched the *Sputnik* in October 1957 and the United States played catch-up, landing the first man on the moon in July 1969. But with no one to conquer and limited funds, the government space agencies soon ran out of competitive steam, jointly establishing the International Space Station in 1998.

Enter the extraterrestrials.

Sir Richard Branson, the thrill seeker for whom each successive Virgin business has provided fresh excitement, and each hostile geographic environment a new challenge, wants to be with his two children on board *Virgin Galactic*'s first flight into space.

Jeff Bezos, the consummate marketer who set out to make Amazon "the world's most consumer-centric company", now wants to "accelerate access to things that inspire, educate and entertain" by providing his customers with safe, low-cost travel into space.

And Elon Musk, the prolific inventor who has engineered everything from PayPal's financial systems to Tesla's electric cars, wants to see the spacecraft he designs be the first commercial cargo ships to deliver astronauts to the international space station, and one day to Mars.

RICHARD BRANSON

Clarrie Gardner was just ten years old in 1925 when an Italian aviator flew over his family home on the fringe of the Nullarbor Plain in outback Australia. "It was magic. From that moment I wanted to fly". And he did, flying 48 missions during the Second World War as a bomber pilot, including 14 in the Battle of Berlin, and earning the RAAF's highest honour, the Distinguished Flying Cross and Bar.

In 2007, Clarrie had just turned 92 when his granddaughter Angela, a Virgin staff member, mentioned her grandfather's enduring fascination with flight to Richard Branson. "Tell him there'll be a free seat on *Virgin Galactic* for him on his 100th birthday", said Branson, "it will be just fantastic to have him on board". Angela, like countless others before her, was captivated by Branson's easy charm and infectious enthusiasm. And, Clarrie, like countless others before him, was forever more a Branson fan.

ଓଓଓ

When Richard Branson's mother decided that she was going to make her children independent, she was not mucking around: while other four-year-olds were watching TV, Branson was deposited in the

countryside and told to find his own way home. And it worked. Sent
to a series of boarding schools from the age of eight, his autobiography
records that he excelled at sport at the first, was caught late at night on
the way back to his dormitory - from the bedroom of the headmaster's
daughter - at the second, and compensated for his lack of academic skills
by cheating in ancient history exams at the third. Bidding him farewell
from Stowe School on the eve of his 17th birthday, the headmaster said:
"Congratulations Branson, I predict that you will either go to prison or
become a millionaire".

In fact, Branson was already en route to both. Even before leaving
school, he had begun laying the groundwork for his first venture, a
countercultural magazine aimed at 16-25-year-olds, for which he solicited
interviews and advertisements from a public phone box at the entrance to
his school.

And he was already a consummate salesman. By the time the first edition
of *Student* appeared on January 26, 1968, Branson had raised enough
advertising revenue to enable him to distribute 50,000 copies of the
magazine free, and subsequent editions carried interviews with everyone
from Mick Jagger to John Lennon, boosting circulation to 100,000.
The magazine was such a success that the BBC invited the 21-year-old
Branson to present his story as part of a documentary series called *People
of tomorrow*.

And then, shades of things to come, he used it to build more businesses,
starting with the Student Advisory Centre, which offered services ranging
from counselling potential suicides to dispensing advice on where to
find medical practices willing to provide safe and affordable abortions. It
also led to his first scrape with the law. Arrested under the 1889 Indecent
Advertisement Act for printing the term venereal disease in his publicity
brochures, he was rapped gently across the knuckles by a judge who very
reasonably saw the law as archaic.

But if he was a consummate salesman, he was also a born businessman.
Tiring of *Student* magazine, he used its last edition to launch the very first

Virgin company, a mail-order business selling Britain's first discounted pop records. And then, when a postal strike threatened to derail Virgin Mail Order, he moved on to establish the Virgin Record Shop, where he discovered, seemingly by accident, that the goods and services tax levied by the British government could be miraculously avoided by taking a van full of records, ostensibly destined for sales tax-free Belgium, to and from France on the cross-Channel ferry.

But not for long. After four trips and net savings of £20,000, the Virgin Record Shop was raided by Customs and Excise and a contrite Richard Branson spent the night in jail before being bailed out by Mum, who also guaranteed his undertaking to pay both the tax and a £40,000 fine.

And Branson moved on. If we are going to be in the record selling business, he asked, why not produce them as well? With his cousin, Simon Draper, and the rest of the Virgin team in tow, Branson acquired a country manor house in Oxfordshire, set it up as a recording studio, and picked a winner: Mike Oldfield, a backing musician and wannabe composer rejected by mainstream studios, recorded an instrumental album for Virgin Records that sold 16 million copies and stayed on Britain's best-selling list for the next five years.

That single recording, *Tubular Bells*, not only paid off Branson's debts, but also enabled him to recruit a string of stars to his recording studio, including Boy George and, for better or worse, the Sex Pistols, whose venomous rendition of God Save the Queen, blasted toward the House of Commons from a barge on the Thames during the celebrations of Queen Elizabeth's silver jubilee, provided yet another boost to Virgin's anti-establishment image.

Tubular Bells success also set the scene for all that was to follow. If one could move so easily from flogging records to producing them, what about books and games? By 1984, Virgin Records, Virgin Music, Virgin Books and Virgin Games, as well as the first Virgin Megastore, were all on the scene. And the three defining pillars of the Virgin culture were all firmly in place.

First, and foremost, Virgin businesses had to be fun. They were light-hearted, full of creative flair and style, always innovative and always willing to break the establishment mould.

Second, they had to offer a serious challenge. For Branson it was the challenge of creating a brand-new business, and attracting the best people to run it. For those people, it was the challenge of building a business in which they now had a personal stake, while still remaining at heart a part of the overall Virgin team.

And, third, they took risks. Nothing great was going to occur without taking risk. In Branson's famous words: "Screw it, let's do it!"

And Branson was about to take his biggest risk yet.

ᘒᘒᘒ

Enthralled by the prospect of mounting a challenge to British Airways' virtual monopoly over the London-New York route, Branson acquired a second-hand 747, filled it with friends, celebrities, champagne and fine food, and took off across the Atlantic. With a fleet of one, he told BBC's John Wilson: "We would either have the best safety record in the world, or the worst".

Over the course of the next five years, Virgin Atlantic acquired more planes and more destinations, and Branson promoted them with ever more hair-raising stunts: first crashing then smashing the speed record for a sea crossing of the Atlantic, then traversing both the Atlantic and the Pacific in hot air balloons before crashing into both the Algerian desert and the Pacific Ocean in attempts to circumnavigate the globe.

He also flirted for the first and only time with the Stock Exchange, taking Virgin Group public in 1985 and then buying it back two years later, bleeding from the experience of regular reporting to shareholders.

And British Airways executives were also after Branson blood. Accustomed to seeing off competition from upstart airlines, they were not amused by either the competition or the "grinning pullover" whose stunts were upstaging their massive advertising budget. In what was to become known as the "dirty tricks" campaign, they set about undermining both Branson's credibility and Virgin's credit rating, to the point where both were in danger of going under.

Discovering for the first time that business wasn't just about fun, Branson addressed the credibility issue by suing British airways for libel, netting £500,000 and a public apology. But his plummeting credit rating was a much tougher call. Faced with little or no choice, he made the ultimate sacrifice, selling the jewel in his crown, Virgin Records, to Thorn EMI for £560 million. And he cried, he says, all the way to the bank, for what felt like the loss of a child.

Cashed up for the first time in his career, Branson embarked on a new phase of empire-building, creating more and more Virgin businesses and passing each one on to a loyal lieutenant to run. Virgin mobile phone companies, health clubs and retail outlets sprouted around the globe. Virgin was no longer just a superb brand: it had become a way of life. And Branson, as he thumbed his nose at one staid old establishment company after another, had become a popular hero, touted as a future prime minister, the man who could do no wrong.

And then, at the height of his success, a new - responsible, respectable, but a tad less exciting - Branson began to appear.

ଝଝଝ

On the one hand, he began buying out failing government businesses that - although undoubtedly important and potentially valuable - hardly fitted Virgin's anti-establishment mould. Virgin Trains? Even when painted lipstick red they were scarcely likely to excite Virgin fans. And Virgin Money? Selling the group's finance arm, Virgin One, to the Royal Bank of Scotland, and then buying back the profitable bits from the British government after the global financial crisis, was certainly a coup, but hardly vintage Branson.

And on the other, he began to look for ways "to not just build businesses, but also to try and make a difference" at both a social and an environmental level. And, as usual, Richard Branson didn't do it by halves.

On the environmental front, he established the $25 million Virgin Earth Challenge to encourage the development of technologies for the removal of atmospheric carbon dioxide, and pledged that he would invest all of the profits from his transport businesses - expected to total $3 billion over ten years - in the search for sources of sustainable energy.

And on the social side, he created Virgin Unite, a not-for-profit foundation that aims to use Branson's contacts and Virgin's resources to help make businesses, governments and the social sector work more effectively together to address major social issues. One of Virgin Unite's first initiatives, The Elders, comprises a group of very senior statesmen, chaired by Nelson Mandela, who work behind the scenes to resolve international conflicts.

By 2012, Branson was spending 70% of his time, and bringing all of his entrepreneurial skills, to these and other non-profit public good ventures. But, fortunately for those who hanker after the swashbuckling Branson of old, the remaining 30% is devoted to a venture of which Branson says: "It's going to be ridiculously exciting. It's the start of a whole new era".

ଓଓଓ

In many respects that era started almost 100 years earlier, in 1919, when French entrepreneur Raymond Orteig offered a $25,000 prize to the first person to make a nonstop flight across the Atlantic.

History relates that the Orteig prize was ultimately won seven years later by Charles Lindbergh. But more important, from the viewpoint of Orteig's philosophical descendant and space entrepreneur Peter Diamandis, was the fact that the very existence of the prize had stimulated investment of almost 20 times the prize money in the development of aircraft technology. Diamandis resolved to provide a similar boost for space research, orchestrating a $10 million prize - the Ansari X Prize - for the first privately built spaceship, capable of carrying three or more people, to penetrate the space barrier, 100 km above the surface of the earth, twice within a period of two weeks.

That prize was won in 2004, eight years after its announcement, by *SpaceShip One*, designed by the legendary Burt Rutan, the space engineer who had earlier designed the first aircraft to make a nonstop circuit around the globe without refuelling. And in 2005, Rutan and Richard Branson announced a joint venture - The Spaceship Company - to build a fleet of commercial launch aircraft and suborbital spaceships.

Seven years on, both goals have been achieved. By the beginning of 2012, *SpaceShip Two* had made 30 atmospheric test flights, half of them being launched from its three-hulled carrier vehicle, *White Knight Two*. With room for six passengers and two pilots, *SpaceShip Two* will be released from *White Knight Two* at 50,000 feet, ignite its rocket engine, and soar to 100 km above the surface of the earth, where passengers will experience five minutes of weightlessness before the spacecraft begins its descent, folding its wings back into the shape of a shuttlecock to slow its fall. At $200,000 a ride, there are already over 500 customers on the waiting list.

And with typically brilliant branding, Branson proclaims: "Space is Virgin territory".

ßßß

But hype aside, from Branson's perspective, the progress toward liftoff has been painfully slow. Every year since 2007, he has claimed that *Virgin Galactic*'s first commercial flight is just 18 months away, and every year it has been delayed. Some of those on the original passenger list, including his father, will no longer be on board. But few doubt that the launch day will come, and when it does, Branson and his two adult children will undoubtedly be there, celebrating yet another remarkable voyage into the unknown.

And what about Squadron Leader Clarrie Gardner, the Second World War bomber pilot, who was still dreaming about flying into space with Branson two weeks before he died in 2012 at the age of 97?

He'll be there too - at least in spirit - along with millions more of Richard Branson's admiring fans.

JEFF BEZOS

The Class of 2010 sat spellbound in the University Chapel at Princeton University as the founder and CEO of Amazon delivered the graduation address: "We are what we choose".

Recalling an incident in his childhood when he had reduced his grandmother - a heavy smoker - to tears with a clever but thoughtless calculation of the likely reduction, at two minutes per puff, in her lifespan, he said:

> What I want to talk to you about today is the difference between gifts and choices. Cleverness is a gift, kindness is a choice. Gifts are easy - they're given after all. Choices can be hard. You can seduce yourself with your gifts if you're not careful, and if you do, it'll probably be to the detriment of your choices.

And he went on to ask the graduands:

> How will you use your gifts? What choices will you make? Will inertia be your guide, or will you follow your passions? Will you wilt under criticism, or will you follow your convictions? Will you follow dogma, or will you be original? Will you play it safe, or will you be a little bit swashbuckling?"

Needless to say, the Class of 2010 knew the right answers to those questions. They all knew the Amazon story.

And Jeff Bezos had made every one of those choices.

ജ്ഞ

Jeff Bezos was just 30 years old when he faced the first big choice: "Will inertia be your guide, or will you follow your passions?"

It was a question that Bezos had not previously needed to confront. With loving parents, doting grandparents, good schools and great grades, he had sailed through electrical engineering and computer science at Princeton University and into a series of high-powered Wall Street jobs. By 1994, he was senior vice-president at D.E. Shaw, leading the search for new business opportunities in a firm renowned for devising innovative trading strategies.

And then he saw a statistic that amazed him. The Internet, long the province of government and academia, was growing at 2,300% a year, but with scarcely any commercial activity. From Bezos' perspective, it looked like a land-grab waiting to happen.

In characteristic style, Bezos crunched the numbers, looking for businesses where the Internet might offer customers significant benefits relative to existing marketing methods. He soon homed in on mail-order products, then narrowed the field to books. With millions of titles, far too many for a mail-order catalogue, but with inventory lists from major distributors already available on CDs, book retailing was a business custom-made for the Web! And he crunched the downside: only 1 in 10 fledgling Internet businesses were successful. But he knew his odds would be better than that.

He consulted his wife, Mackenzie, who said: "Go for it", questioned his boss, David Shaw, who sowed seeds of doubt: "That sounds like a really good idea, but it would be an even better idea for someone who didn't already have a good job". Then he made his own decision. Given the choice between inertia - the security of a highly paid Wall Street job - and the excitement of exploring new online frontiers, a chance perhaps to change the world, he chose to follow his passions.

Two months later, in July 1994, the Bezos family were on the road to Seattle: Mackenzie driving, family dog in the back, and Jeff hunched in the passenger seat tapping out the business plan for a company with such amazing potential that he later named it Amazon.

And it wasn't too long before Amazon began to live up to its name. Operating from the garage of his rented home, Bezos and two programmers wrote the prototypic Amazon code, tested it on friends and acquaintances, and opened it up to the public just one year after his arrival in Seattle. And within a month, without a single advertisement, they had sold books in every state of the United States and 45 other countries. As he told Joshua Quittner of *Time Magazine*: "Within the first few days, I knew this was going to be huge".

Two years later, Amazon was listed on NASDAQ, and by 1999, when *Time Magazine* named Bezos Person of the Year, the company had over $1 billion in sales and a market capitalisation more than 100 times that at the IPO. Bezos' parents, who had contributed $300,000 of the initial $1 million seed capital despite his dire predictions of potential failure, were billionaires, at least on paper.

But losses were also astronomical - over $700 million in 1999 - and the shareholders were becoming restless. With margins down and cash burn-up, market analysts were almost unanimous in the view that Bezos was growing too fast. Amazon, one said, should change its Web address to Amazon.toast!

And Bezos was facing his second big choice: "Will you wilt under criticism, or will you follow your convictions?"

The answer was never in doubt. Right from the start Bezos had stuck by two simple principles, one short term, the other decidedly long.

His short-term position was that shared by many CEOs with stakes in the dot. com boom: "Get large or get lost". In Bezos' opinion, there would only be one first-mover opportunity in online retailing, and he intended to grab as much of the market as he could get - from books to music, to toys, to groceries, to anything that anyone wanted to buy - while that opportunity lasted.

But his long-term position was unique. Bezos was determined to ensure Amazon's longevity by making it the world's most customer-centric company, and that meant continuing to invest in offering customers the widest selection, lowest prices, and most convenient delivery.

And that's what he did, powering right through the dot.com crash that wiped $5 trillion off US technology stocks, introducing more and more new products and new customer-friendly technologies, and emerging in 2003 as a profit-making operation with 400 retail partners and sales approaching $10 billion.

Which led to the third big choice: "Will you follow dogma, or will you be original?"

What do you do when you're 40 years old and have just finished building the biggest online store on Earth. Defend the patch? Wrong. Bezos opened it up, in three remarkable ways.

First, he not only invited third-party sellers to market their products, for a small commission, on Amazon's Web pages in competition with Amazon, but also offered Amazon affiliates the opportunity to earn commissions by placing links to Amazon on their Web sites. Either way, Amazon had more and more customers and more and more opportunities to sell them products that they had not yet realised they liked.

Second, he moved into cloud computing, establishing Amazon Web Services to sell access to Amazon's vast data storage, thousands of servers and associated software. Companies no longer generate their own electricity, he argued, so why should they build their own data centres? Why not treat data storage as a service? And that argument appealed to organisations ranging all the way from computer-hungry start-ups to entertainment giants like Netflix, whose video streaming service accounts for 25% of US Internet traffic.

And third, he went into competition, with himself. On November 19, 2007, the man who'd made his fortune selling hard copy books rolled out the Kindle e-reader, accompanied by 97,000 e-books at bargain basement prices. Less than six hours later, the Kindle was out of stock. And four years later, the product that Bezos called "the culmination of the many things we've been doing for fifteen years" appeared. The Kindle Fire Tablet wasn't just an e-reader, it was a media service, a mobile portal to Amazon's massive cloud of books, music and movies.

As he told Steven Levy of *Wired* magazine: "As a company ... we like to disrupt even our own business".

By 2011, Amazon was not just the world's largest online retailer, but also a major producer of consumer electronics and the largest provider of cloud computing. With over 150 million customers and 60,000 employees, it had revenues of $48 billion and a market capitalisation of over $100 billion.

And Bezos asked himself the fourth big question: "Will you play it safe, or will you be a little bit swashbuckling?"

In fact, he'd asked himself that question back in 2000, but given the state of the stock market at the time - Amazon's market capitalisation had fallen more than 90% in a year - it was probably just as well that he didn't tell Amazon shareholders his answer.

ଽଽଽ

Like almost every child who watched Neil Armstrong step onto the moon, Bezos was fascinated by the exploration of space. But unlike most others, he didn't want to be an astronaut: he wanted to be a space entrepreneur.

And that little bit of swashbuckling is just what began in September 2000, when Bezos very quietly founded Blue Origin, a private company whose goal is to develop technologies to enable private human access to space at dramatically lower cost and with increased reliability.

Remarkably, the existence of Blue Origin remained secret until 2003, when Bezos' exploration of potential launching sites in isolated parts of Texas was cut short as the helicopter he was travelling in crashed upside-down into a creek bed. Trapped in the wreck, Bezos and his colleagues were lucky to be alive, but the cat was well and truly out of the bag. Just what was the CEO of Amazon doing buying up vast tracts of land in Texas?

In fact, detailed information on Blue Origin's secretive activities is still in short supply, but what is available suggests that in many respects Bezos' approach is parallel to Branson's. Both hope to begin by exploiting the suborbital tourism market, and both plan to deploy reusable launch vehicles to propel spacecraft carrying up to six passengers into suborbital flight, providing them with a few minutes of weightlessness before returning to earth.

But whereas Branson's launch vehicle is an aircraft - albeit an unconventional one - Bezos will launch his *New Shepard* spacecraft - named after NASA astronaut Alan Shepard, the first American to enter suborbital space - from a vertical takeoff vertical landing rocket that has been described as resembling a stubby cigar.

Unfortunately for Bezos, that cigar was almost stubbed out in August 2011, after just one successful test flight, when a flight instability at an altitude of 45,000 feet caused automated safety systems to shut off thrust, leading to its destruction.

Bezos was undeterred: "Not the outcome any of us wanted, but we're signed up for this to be hard. We're already working on our next development vehicle". And, true to his word, in October 2012 Blue Origin successfully test-fired not only a new high-performance liquid hydrogen-powered rocket engine but also a revolutionary launch pad escape system, capable of rocketing the passengers and crew away to safety in the event of any failure in propulsion.

But he's also cautious. Unlike Richard Branson, he's not about to start taking flight deposits: the motto of Blue Origin is Gradatim Ferociter, Latin for "Step-by-Step, Ferociously".

ଧ୍ୟଧ୍ୟ

Bezos concluded his talk to the Princeton Class of 2010 with a prediction: "When you are 80 years old, and in a quiet moment of reflection narrating for only yourself the most personal version of your life story, the telling that will be most compact and meaningful will be the series of choices you have made. In the end, we are our choices. Build yourself a great story".

One thing's for sure, when Jeff looks back at the age of 80, he should be proud of both his choices and his story.

ELON MUSK

Elon Musk was a free spirit from day one. Whether it was the 6-year-old Elon walking halfway across the South African city of Pretoria to pay a forbidden visit to his cousins, the 10-year-old Elon buying and programming his first computer, or the 17-year-old Elon leaving home and country against his father's wishes to make a new life in North America, there was never any doubt that he would pursue his dreams, relentlessly.

And as he pursued his studies, first at Queen's University in Ontario and later at the University of Pennsylvania, where he completed an economics degree at the Wharton School and a second degree in physics, those dreams began to crystallise: "I tried to think, what are the really big problems that face the world, that will most affect the future of humanity? And the three that I thought were the most important were the Internet, transition to a sustainable energy economy, and space exploration, particularly making life multi-planetary. Those were the things that, if I had the opportunity, I would like to get involved in".

And he did, in all three, with a vengeance.

ଓଓଓ

In the summer of 1995, just as Amazon was going online in Seattle, Elon Musk moved to California to start a PhD in high-energy physics at Stanford University. He had seen it as a starting point for a career in sustainable energy, but now, surveying the scene in Silicon Valley, he became concerned that the surging wave of Internet commercialisation would pass him by. Two days after his arrival at Stanford, Musk dropped out to found an Internet company that he named Zip2 Corporation.

Like Amazon, whose entry to the Internet had been hugely facilitated by the availability of book distributors' lists on CD-ROM, Zip2 was an opportunistic play aimed at being first to translate an old-world business onto the Web. Working in partnership with major media companies, including the *Chicago Tribune* and the *New York Times*, Musk simply spliced commercial business directories, available on CD-ROM, with newly emerging digital maps to produce the Internet's first door-to-door restaurant and city guides.

From Musk's perspective, that was just the start - he was already dreaming of building a major Internet brand - but he was about to learn a hard lesson. With upward of $40 million of venture capital money invested in Zip2, Musk's equity had been diluted to just 7%, and the VCs had a decidedly shorter-term view of its potential. Installing one of their number as CEO, they sold out for just over $300 million - the then highest price paid for an Internet company - and Musk walked away with $22 million, plus a sore head: "What they should have done is put me in charge. Great things will never happen with VCs or professional managers".

But he didn't let the headache slow him down.

ଢ଼ଢ଼ଢ଼

Musk's approach to choosing the focus for his next Internet venture was both simple and salutary: "Where", he asked, "is there still room for a lot of innovation on the Internet?"

Put that way, the answer was obvious: "I chose the financial services sector because money is just an entry in a database. You don't need any big infrastructure upgrade". And so was the opportunity: "The idea was to aggregate all of your financial services seamlessly in one place and make it really easy to use so you don't have to go to multiple financial institutions to take care of your mortgage, your credit cards, your banking relationship, insurance, mutual funds".

Inspired by the concept of building a global financial services company, Musk put $10 million of his Zip2 gains into his new venture, named X.com, and attracted more from Sequoia and other venture capital firms. But the real value, from the investors' viewpoint, was in X.com's ability to transfer money by e-mail, an attribute that was further enhanced when X.com acquired Confinity, a cryptography company whose Web site enabled users to reconcile electronic payments and update their bank accounts.

Appointed CEO of the merged company, Musk drove the development of a series of novel e-mail payment technologies, including an inexpensive means of authenticating customers' bank accounts by making pairs of random deposits, of less than a dollar, to create unique four-digit pin numbers. But his frequent clashes with Confinity founders Max Levchin and Peter Thiel soon led to his replacement by Thiel, who renamed the company PayPal and two years later sold it to eBay for $1.5 billion.

Elon Musk's share was $165 million. The time had come to pursue the rest of those dreams.

ଛଛଛ

In Musk's view PayPal, like Zip2, had been sold long before it reached its true potential. Now, with sufficient cash in the bank to call his own shots, he was determined to not only maintain control of any future company he founded, but also to maintain its focus on the long term. And both sustainable energy and space fell squarely into that category.

In the case of sustainable energy, he identified two clear targets. One was to replace gasoline-powered cars with electric vehicles, the other to replace coal with solar power as the major source of electricity. Musk expects both outcomes to occur within 40 years.

In 2003, after failing to persuade the inventors of an impressive lithium ion battery-powered car called the TZero to join him in forming a production company, Musk and a colleague, engineer JB Straubel, and a second group of TZero suitors led by e-reading pioneer Martin Eberhard, joined forces to found Tesla Motors.

Installing Eberhard as CEO, but mindful of maintaining control, Musk led Tesla's first three capital raisings, personally investing a total of $70 million as well as taking a leadership role in the design and engineering of the Tesla Roadster, the first battery-powered sports car. Then, in 2008, with the company buffeted by internal management issues and depressed capital markets, he took over personally as CEO and head of product design.

The first of those products, the $100,000 Roadster sports car, came to market in 2008, with a Ferrari-like performance and fuel costs less than one-tenth of a comparable gasoline-powered car. Which shows, said Musk "that you don't have to give up something that is fun to be conscious of the Earth".

But Musk's ultimate goal - to produce affordable electric vehicles for mass markets - was also well on track. The $50,000 model S sedan, with optional battery packs ranging up to 300 miles, was launched in 2012, and a $30,000 version is on the way. Meanwhile, both Daimler and Toyota - now also significant investors in Tesla - are using Tesla power trains in their latest electric vehicles.

Will it happen? The November 2012 announcement by Edward Loh, Editor-in-Chief of Motor Trend, certainly suggests so: "Musk has often stated that his goal wasn't to build the world's best electric car, but the world's best car that just happens to be electric. Well, we believe he has, which is why the Tesla Model S is Motor Trend's 2013 Car of the Year".

And what about the other side of the equation, the electricity supply? Musk has a finger in that pie as well. In 2006, he invested $10 million in Solar City, a solar panel installation company that just happens to be run by his cousins, Lyndon and Peter Rive. By allowing its customers to lease solar panels rather than paying for them upfront, and profiting further from plummeting global prices for photovoltaic cells, it has grown rapidly to become the largest installer of residential solar systems in the United States.

As he once dreamed, Musk is successfully addressing both sides of the sustainable energy equation. But, despite everything that he has poured into sustainable energy, it's nothing compared to the time, money and effort he's investing in space!

಄಄಄

As for Tesla, Musk's space odyssey began soon after the PayPal sale. And, as for Tesla, Musk led the early financing rounds, ultimately investing upward of $100 million in the new company, SpaceX. And again, as for Tesla, he had a very clear vision of what he wanted to achieve: to make spaceflight routine and affordable.

To Musk, that meant reducing the cost of launch rockets by at least a factor of ten, while simultaneously increasing their cargo-bearing capacity by a similar margin. Ultimately, he reasoned, it would require reusable rockets - something that no national space program had ever achieved.

Knowing nothing about space engineering Musk hired the best, interviewing each candidate personally not only to ensure that they were willing to sign on to his extraterrestrial vision, but also to satisfy himself of their ability to work happily in a close-knit multidisciplinary team ranging all the way from technologists to marketers. He called it his "no assholes policy".

And then, seemingly belying his own words, he proceeded to set them tasks that were unprecedented relative to the achievements of national space programs and their commercial suppliers, who had hitherto operated on a virtually limitless cost-plus basis. And as self-appointed chief designer and CEO, he demanded that the company's rocket engines be designed for reusability from the start, at one-tenth of historic cost.

Like a boy playing with a Lego set, Musk designed a series of rockets - starting with *Falcon 1*, which in September 2008 was the first privately developed rocket to make it into Earth orbit, and culminating with *Falcon 9* - all of which used and reused common components. And sitting on top of all of them was the *Dragon*, a multipurpose spacecraft designed initially to carry cargo and later to become the module for taking up to seven people into space at a fraction of the cost currently charged for trips on the Russian *Soyuz* spacecraft.

On May 25, 2012, a SpaceX *Dragon* spacecraft launched from a *Falcon 9* rocket became the first privately developed vehicle to dock at the International Space Station. For 1,800 elated SpaceX employees it was the culmination of three nail-biting days since the launch; for Elon Musk it was the vindication of ten years personal commitment, often in the face of trenchant criticism and sometimes frank disbelief.

So, could they do it again? Absolutely. Five months later, on October 10, a second *Dragon* arrived at the space station bearing crew supplies and scientific experiments, the first of 12 planned resupply missions under NASA's $1.6 billion Commercial Supply Services contract with SpaceX. And on October 28, 2012, the *Dragon* spacecraft returned to Earth with scientific samples that had been stored in the space station's freezers since the retirement of the space shuttle.

ଷଷଷ

So, where next? Remember those college dreams? And remember the rider on number 3: "space exploration, *particularly making life multi-planetary*"? Well, Elon's serious - especially about the lovely red planet, Mars.

> I think it's extremely important that life become multi-planetary. Think of the history of life on Earth. Forget about the parochial concerns of humanity. What would any intelligent species say were the really important elements?

And he answers for them:

> There was the advent of single-celled life, then multi-celled life, the development of plants, then animals, the transition from life in the oceans to life on land. On that list, the extension of life to multiple planets will be at least as important as life going from oceans to land, and arguably more important.

Why? Musk sees it partly as a simple insurance policy, ensuring the survival of humanity in the face of natural or man-made disasters, and partly as an expression of human nature at its best. As he put it to Marlow Stern of *The Daily Beast*: "Do we want a future where humanity is a space-going civilisation that's out there, understanding the stars, exploring the universe, and doing exciting bold things? Or do we want a future where we are forever confined to earth until the eventual disaster takes us out? I think we want to be out there exploring the stars".

How? "Well, it's extremely difficult, but it's possible, just barely, to create a self-sustaining ecosystem on Mars. That's the only viable place". But first, you need to "reduce the cost of moving to Mars to around the cost of a middle-class home in California - maybe to around half a million dollars" And to do that, Musk needs to reduce the cost of space travel at least 100-fold.

When? By the middle of the century: "It would be a good place to retire".

SPACE ON STEROIDS

These three aren't just invading "outer" space, they're invading everybody's. If anyone ever told them about sticking to their knitting, they weren't listening. They are constantly on the lookout for new opportunities, and have no trouble finding them. As Richard Branson puts it: "Business opportunities are like buses. There's always another coming along".

But none of them are prepared to take on just any business. All three seek to create very big businesses for which there is a very serious need. And when it comes to the question of defining "serious need", they have no qualms about relying wholly and solely on their own judgement. For Branson, it's sectors "where things are not being run well by other people". For Bezos, it's "what the customer needs" (which may or may not be what the customer thinks they want). And for Musk, it's what's important for "the future of humanity".

Space travel ticks all three boxes.

First, there seems to be little doubt that they can do it better than government. According to NASA, Amazon Web Services took 5 hours to process 180,000 Saturn photographs that would have taken 15 days in-house, and the successful docking of a SpaceX *Dragon* with the International Space Station was "absolutely incredible".

Second, there's no doubt about what the customers want. *Virgin Galactic* already has $100 million in advance bookings, and the current SpaceX contract with NASA is worth $1.6 billion.

And third, there's the future of humanity thing. As Musk puts it: "It's important that we attempt to extend life beyond Earth now. It is the first time in the four-billion-year history of Earth that it's been possible, and that window could be open for a long time - hopefully it is - or it could be open for a short time. We should err on the side of caution and do something now".

ଧଧଧ

And what of the risks?

Fortunately, not one of these three is the least bit daunted by high levels of risk. Their spectacular crashes in hot-air balloons (Branson), helicopters (Bezos) and high-performance sports cars (Musk), and their willingness to bet the bank on businesses, such as Virgin Atlantic, Amazon and Tesla, that others regarded as unviable, are all testament to that.

As SpaceX's VP of Propulsion Development, Tom Mueller, commented to Andrew Chaikin of *Air and Space Magazine*: "There are a thousand things that can happen when you go to light a rocket engine, and only one of them is good".

And that's the one on which Branson, Bezos and Musk are laying their bets.

KEY SOURCES

RICHARD BRANSON

Chris Anderson, "Richard Branson: Life at 30,000 feet", TED Conversation, October 13, 2007.

Jason Ankeny, "Richard Branson on building an empire", *Entrepreneur.com*, June 19, 2012.

Richard Branson, *Losing my virginity: how I've survived, had fun, and made a fortune doing business my way*, Times Books, 1999.

Richard Butler, "Richard Branson: 'Screw it, let's do it'", in R.W. Butler and R.A. Russell (eds), *Giants of Tourism*, CAB International, 2010.

Alan Deutschman, "The enlightenment of Richard Branson", *Fast Company*, September 1, 2006.

Jon Metrikas and Suzy Foskett, "Clarence Charles Gardner, DFC & Bar, pilot, businessman, July 19, 1915 - July 20, 2012". *The Age*, September 25, 2012.

John Wilson, "Sir Richard Branson", *Meeting Myself Coming Back (Series 4), BBC Radio 4, Archive*, June 9, 2012.

JEFF BEZOS

George Anders, "Inside Amazon's idea machine: How Bezos decodes the customer", *Forbes Magazine*, April 23, 2012.

Chip Bayers, "The inner Bezos", *Wired*, March, 1999.

Jeff Bezos, "We are what we choose", *Graduation Speech, Princeton University*, May 30, 2010.

Leonard David, "Amazon.com's Jeff Bezos relaunches secretive private spaceship website", *SPACE.com*, November 18, 2011.

Steven Levy, "Jeff Bezos owns the Web in more ways than you think", *Wired*, November, 2011.

John H. Ostdick, "E-vangelist: after changing the retail industry and now shaking up the publishing world, the sky is the limit for Jeff Bezos' widening empire as Amazon takes to the cloud", *Success*, August, 2011.

Joshua Quittner, "An eye on the future", *Time Magazine*, December 27, 1999.

ELON MUSK

Max Chafkin, "Entrepreneur of the year, 2007: Elon Musk", *Inc. Magazine*, December 1, 2007.

Andrew Chaikin, "1 visionary + 3 launchers + 1500 employees = ? Is SpaceX changing the rocket equation?", *Air and Space magazine*, January, 2012.

Hannah Elliott, "Elon Musk on the biggest week of his life", *Forbes*, May 25, 2012.

Paul Harris, "Elon Musk: 'I'm planning to retire on Mars'", *The Observer*, August 1, 2010.

OnInnovation, "Full length interview with Elon Musk", *The Henry Ford*, June 2008.

Marlow Stern, "Elon Musk and the revenge of the electric car", *The Daily Beast*, April 25, 2011.

Ashlee Vance, "Elon Musk, the 21st century industrialist", *Businessweek*, September 13, 2012.

.

An individual with an epic ambition to change the world, who ...	Richard Branson Born: 1950, Blackheath, England Education: Stowe School, Buckingham Organisation: Virgin Group, Virgin Galactic	Jeff Bezos Born: 1964, Albuquerque, USA Education: BS, Princeton University Organisation: Amazon, Blue Origin	Elon Musk Born: 1971, Pretoria, South Africa Education: BA (Physics), BS (Econ), University of Pennsylvania Organisation: Tesla Motors, SpaceX
.. sees and seizes opportunities for change ..			
Opportunistic: aggressively seeks and adopts new ideas	When Richard Branson founded Virgin Atlantic to occupy the space vacated by Freddie Laker's defunct airline in 1984, the head of American Airlines said: "What does Richard Branson know about the airline business? He comes from the entertainment business".	Seeing the Internet as an opportunity for a new sphere of business that would effectively cut out the middleman, Jeff Bezos immediately began considering ways to create ...	Accepted into Stanford's PhD physics program, Elon Musk dropped out after two days to join the Internet landgrab. He had no plan, no money and no friends or family in California, but ...
& Visionary: intuitively grasps the big picture and how it might evolve	"But that", said Branson: "was exactly what the airline business needed".	... "earth's most customer-centric company: to build a place where people can come to find and discover anything they might want to buy online".	... "It just became clear that the Internet was going to change the world in a major way".
.. senses the way forward ..			
Innovative: thinks creatively, ignores boundaries, disrupts the status quo	"Freddie Laker gave me a great piece of advice on setting up my own airline: 'You'll never have the advertising power to outsell British Airways. You are going to have to get out there and use yourself'"	Placing an empty chair at the conference table, Bezos tells his managers to imagine that it is occupied by their customer: "the most important person in the room".	Musk named his electric car company after the electrical engineer and prolific inventor, Nikola Tesla, because "we use an AC induction motor, which is an architecture that Tesla developed" ...
but Pragmatic: recognises constraints, devises practical solutions, creates value	"I've followed that advice ever since. I've been very visible and made a fool of myself on more than one occasion".	"Having a culture that is heads-down focused on the customer instead of the external world makes a company that is more resilient to external influences".	... but models himself on Tesla's one-time boss and equally prolific inventor, Thomas Edison, because "Edison brought his stuff to market and made those inventions accessible to the world".

	Branson	Bezos	Musk
Persuasive: articulate and convincing communicator, consummate networker	Branson built his companies on the basis of strong partnerships, often with family and friends, and brought them with him as he moved from business to business, ...	Promoting Amazon as a company that is hard-wired for innovation, Bezos is able to recruit exceptional talent	According to Max Levchin, who co-founded PayPal with Musk and Peter Thiel, "One of Elon's greatest skills is the ability to pass off his vision as a mandate from heaven" ...
& Empowering: attracts talent, inspires loyalty, rewards excellence	... inspiring the loyalty of the Virgin Group's 50,000 staff, and repaying it with complete trust in their ability.	... and offer these bright minds the chance to both "have fun" and "make history".	... and attract talented individuals, often from competing firms, by offering them the opportunity to "do something bold and new".

.. and pursues the dream ..

	Branson	Bezos	Musk
Focused: passionate and highly energetic perfectionist, totally committed to an overriding vision	"I have always lived my life by making lists - lists of people to call, lists of ideas, lists of companies to set up, lists of people who can make things happen. Each day I work through these lists, and that sequence of calls propels me forward".	When Bezos told his engineers that their target for the Kindle was an e-book reader that could download any book in the world in 60 seconds or less, he was thinking solely of his customers. The technical details were up to the engineers.	"I know my rocket inside out and backwards".
& Confident: driven by unconditional self-belief, assumes absolute authority and accountability	"My interest in life comes from setting myself huge, apparently unachievable challenges and trying to rise above them".	When asked how much he wanted to spend on the project, he responded: "How much do we have?"	SpaceX will launch satellites into orbit for "as little as a quarter of the going rate".

.. regardless of the odds ..

	Branson	Bezos	Musk
Resilient: flexible, thrives on change and uncertainty, learns from mistakes	"One thing I'm quite good at is picking myself up quickly and battling again".	"If you are going to do large-scale invention, you have to be willing to do three things: you must be willing to fail; you have to be willing to think long-term; and ...	2008 was Elon Musk's year of horrors. SpaceX's rocket refused to fly, he was in the middle of a very messy and public divorce, and Tesla, wracked by internal dissent and production delays, was running out of cash.
& Courageous: bold, intelligent risk-taker, undaunted by criticism, determined to succeed	Knocked back for a $10 million loan to put video screens in the economy section of Virgin Atlantic planes, he asked Boeing and Airbus if they would supply them for free if he bought ten new planes: "It was easier to get $4 billion credit than borrow $10 million".	... you have to be willing to be misunderstood for long periods of time".	With venture capital markets almost entirely dried up, Musk put every cent he had left into Tesla. Asked later how much skin he had in the game, he replied: "All of it".

Part II

HIGH TECHNOLOGY

THERE WAS A TIME WHEN we could all keep up.

Both the principles and the practical implications of the agricultural revolution - the transition from a nomadic lifestyle of hunting and gathering to one of planting and harvesting grain in settled farming communities - were probably evident to all concerned. But how many residents of 18th-century Great Britain understood the mechanics of the steam engine - the basis for the industrial revolution - or its implications for their textile and mining industries?

And now, at the start of the 21st century, how many of us are on top of the mélange of chemistry, biology and computing that underpins the potential of personalised medicine, or the interplay of physical, chemical, biological and social factors that determines the climate of our planet? And how few of us have the vision to see and seize the opportunities to use that science to change the world?

How can we capture the economic, social and environmental benefits of science we don't even know?

੬੬੬

The prospective relationship between science as an intellectual pursuit and its application for the benefit of mankind was first enunciated by the 17th-century parliamentarian, philosopher and scientist - Sir Francis Bacon.

Famous primarily for his revival of Aristotle's notions of inductive reasoning, or empirical science, he also argued that "the true ends of knowledge" are not "for pleasure of the mind, or for contention, or for superiority to others, or for profit, or fame, or power, or any of these inferior things: but for the benefit and use of life".

Writing in 1626, centuries before the invention of the telephone, genetic engineering or salt water desalination plants, Bacon described a fictional island somewhere in the Pacific where the inhabitants possessed means "to convey sounds in trunks and pipes, in strange lines and distances", "to make diverse new plants, differing from the vulgar, and to make one tree or plant turn into another", and to "strain fresh water out of salt". The sources of these marvels were 12 men "that sail into foreign countries" and "bring us the books and abstracts, and patterns of experiments of all other parts" that can be used to create "things of use and practice for man's life and knowledge".

He called these men "merchants of light".

ଛଛଛ

In the following three chapters we describe the roles of nine modern-day "merchants of light", discoverers and translators of science and technology whose visionary leadership is changing our world.

Three of them, Bill Gates, Larry Page and Niklas Zennström, saw and seized upon emerging microelectronic technologies as the means for converting computers from the massive and exclusive engines of big government, business and academia of the 1960s into desktop tools that all of us, including small children, use easily and instinctively for accessing, managing and communicating information.

On the medical front, George Rathmann, Barry Marshall and Craig Venter translated new and old discoveries from the fields of genetic engineering and microbiology into ways of vastly reducing the costs of treating diseases like diabetes and gastric ulcers, and opened up opportunities for the future development of genome-based personalised medicine.

And Olivia Lum, Zhengrong Shi and Shai Agassi harvested technologies from the laboratories of the world's best chemists, physicists and engineers, and translated them into industries that provide clean water, clean electricity and clean cars for people around the globe.

KEY SOURCE

Francis Bacon, *New Atlantis*, 1626 (Internet Wiretap edition prepared by Kirk Crady, 1993, based on scanner output from *Ideal Commonwealths*, P.F. Collier & Son, New York, ca 1901).

Chapter 5

SPEED BYTES

WHEN STEVE BALLMER, NOW CEO of Microsoft, told his parents in 1980 that he was planning to drop out of his prestigious MBA program to join a tiny company creating software for personal computers, his mother asked: "Why would a person want a computer?"

And she wasn't the only one who had trouble cottoning on to the potential of personal computers to transform all our lives. The world's first commercial microprocessor was created at Intel in 1971, but Intel management failed totally to appreciate its future significance. As Gordon Moore, author of Moore's Law and co-founder of Intel, explained to Robert Cringely of PBS:

> An engineer came to me with an idea for a computer that would be used in the home. And while he felt very strongly about it, the only example of what it was good for that he could come up with was the housewife could keep her recipes on it. And I couldn't imagine my wife with her recipes on a computer in the kitchen. It just didn't seem like it had any practical application at all, so Intel didn't pursue that idea.

And nor did anyone else. It was to be another five years before Bill Gates and Paul Allen leapt to the stunning conclusion that household computers based on the Intel microprocessor would not only have practical applications, but would ultimately lead to a "computer on every desk and in every home".

The potential of the Internet was equally unanticipated. Created in 1982 as a worldwide network of networks, the Internet was primarily used by government and academic research organisations. But it was not until 1998, three years after its first commercialisation, that Larry Page and Sergey Brin emerged from a scrum of putative Internet search providers with the promise of making "all of the world's information easily accessible, free and without bias" to every one of those people on the planet with a computer on their desk or in their home.

And then, in 2005, along came Niklas Zennström and Janus Friis with their remarkable realisation that the combined resources of all of those personal computers, connected via the Internet, could be deployed to provide a telephony network that let "the whole world talk for free".

Not one of these merchants of light invented the technology on which their innovations were based. But each of them saw and grasped the future, before the rest of us knew it was there.

BILL GATES

When Bill and Melinda Gates flew into the tropical Australian city of Cairns just before Christmas 2011, they were certainly not there for the hot, wet and unbelievably sticky summer weather. They were there to see their bananas.

It was just over three years since Bill Gates had resigned his executive role at Microsoft Corporation to devote himself fulltime to the work of the Bill and Melinda Gates Foundation, including its assault on the Grand Challenges in Global Health. And among those many challenges were two of the major health problems facing the children of central Africa: blindness, caused by lack of vitamin A, and stunted growth, due to lack of iron. In Uganda, for example, around 40% of children under the age of 5 are stunted by malnutrition. Their staple diet is bananas, of which Ugandans eat an average of 1 kg a day, but which lack sufficient vitamin A and iron for their needs.

And in tropical Australia, working under the auspices of the Gates Foundation, biotechnology wiz Professor James Dale had figured out how to genetically enrich Ugandan bananas with not just iron, but also up to five times more vitamin A than traditional banana varieties.

Bill and Melinda were there to help African kids grow tall, and see the world.

੪੪੪

Bill Gates himself is unlikely to have suffered from a childhood vitamin deficiency - he was brought up in a prosperous and highly supportive Seattle family - but he did have an insatiable thirst for knowledge. He read voraciously, consuming the World Book Encyclopedia from A to Z by the time he was nine years old, and washing it down with whole shelves of science fiction novels and biographies. He was also extraordinarily competitive, revelling in inventing and performing daredevil feats on water skis or roller skates, and delighting in the vicarious opportunities for world domination and business success offered by board games such as Risk and Monopoly.

But it was the Lakeside School Mothers' Club that really changed the course of Bill Gates' life, when they used the proceeds of their annual rummage sale to acquire a teleprinter terminal and connect it by telephone to a time-share computer owned by a local company. Bill was 13 years old, and for the next four years he spent most of his waking hours exploring the world of computers, finding out what they could and could not do, and learning to program them.

With three of his friends, including future Microsoft co-founder, Paul Allen, Gates taught himself to write programs in BASIC, and then offered classes to others. They called themselves the Lakeside Programming Group. But the costs of accessing the time-share computer rapidly became prohibitive, and Gates soon began to apply his nascent entrepreneurial skills to finding ingenious ways to garner time on other people's computer systems.

And he succeeded. One company offered to give the group free access day and night if they would write a program to handle payroll, including state and federal tax reports. That program was duly delivered by the 16-year-old Gates and his best friend, Kent Evans. Another agreed to give them free time provided that they identified system failures that would justify deferring rental payments on their Digital Equipment Corporation (DEC) computer. Once again, Gates and his fellow students delivered: they not only found problems, but dived into the operating system and wrote reports to DEC on how to fix them. And in the process they became so well known for their expertise with DEC machines that people began to hire them.

By the time Bill Gates finished school, he and Paul Allen, two years his senior but already deferring to Gates' precocious business acumen, had set up a class scheduling program at their school, contributed to the software required to control the Washington State hydroelectricity grid, and established a company, Traf-o-Data, to automatically monitor traffic flows around Seattle.

But even more importantly, in 1971, when Gates was just 15, Paul Allen had seen the future. Buried in a computer magazine, he had spied a tiny article on the Intel 4004 microprocessor - the first prospective "computer on a chip" - and knew "that it would be deeply important".

ೞೞೞ

The "Aha" moment came four years later, during Gates' second year at Harvard.

As Allen revealed to Robert Cringely, Gates was "probably playing poker and losing money - one of the few times that's been the case", when Allen arrived at his dorm with the January 1975 issue of *Popular Electronics* magazine. On the front cover was the vision that Paul Allen had imagined four years earlier: the first personal computer, or at least the first kit that offered hobbyists the opportunity to build their own personal computer. But there was a hitch: it was a personal computer that lacked any semblance of the key thing that would ultimately make it useful - software.

Gates' decision was instant: they had to get on board, and they had to do it fast.

He called Ed Roberts, CEO of Micro Instrumentation and Telemetry Systems (MITS), the man behind the computer kit, and asked if he was interested in their (not yet written) version of BASIC for the Intel 8080 microprocessor, the chip at the heart of MITS Altair 8800.

Roberts was interested, and Gates and Allen scrambled. They spent the next two months writing a BASIC interpreter for the Altair 8800, not using an

Altair or even an 8080 chip - they didn't have either - but on a DEC PDP-10 machine in the Harvard computer centre using a program written by Allen to simulate the MITS computer. When Allen flew to MITS headquarters in Albuquerque, New Mexico, to demonstrate their transformational software he was understandably nervous: it had never been run on an Altair. But it worked! Suddenly, the Altair 8800 was a real computer.

Allen and Gates moved to Albuquerque, signing a contract with MITS that not only gave them a royalty on each copy of BASIC sold, but also gave MITS an exclusive worldwide licence to the software, provided that MITS used its "best efforts" to promote and sublicense the software to other companies. But the arrangements soon foundered on two counts: first, the main buyers of the Altair computer kit were hobbyists, who were more inclined to borrow a copy of the BASIC software from a friend than buy one; and, second, MITS was understandably more focused on selling its own computer kits than helping emerging competitors to acquire the BASIC software.

Gates tackled both issues hard and fast. Writing in February 1976 as general partner of the newly formed "Micro-Soft", he sent an open letter to hobbyists pointing out that he, Paul Allen, and a second Harvard student, Monte Davidoff, had spent the past year documenting and improving BASIC, but could not afford to continue doing so if only 10% of users actually paid for their software. And he pulled the plug on MITS' exclusive license, leading to arbitration that resulted in the Microsoft partnership, now without the hyphen, regaining the right to license BASIC to other companies.

Suddenly, the world was Microsoft's oyster. By 1978, the Albuquerque start-up and its unkempt band of pizza-munching, Coke-swilling hackers were supplying BASIC to all of the new companies building personal computers based on the Intel chip, and busily writing additional software to offer users word processing, accounting and other applications.

At the end of that year, with 25 staff and over $1 million in sales, they decided the time had come to move back home to Seattle.

ଝଝଝ

When IBM decided to go head-to-head with Apple in the PC market in 1980 their first port of call was Microsoft, from whom they sought licences to both the BASIC software package and a disk operating system, CP/M, developed by Californian software company, Digital Research. Unable to supply the latter, Gates referred them directly to Digital Research, but the two companies failed to reach agreement on a deal.

And then Gates made the move that sealed Microsoft's future success. Believing that IBM's clout in the business community would be key to achieving Microsoft's early mantra, "a computer on every desk and in every home ... running Microsoft software", and already committed to providing IBM with BASIC and other software, Gates stepped into the breach, committing Microsoft to developing an equivalent operating system to CP/M.

And they did. Microsoft acquired a CP/M look-alike from a local Seattle company, adapted it to IBM's requirements, and sold it on to IBM, with one condition: Microsoft would be free to license the same operating system, now named MS-DOS, and the same BASIC software package, to the manufacturers of any and all of the IBM PC clones that Gates was certain would soon come streaming over the horizon.

And he was right. No sooner had IBM, with Microsoft and Intel in tow, gained dominance of the PC industry than a tsunami of IBM PC clones came onto the market, battering IBM's market share while enshrining MS-DOS as the standard operating system for the industry. Gates, never slow to seize an advantage, set the seal on that victory by partnering with all comers to develop more and more software compatible with MS-DOS, resulting in what he called Microsoft's virtuous cycle, "where the more software we got, the more people would buy the machine, the higher the volume, the lower the price ... so the whole PC industry really took off around the variety of software packages that we got people to write".

ଧ୧ଧ

But that was nothing compared to the tsunami coming next.

When Steve Jobs was invited to visit Xerox's Palo Alto Research Center in December 1979, he couldn't believe his eyes: "I thought it (Xerox's revolutionary graphical user interface) was the best thing I'd seen in my life. Within ten minutes it was obvious to me that all computers would work like this some day". Fortunately for Jobs, it was not at all obvious to Xerox's senior management, who raised no objection when he returned with his programmers for another demonstration!

Back at Apple, Jobs hired a team of engineers to emulate what he had seen at Xerox, building what he envisaged as the world's first truly user-friendly personal computer: the Macintosh.

But Jobs wasn't the only one to appreciate the significance of the graphical user interface (GUI). Under pressure from his board to regain market share from IBM as quickly and cheaply as possible, he had engaged Microsoft to assist in developing the Macintosh software. And Bill Gates, too, saw GUI as the way of the future.

And thus it was, when the Apple Macintosh was launched early in 1984, that Bill Gates had already announced the imminent arrival of Microsoft's own GUI-based operating system, Windows, as an extension of MS-DOS.

"Imminent" was perhaps a little too strong a word. When Windows finally appeared two years later it was a pale and clunky imitation of the Apple GUI. But Bill Gates had bet the bank on the GUI approach rather than staying with IBM, and he wasn't about to give up.

Following the capital-raising success of Microsoft's IPO in 1986, Gates continued to pour money and resources into developing Windows. Version 3.0, released in 1990, sold 2 million copies in 6 months, and by 2000 annual sales had reached $20 billion. In 2010, 90% of all personal computers were using Windows operating systems.

ﺽﺽﺽ

In 2000, Bill Gates gave up his position as CEO of Microsoft in favour of his right-hand man, Steve Ballmer, and merged his family's two philanthropic foundations to form the Bill and Melinda Gates Foundation. And in 2008, he retired from his remaining management position at Microsoft, as Chief Software Architect, to work full-time for the Foundation.

In his 2012 annual letter from the Foundation, he wrote: "Throughout my careers in software and philanthropy - and in each of my annual letters - a recurring theme has been that innovation is the key to improving the world. When innovators work on urgent problems and deliver solutions to people in need, the results can be magical".

Which is why Bill and Melinda were in Cairns, inspecting bananas.

LARRY PAGE

When Eric Schmidt replaced Sergey Brin as chairman of the board at Google in March 2001, Brin's explanation to Vanessa Hua of the *San Francisco Chronicle* went down in history: "Basically, he's going to be a bit of a chaperone, providing adult supervision". Several months later, Brin and co-founder Larry Page further consolidated their child-minding arrangements, with Schmidt replacing Page as CEO, and the two co-founders becoming joint presidents of the company.

It was hardly a conventional approach for a pair of 28-year-old entrepreneurs who had already succeeded, in just three years, in taking their company from a Menlo Park garage to a firm with 200 employees, supported by $25 million in venture capital, and offering "uncannily relevant" Internet searches in 26 languages.

But, as Larry Page explained three years later in his IPO letter to potential shareholders:

> Google is not a conventional company. We do not intend to become one. Our goal is to develop services that significantly improve the lives of as many people as possible. In pursuing this goal, we may do things that we believe have a positive impact on the world, even if the near term financial returns are not obvious.

Remarkably, despite the caveat, investors in the IPO valued his six-year-old enterprise at $23 billion.

ଷଷଷ

Larry Page's decision to do a PhD in computer science at Stanford University was hardly surprising: after all, his mother was a computer programming instructor and his dad, a computer science professor, introduced him to his first computer at the age of six.

But what of his introductory tour of the Stanford campus, conducted by none other than his future business partner, Sergey Brin? That was surely quite some coincidence, though perhaps equally unsurprising. Both young men were attracted to Stanford for the same reasons: they both wanted to do great science, and they both wanted to do it in an environment where the creation of technology companies like Cisco and Sun Microsystems, dedicated to converting scientific discoveries into practical benefits for the outside world, was not just accepted but positively encouraged.

Within a year of Page's arrival at Stanford, he and Brin were cooperating on a research project that combined Page's curiosity-driven interest in mapping the links between Web sites with Brin's expertise in data mining: how to convert the outputs of Internet search engines from meaningless lists of Web sites into something relevant?

The solution, they argued in their 1998 research paper, "The Anatomy of a Large-Scale Hypertextual Web Search Engine", was to rank the Web sites returned by a search according to the number and quality of their back-links, or referrals, from other sites.

Tested on other Stanford students, that simple and elegant solution proved exceptionally popular, if computationally expensive. The PageRank algorithm, later to be named Google (after googol, or 10 to the power of 100), was soon running 10,000 searches daily on a network of personal computers that Page had cobbled together in his dorm, and tying up a substantial part of Stanford's total computing capacity. After investing the last of their capital in extra disk storage, and getting some fairly clear wind-up signals from the University, Page and Brin wisely decided that it was time to find a buyer for their algorithm and get back to work completing their PhDs.

But things weren't quite that easy. The most obvious buyers were the more established search companies, like Yahoo and Excite, whose search algorithms were clearly inferior to PageRank, but who nevertheless saw little point in acquiring it. Search was generic, they argued, and would never be a serious money maker. Without exception, they rejected Google out of hand.

On the verge of giving up, Page and Brin approached Stanford professor and serial entrepreneur David Cheriton, who invited them to his home to meet his business partner and Sun Microsystems founder, Andy Bechtolsheim. And Bechtolsheim was, to say the least, impressed: "It was immediately clear that this was a very, very good idea. In fact, I think it was the best idea I've seen in my entire life. I rushed out to my car, pulled out my cheque book and wrote them a cheque on the spot". That cheque, for $100,000, was soon matched by Cheriton and a handful of other angel investors, including Jeff Bezos, who collectively brought the total to $1 million.

Inspired by Bechtolsheim's interest, Page and Brin dropped out of Stanford in 1998, incorporated Google, and opened a bank account - a necessary precursor to cashing Bechtolsheim's cheque! And nine months later, with Google rapidly gaining recognition in the IT community as the search engine that returned genuinely relevant results, they raised a further $25 million from venture capitalists John Doerr and Michael Moritz.

ৎৎৎ

From the start, Page and Brin were committed to the concept of making Google a force for good, of making the world a better place. Indeed, their early motto, "Don't be evil", remains the highly respected mantra of the company today. Google, they said, would connect people and information, providing users all around the world with unbiased search results, for free. But, as Google's early investors were not slow to point out, they couldn't keep doing that unless they found a way to make some money.

The most obvious solution was advertising, but from Page and Brin's perspective it was also the most distasteful, both aesthetically and practically. They disliked the idea of cluttering Google's homepage with traditional banner advertisements and other items - such as news and sporting results - designed to keep users logged onto the page, which they saw as directly counter to their own goal of providing fast and efficient search results. They wanted the Google experience to be enjoyable, and bombarding users with flashy ads did not fit the bill.

The answer, when they found it, was someone else's idea. Bill Gross, founder of GoTo.com, had come up with an idea that was as simple and elegant an approach to advertising as Page's PageRank algorithm was to search: the search query, he realised, was not only a way of describing the information the user was seeking, but also a pointer to the products that he or she might be interested in buying. All that was needed was to match the advertisements with the search.

After seeking, and failing, to do a deal with Gross, Page and Brin took the easy way out. By reverse-engineering his concepts, they developed the software that was to become the cornerstone of Google's advertising strategy from 2000 onward. That strategy is based on three very straightforward principles.

First, consistent with the co-founders' belief that the best search is a fast search, the homepage has remained strikingly simple - just the company logo and a search box - with nothing to distract users from composing an effective query.

Second, although the ranking of the search results is automatically determined by the search algorithm, and cannot be influenced by advertising, advertisers can buy the right to display a small text advertisement in a separate box on the search results page for any search involving a key search term.

Third, the owners of web pages can generate revenue by showing relevant advertisements alongside content on their Web sites, and receiving payment when a user clicks on the advertisement and/or buys a product.

The upshot has been better for users, better for advertisers, and certainly better for Google. Between 2001 and 2010 Google's annual advertising revenue increased from less than $100 million to almost $30 billion. And Bill Gross, the man who dreamt up the idea of search-based advertising, didn't do too badly either. He settled out of court for 2.7 million shares in Google.

ৡৡৡ

As Page predicted, Google's 2004 IPO was far from conventional. Almost derailed by the co-founders' candid interview with *Playboy* magazine on the eve of the listing, the IPO was run as a "democratic" auction, ultimately resulting in an opening price of $85, 20% or more below initial expectations. And to make sure that everyone knew where he and Brin were coming from, there was Page's IPO letter to shareholders, with its Warren Buffet-inspired title "An Owner's Manual".

That manual, while recognising that the economic engine of the company was search-based advertising, also made clear that the founders did not intend to stand still: "Our business environment changes rapidly and needs long term investment. We will not hesitate to place major bets on promising new opportunities". And, to address those opportunities, "We encourage our employees, in addition to their regular projects, to spend 20% of their time working on what they think will most benefit Google".

Over the following six years, the triumvirate of Page, Brin and Schmidt pursued many new opportunities and placed some very large bets, some on internal innovations like Gmail, Street View and Google Books, and some on externally developed platforms such as the Android mobile phone operating system, online video distributor YouTube and leading navigation service Google Maps.

But the outcome of those bets wasn't always as they had hoped.

Google Maps and Gmail soon encountered privacy issues, copyright problems emerged with Google Books, and antitrust investigations loomed as competitors accused Google of abusing its search power to promote the other products in its portfolio. And worst of all, they weren't earning anything. By the end of 2010, $28 billion of Google's revenues, 96% of total earnings, were still driven by search-based advertising. Total revenues from all other sources were just over $1 billion.

Google, as Microsoft CEO Steve Ballmer described it, seemingly unconscious of the irony, was still "a one trick pony".

ဪဪဪ

On January 20, 2011, Eric Schmidt announced that he was stepping down as Google CEO in favour of Larry Page. But his farewell tweet "Day-to-day adult supervision no longer needed!" certainly didn't mean that Page could afford to neglect Google's ongoing growing pains.

First, there was China. Early in 2010, when Google responded to cyber-attacks on the Gmail accounts of Chinese human rights activists by threatening to shut down its Chinese operations, its share of the Chinese search market was over 30%. Two years later, with most Chinese Google searches being provided from Hong Kong, uncensored but heavily compromised by the Chinese government's filtering system, Google's share of page views was down to just 5%. Unwilling to compromise on Google's "Don't Be Evil' mantra, Page needed to find another way to increase his share of the Chinese market without falling foul of the government censors.

Second, there was the threat to Google's dominance of search - and its associated advertising revenues - from the increasing proportion of searches being conducted using smartphones. Google's initial move, the widespread licensing of the Android operating system, provided a first line of defence, but now Apple had counter-attacked with its own search engine, the voice-activated Siri, and tackled the mobile search market at its heart - location-based searches for products and places - by removing Google Maps from its new iPhones. And Microsoft, with Bing and Nokia in tow, and Facebook, with new socially oriented search opportunities, were closing in. Page needed to find a way to strengthen his hold on Google's core market.

And third, there was the fear that Google might be losing its hard-won reputation as the place for young technologically savvy go-getters to work. Page needed to restore the excitement and innovation of Google's start-up days.

He tackled all three issues head-on.

In China, aggressive licensing of the Android operating system gave Google a foothold over more than half of the nation's mobile phone market, and the potential for massive new advertising revenues.

At home, the 2012 purchase of Motorola Mobility for $12.5 billion provided not only a vast patent estate around mobile phone technology, but also the capability to push back on the squeeze from Apple and Facebook by producing innovative smartphones and tablets bundled with its own mapping and social networking applications.

And at work, he sought to reassert Google's reputation as a family of the best and brightest minds: "It's important that the company be a family, that people feel that they're part of the company, and that the company is like a family to them ... If you're changing the world, you're working on important things. You're excited to get up in the morning". In 2012, Google was ranked Number 1 of the "100 Best Companies to Work For" by *Fortune* magazine.

ଌଌଌ

And he continued to dream. Back in 2000, Page had described the perfect search engine as something that "understands exactly what you mean, and gives you back exactly what you want".

In his 2012 update to shareholders, the same philosophy seemed to be at work, albeit on an even grander scale: "Top of my priority list has been creating a simpler, more intuitive experience across all our products so users get exactly what they need, right when they want it". And at Google X, the company's top-secret research lab, scientists are working on robots that will understand exactly what you want, and do exactly what you want, whenever you want it, be it chauffeuring your car, cooking your dinner, or standing in for you at the office on days when you feel like staying home.

NIKLAS ZENNSTRÖM

As a small boy, Niklas Zennström spent his summer holidays cruising among the 24,000 islands of the Stockholm Archipelago, and later racing there against other youngsters in Laser dinghies. He loved the competition, the beautiful and unspoilt environment of the Baltic Sea, and the freedom to let his imagination roam: "The two races I've dreamed about since I was a kid are the Fastnet and the Sydney-Hobart", the two classic offshore races of the yachting world.

Thirty years later, Zennström got serious about that childhood dream, working with naval architect Rolf Frolijk to design his 72' offshore racing yacht *Rán 2*, and handpicking his 20-member crew. As he commented to Carla Anselmi of *Yacht OnLine*: "Sailing is a team sport. To have a successful campaign you need to create a team rather than a crew. It's not that much different to putting together a team for a technology start-up. It's important not to have any prima donnas aboard, just team players with well-controlled egos".

That very practical business approach to sailing has delivered Zennström the first half of his dream, twice, with Fastnet wins in 2009 and 2011. The second half, the Sydney-Hobart, has so far eluded him, but if his business success is any guide, it won't do so for long.

ଔଔଔ

Zennström was a serious child and a model student, taking degrees in business administration and engineering physics at Uppsala University before spending his final year at the University of Michigan. His first job, in 1991, was with Tele2, an offshoot of Swedish investment conglomerate Kinnevik, which was seeking to challenge Europe's largely government-owned telecom monopolies.

Apart from a brief interlude with a competing telecom consortium, Zennström spent the next nine years moving around Europe and up the ranks of Tele2, helping to build it into one of Europe's leading telecom operators. And, along the way, he hired his future business partner, Danish high school dropout Janus Friis, met and married his wife, Catherine, and became intrigued by the business opportunities offered by P2P, or peer-to-peer, the direct exchange of information between individual users over the Internet.

In early 2000, Zennström took the plunge, supported by his wife's earnings while he and Friis began exploring the prospects for P2P from the kitchen/

office of the Zennströms' Amsterdam apartment. Asked ten years later about his worst ever mistake, he told CNBC: "I try not to dwell on big mistakes, but … I guess one big mistake I did was not to start my own company earlier. I spent nine years working for others before starting KaZaA in 2000".

On the other hand, it was at Tele2 that he first encountered the idea of challenging inefficient and overpriced incumbent companies, made the acquaintance of both his wife and Janus Friis, and discovered the extraordinary talents of a trio of hard-drinking Estonians.

ଷଷଷ

Zennström and Friis did not have a fixed business plan, but they were keenly aware of the mounting demand among Internet users for tools enabling them to exchange very large files - music, films, etc - in real time, and they were convinced that the solution would ultimately lie in enhancing the capacity of P2P. But first, they needed an inexpensive and user-friendly way to overcome the bandwidth and storage capacity costs inherent in transferring such large files to and from central servers. That, they realised, was a software issue, and neither of them were programmers. Fortunately, they knew exactly where to turn.

The collapse of the Soviet Union in 1991 had left Estonia an independent nation, with just 1.5 million inhabitants and two rather unusual assets: Tallinn University of Technology's Institute of Cybernetics and a remarkably innovative, technology-oriented society. Software, it seemed, was in their genes. And three of the smartest among them were the principals of Bluemoon Interactive, Jaan Tallinn, Ahti Heinla and Priit Kasesalu, suppliers of innovative software to, among others, Tele2.

Tallinn and his colleagues rose to Zennström's challenge, developing software that recruited the personal computers of all of its users into a self-organising network that employed the total computing capacity and high-speed Internet connections of its components, rather than a central server, to transfer files from one user to another. That software package, FastTrack, was to form the basis of all of Zennström and Friis' subsequent

P2P ventures. As Zennström put it: "These guys are the best software developers I have ever seen in my life".

ଽଽଽ

FastTrack's first outing was as the core of KaZaA, a file-sharing service launched by Zennström and Friis in September 2000. It was just a month since Napster, a music exchange program that offered its users free access to around 300,000 titles, had been forced to close down its central server following legal action by the Recording Industry Association of America. Now KaZaA, with no central server to close down, was offering a quick and easy means to download any file a user wanted, be it music, film, software or games. Within a year, and without spending a cent on advertising, KaZaA was the most downloaded program on the Internet.

With KaZaA users around the globe illegally downloading over a million files per hour, and the recording and film industries baying for blood, courts in the United States and Europe were ambivalent. Some saw KaZaA as legally liable for the actions of its users, others ruled that the provision of file-swapping tools was no different to selling video recorders or photocopiers, both of which could equally well be used for infringing copyright.

But the legal pressure was intense. In 2002, Zennström and Friis sold KaZaA to an Australian Internet company, Sharman Networks, and moved on to tackle an even more disruptive P2P opportunity. It was time to take on the telcos.

For Zennström and Friis, the transition from circuit-switched telephony services to Internet telephony was long overdue. Better still, there were no copyright issues. On one side were the established telecoms, with revenues in excess of $1 trillion, but with infrastructure costs to match. On the other were the emerging Internet phone companies, taking advantage of increased broadband capacity and standard Voice-over-Internet protocols to enter the market, but also constrained by poor sound quality and the significant infrastructure costs associated with each additional user.

The solution seemed simple. FastTrack, which the partners had wisely licensed, but not sold, with KaZaA, could be redeployed to build a computer-based telephone network in which all necessary infrastructure was provided by the users' own computers, with new customers not only being added at no cost, but also simultaneously increasing the overall power of the network.

The outcome was Skype. By effectively converting any personal computer with a high-speed broadband connection into a telephone, Skype allowed users to conduct high-quality audio, and, ultimately video, conversations over the Internet. And thanks to the programming team back in Estonia, it was extraordinarily easy to use: one-touch dialling, instant messaging and file transfers all rolled into one. And best of all, it was free.

Not surprisingly, Skype went viral, growing exponentially from 1 billion minutes of call time in its first year to 10 billion in the next. As Zennström put it: "I think charging for calls belongs in the last century".

In 2005, Skype was sold to eBay, who had hoped that "skyping" between buyers and sellers would accelerate online sales. It was a massive endorsement of Zennström's strategy, and an equally massive payout - $2.9 billion. Too big, as it turned out, for the banking system: "We agreed that the money should be transferred from eBay to a special account and then to be split between the sellers. But the transfer did not succeed completely. It was a Friday and the Bank of England did not possess enough cash".

Unhappily for eBay, despite continued expansion in the Skype user base, the anticipated increase in sales did not materialise, and four years later eBay sold 70% of the company for $1.9 billion. Among the consortium of buyers were Zennström and Friis, who used a combination of cash and leverage to acquire a 14% equity stake. The leverage was FastTrack, the underpinning technology that they had once again licensed, but not sold, in the initial sale to eBay!

But the new owners didn't hang around long. Dangling the bait of a forthcoming IPO in an IT market hungry for quality Internet telephony, they were no doubt surprised and delighted by Microsoft's April 2011 offer of $8.5 billion. This time, FastTrack was included in the deal.

༊༊༊

And what of the Estonians? Zennström is at pains to point out that they are typical of the many ambitious young entrepreneurs around the world with the potential to grow successful online companies. In 2006, he established Atomico, a venture capital fund that he hopes will encourage other young entrepreneurs from countries like Estonia to expand internationally. Headquartered in London, its other offices are in Beijing, Istanbul, Tokyo and Sao Paulo.

Atomico's portfolio focuses on emerging trends in a world where innovations are coming thick and fast. In the world of IT, Zennström says: "The winners who emerge will be swift and nimble in response to consumer demand. It's not the big who beat the small, it is the fast who beat the slow".

༊༊༊

And throughout all of that, Zennström has never forgotten his childhood sailing paradise off the Stockholm archipelago. Assaulted by discarded Second World War weaponry, agricultural runoff and illegal fishing, the Baltic Sea is under serious threat. But help is at hand.

In 2007, Zennström and his wife Catherine established Zennström Philanthropies with the aim of pursuing issues relating to human rights and climate change, and helping to restore the health of the Baltic Sea by limiting fisheries to maximum sustainable yields and promoting cooperation between neighbouring nations.

POWER OF PARTNERSHIPS

The seeds of the formidable tools created by Gates, Page and Zennström have been with us for centuries.

Microsoft Office is simply the latest reincarnation of the abacus and the printing press, the slide rule and the typewriter; Google is the direct descendant of the Great Library of Alexandria and the Encylopaedia Brittanica; and Skype is the benefactor of the rich history and universal application of the telegraph and the telephone. And the digital technology on which all of them are based can be traced to the Analytical Engine of 19th-century English mathematician Charles Babbage and the programming skills of his assistant, Countess Ada Lovelace.

Both the means and the needs were there, but the connecting dots were invisible to all but these three men and their long-term partners in business and technology.

So, how important were the partnerships?

There is no doubt that Gates, Page and Zennström are all hard-wired for speed. Whether on skis, kitesurfers or yachts, they are all men of action, men who combine burning business ambition with strong strategic and technological skills and fanatical work ethics. Perhaps any one of them could have made it alone.

But there is also no doubt of the impact of their partners, the dreamers and visionaries whose ultimate measures of success have always been less about the money they made than the value that their work created. In their words:

Janus Friis: "To me it is not important to turn our ideas into large commercial successes. The important thing is that the ideas are accepted and used by a lot of people".

Paul Allen: "In my own work, I've tried to anticipate what's coming over the horizon, to hasten its arrival, and to apply it to people's lives in a meaningful way".

Sergey Brin: "We've let a thousand flowers bloom; now we want to put together a coherent bouquet".

They too have realised their dreams.

KEY SOURCES

BILL GATES

Academy of Achievement, "Interview: Bill Gates", March 17, 2010.

Elizabeth Corcoran, "Bill Gates unfiltered", *Forbes Q&A*, June 23, 2008.

Robert X Cringely, "Triumph of the Nerds", *PBS*, June 1996.

Robert A Guth, "Raising Bill Gates", *The Wall Street Journal*, April 25, 2009.

Stephen Matchett, "Yes we have lots of bananas", *The Australian*, December 22, 2011.

"The Whiz Kid becomes the Biz Kid", *Success Magazine*, 1985.

LARRY PAGE

Anonymous, "Technology giants at war. Another game of thrones". *The Economist*, December 1, 2012.

Ken Auletta, "Searching for trouble", *The New Yorker*, October 12, 2009.

Vanessa Hua, "Novell, Sun Micro vet Schmidt joins Google", *San Francisco Chronicle*, March 27, 2001.

Adam Lashinsky, "Larry Page: Google should be like a family", *CNN Money*, January 19, 2012.

Larry Page, "2004 Founders' IPO Letter", *Securities and Exchange Commission Registration Statement*, August 13, 2004.

Larry Page, "2012 update from the CEO", *Google Investor Relations*, 2012.

NIKLAS ZENNSTRÖM

Carla Anselmi, "Niklas Zennström: my love for sailing", *Yacht OnLine*, August, 2009.

James Ashton, "Sails set for the next big thing", *Sunday Times*, June 6, 2010.

Pete Cashmore, "Documented@Davos: Niklas Zennstrom, Skype and Atomico", *Mashable*, January 29, 2012.

Ebbe Munk, *Why were Janus Friis and Niklas Zennström successful with Kazaa and Skype*, Aarhus School of Business, 2006.

David Rowan, "What I've learned, by Skype's Niklas Zennström", *wired.com*, November 6, 2010.

"Skype co-Founder reflects on past success, looks for next big investment", *CNBC.com*, May 4, 2011.

An individual with an epic ambition to change the world, who …	Bill Gates	Larry Page	Niklas Zennström
	Born: 1955, Seattle, Washington State, USA Education: Harvard University Organisation: Microsoft	Born: 1973, East Lansing, Michigan, USA Education: BSc (Computer Engineering), University of Michigan; MSc, Stanford Organisation: Google	Born: 1966, Järfälla, Sweden Education: BSc (Business Admin), MSc (Eng Physics), Uppsala University Organisation: Skype
.. sees and seizes opportunities for change ..			
Opportunistic: aggressively seeks and adopts new ideas	Telephoned Ed Roberts, the man behind the Altair 8800 - the world's first microcomputer - to offer a BASIC software package that he and Paul Allen had not yet written, …	Observing that Web sites with most back-links, or referrals, from other sites were also likely to be of most relevance to users, Page saw the opportunity to build an Internet search engine that could …	"We realised that P2P with a distributed base could be used for lots of applications, so we decided to create the technology and build the business from there".
& Visionary: intuitively grasps the big picture and how it might evolve	… because he knew that one day there would be "a computer on every desk and in every home", and they just had to be in at the start.	… "make all the world's information easily accessible, free and without bias", …	"Our vision was to create a business that could fundamentally transform the telecommunications industry", …
.. senses the way forward ..			
Innovative: thinks creatively, ignores boundaries, disrupts the status quo	Microsoft was built upon "the idea of creating a software industry around the personal computer".	… by employing the user's search query as the basis for targeted advertising. …	… by replacing expensive and centralised infrastructure with the power and connectivity of millions of personal computers, with zero additional cost per user, and …
but Pragmatic: recognises constraints, devises practical solutions, creates value	"You had the platform of the personal computer, and that spurred the desire for more applications, and that drove the need for more computers".	… to the ultimate benefit of the user, the advertiser, and Google's burgeoning bottom line!	… "letting the whole world talk for free".
.. attracts the necessary resources ..			
Persuasive: articulate and convincing communicator, consummate networker	Gates wanted Steve Ballmer to drop out of Stanford business school and join him at Microsoft, but knew it wouldn't be easy: "I tried to get his parents on my side, but that didn't work, so I got my parents to take him out to dinner. And I made him a very generous offer" …	Asked in 1999 just how big he expected Google's revenues to be, Page piqued the interest of venture capitalist John Doerr with an outrageous estimate of "$10 billion", a target that was met in less than ten years, …	During the height of the global financial crisis he raised $165 million for an IT venture capital fund, and invested it …

& Empowering: attracts talent, inspires loyalty, rewards excellence	... perhaps enhanced by Microsoft's hiring philosophy: "Come as you are. Do what you love".	... with a little help from his friends: "The significant employee ownership of Google has made us what we are today. Talented people are attracted to Google because we empower them to change the world".	... in young entrepreneurs from around the world, "founders who are passionate about what they're doing and have an idea to change the world, and want to make something big".
... and pursues the dream ..			
Focussed: passionate and highly energetic perfectionist, totally committed to an overriding vision	While chasing a major IBM contract Gates virtually lived in his office ...	Reappointed CEO in 2011 after a decade of "adult supervision" from Eric Schmidt, Page's top priority was to sharpen Google's focus on "the big bets that will make a difference in the world". He eliminated dozens of projects ...	"Like Volvo and IKEA and others, we realized that we have to go outside our home market. We didn't think about one market - the world is our market".
& Confident: driven by unconditional self-belief, assumes absolute authority and accountability	... and did the deal for peanuts because he knew that the big bucks would follow as other manufacturers followed IBM into the market.	... but left himself plenty of room to move: "I don't think we're going to run out of important things to do. There are many, many problems in the world that need solving".	"Think globally. If you don't think big, it's unlikely you'll become big. We made sure from day one that Skype was an international business - we were incorporated in Luxembourg, we had software developers in Estonia, we moved to London. The internet has no country boundaries".
... regardless of the odds ..			
Resilient: flexible, thrives on change and uncertainty, learns from mistakes	When IBM sought Microsoft's help in wresting control of the PC market from look-alikes by developing a new proprietary operating system, Gates realised that Microsoft's position would also be substantially weakened ...	In 2010 Google suffered a cyber attack originating in China and involving the hacking of the Gmail accounts of Chinese human rights activists, ...	"It took a year to raise money for Skype: we went to 26 different venture capitalists, asking for 1.5 million euros and prepared to give away a third of the company. But no one wanted to invest".
& Courageous: bold, intelligent risk-taker, undaunted by criticism, determined to succeed	... and terminated Microsoft's relationship with the computer giant in favour of betting his company on Windows.	... and retaliated by redirecting search queries from Google.cn to its uncensored site in Hong Kong.	Eight years later, they sold Skype to Microsoft for $8.5 billion. "If you're playing a sport, either you play defense or you play offense. And usually the ones that win the most are ones who are playing offense".

Chapter 6

FROM HELIX TO *HELICO*

OVER THE COURSE OF THE past 60 years the life expectancy of the world's population has increased by an average of 20 years, but at a huge cost. Eighty per cent of aged individuals - those in the process of living that extra 20 years - suffer from chronic illnesses such as diabetes, cancer, and heart disease, whose treatment accounts for up to 75% of total health care expenditure in many developed nations.

Where should we turn to find more effective and less expensive treatments for crippling diseases such as diabetes, peptic ulcers and cancer?

Enter the merchants of light.

The bacterium now known as *Helicobacter pylori* was first observed in association with gastric ulcers late in the 19th century, but it was not until a century later, when Australian physician Barry Marshall finally convinced the medical establishment of the link between the bacterium and the disease, that expensive and often ineffective gastric acid-reducing drugs were finally replaced with simple and effective antibiotic treatments.

James Watson and Francis Crick first deduced the structure of DNA in 1953, but it was another 20 years before Herbert Boyer and Stanley Cohen figured out how to transfer genes from one organism into another, opening the way for big pharma executive George Rathmann and others to use genetic engineering techniques to convert microorganisms into factories to manufacture vastly valuable medicines used in the treatment of cancer and kidney disease.

And although Fred Sanger sequenced the entire 5,000-letter code of bacteriophage Phi-X174 in 1977, it was not until 2001, almost half a century after Watson and Crick's landmark discovery, that US researcher Craig Venter and his competitors published the first examples of the 3-billion-letter human genome, with its promise of untold opportunities in personalised medicine.

GEORGE RATHMANN

October 1980 could hardly have seemed the best time to quit the pharmaceutical juggernaut for the nascent biotechnology industry.

The drug industry was on the threshold of a new era in pharmaceutical discovery, buoyed by its evolving ability to fine-tune the structures of drug molecules to fit specific target sites - usually proteins such as enzymes or cell-surface receptors - in the human body. And the success of the antiulcer drug cimetidine, an early example of rational drug design and the first-ever "billion dollar drug", had reaffirmed the widely held view that the magic bullets of the future would continue to be small chemically synthesised or naturally occurring molecules such as aspirin or penicillin.

The promise of the biotechnology industry, on the other hand, was to use genetically engineered bacteria as factories to produce much larger molecules, including human hormones, to supplement supplies of naturally occurring proteins. But biotechnology's front-runner, human insulin, was still two years away, and no one knew for sure whether the wonder of recombinant DNA technology could be successfully converted into pharmaceutically useful products.

But George Rathmann jumped anyway, giving up his senior executive position at Abbott Laboratories - then one of the world's leading exponents of drug design - to take on the role of president and CEO of a Californian biotechnology company with no money, no staff, and no products - but lots of ideas. His starting salary at Applied Molecular Genetics, later known as Amgen, would be just two-thirds of his remuneration at Abbott - and then only after he raised the money.

His boss at Abbott, Jack Schuler, told him "George, you are making the biggest mistake of your life".

ᏂᏂᏂ

In one respect at least, George Rathmann was probably destined for biotechnology. His mother, born Edna Blatz, came from one of America's best-known brewing families, and his own youthful ambition was to become a medical researcher and use his skills to save human lives.

But after being denied entry to postgraduate medical school as an 18-year-old, he chose instead to follow in the footsteps of his older brother and brother-in-law - both of whom were industrial chemists - and switched to a PhD program in physical chemistry.

His timing was good. Inspired by the success of nylon and other synthetic polymers, chemical companies such as Dow, Dupont and 3M were vigorously competing for research talent, and Rathmann was besieged with job offers even before completing his PhD at Princeton in 1952.

According to Rathmann, the thing that most attracted him to 3M, of Scotchgard fame, and kept him there for the next 20 years, was the company's extraordinary emphasis on innovation, and the recognition that the next big thing was as likely, if not more so, to emerge from the curiosity-driven ideas of individual researchers as it was to be driven from the top.

Like Google 50 years later, 3M had a policy that researchers at all levels should spend a significant part of their time pursuing their own research agendas. As Rathmann later put it: "There is no better culture than 3M to learn about risk-taking and translating science and technology into commercially successful products". And he in turn was soon recognised for his talents at both encouraging innovative thinking and picking the resulting winners. He rose through the ranks of management, thriving on cycles of risk and reward, to lead a new division of the firm devoted to X-ray technologies and their application in health care.

And that brought him full circle, back to his boyhood dream of saving lives. It was time for a change.

In 1975, after a short and unhappy sojourn as president of a failing medical products business, Rathmann moved to Abbott Laboratories as vice-president of R&D in the diagnostics division. As he told Leo Slater of the Chemical Heritage Foundation: "I took a huge step in the direction of back to science, and loved it. I knew that there were plenty of opportunities in this field. I could see the numbers and I could tell how far it was going to go". And over the course of the next five years he delivered, boosting the returns of the diagnostics division with a raft of products built on the back of innovative R&D.

But the most exciting prospect of all for Rathmann was the new frontier of recombinant DNA technology, with its fascinating combination of therapeutic opportunity and technological uncertainty. Like Rathmann, many senior executives within Abbott were interested in pursuing the application of biotechnology to diagnostics, but the safeguards with which they sought to surround the new technology were such that Rathmann soon formed the view that the cutting-edge research needed to create new products from biotechnology could not be undertaken within the conservative and risk-averse confines of a traditional pharmaceutical company.

So, it wasn't too surprising that George Rathmann, when approached to take on the CEO job at Amgen, didn't spend too long making up his mind.

ଷଷଷ

The contrast could not have been more stark. When Rathmann arrived at Amgen in 1980, the company's resources comprised little more than

$50,000 - a venture capital investment that would be worth $700 million in another ten years - and a scientific advisory board of stellar scientists with equally stellar - but often divergent - ideas.

Rathmann's first job was to raise enough money to recruit a team of researchers and take off in pursuit of Genentech, the rapidly growing biotechnology company founded by genetic engineering pioneer Herb Boyer and others just four years earlier. And in a performance that he was to repeat many times, earning himself the nickname Golden Throat, he raised $19 million in just four months, including $5 million from his former employers at Abbott.

Raising the money was one thing. What to do with it was another. In line with the many and varied interests of its scientific advisory board, Amgen flirted with everything from human health to agriculture and industrial chemistry. At one stage, they even contemplated the idea of producing biosynthetic dyes for blue jeans.

It didn't take Rathmann long to decide that the company needed to focus on a much smaller number of projects, and that they had to be projects with the potential to deliver products. But at the same time, harking back to the lessons that he had learnt at 3M, they had to be projects to which his scientists were committed. His job, he said, was to raise the money to let them get on with theirs.

And raise it he did. Although already plagued by negative investor reaction to a string of early project failures, Rathmann's infectious enthusiasm for biotech was such that Amgen's 1983 IPO netted the company $42 million, and enabled him to focus on a handful of projects that he saw as having massive market potential. One of them was erythropoietin, or EPO, a hormone produced in the kidney that was thought to trigger red blood cell production. Another was granulocyte colony-stimulating factor (G-CSF), which was thought to facilitate the production of disease-fighting white blood cells.

Rathmann's focus, and his researchers' commitment, paid off. In October 1983, Amgen scientist Fu-Kuen Lin cloned the EPO molecule, and shortly afterward Amgen announced that it had produced EPO by splicing the gene into bacteria, yeast and mammalian cells. Meanwhile, Rathmann raised more development capital through licensing deals with a Japanese company, Kirin, who paid $12 million for the rights to the Japanese market, and Johnson & Johnson, who secured the rights to most markets in Europe and the United States. The exception, prophetically, was the US market for treatment of anaemia in patients on kidney dialysis, a side effect of which is lowered EPO production in the kidney, resulting in the need for frequent and painful blood transfusions.

In January 1987, Amgen reported positive results in 25 kidney dialysis patients, and in October of that year the company was awarded a patent covering the human gene that produces EPO as well as its production in large quantities by splicing the isolated gene into the ovarian cells of hamsters. Two days later, Amgen filed an application with the US Food and Drug Administration (FDA) seeking approval for the use of its genetically engineered EPO, Epogen, to treat chronic anaemia in kidney dialysis patients. Meanwhile, Rathmann, betting the bank on his success, had already started building the manufacturing facility.

Two years later, the FDA approved Amgen's application, with the added bonus of orphan drug status - because there were less than 200,000 kidney dialysis patients in the United States - giving exclusive marketing rights for an extra seven years. Amgen shipped its first batch of recombinant EPO to UCLA Medical Centre the very next day.

But Amgen was far from alone in chasing EPO. On the other side of the country, Genetics Institute, while not yet successful in producing recombinant EPO, had successfully purified small quantities of the hormone from human urine, and in June 1987, four months before the Amgen patent, Genetics Institute was granted a patent over the molecular structure of EPO, potentially including Amgen's recombinant molecule. Amgen's patent, on the other hand, specifically covered the manufacture and purification of recombinant EPO.

There was plenty at stake. Not only were the potential sales huge, but both companies had also licensed their product to major national and international pharmaceutical companies. Each company sued the other.

In late 1989 the Federal District Court in Boston ruled that both companies had valid patents, and both were infringing the other. The obvious path forward, and that strongly favoured by investors and market analysts, was for them to cross-license their intellectual property and share the market. As Rathmann put it, everybody said: "You should spend your money on R&D, not on litigation".

But Rathmann wasn't having a bar of it. After spending $250 million in development he was not going to give up half the returns for the sake of a few million dollars in legal fees. Pointing out that the Genetics Institute patent offered no path to large-scale production of EPO, he called the lawsuit "blackmail" and refused to sign a cross-licensing deal.

And he was right. In March 1991 the Federal Appeals Court gave Amgen a complete monopoly over the production and sale of EPO in the United States. By 1996, annual Epogen sales surpassed $1 billion.

Meanwhile, with Amgen's future secured by both Epogen and its G-CSF counterpart, Neupogen, and his own retirement secured with over $100 million of Amgen stock, George Rathmann had decided that it was time to move on, chair a board or two, play with the grandchildren, and smell the roses.

But it didn't last long.

Recruited to lead Seattle start-up ICOS Corporation, Rathmann's legendary money-raising capacity was back on show, starting in 1990 with a $5 million investment from Bill Gates and culminating in 1998 with $75 million from Eli Lilly to help develop Cialis, an innovative treatment for erectile dysfunction - and Rathmann's third blockbuster drug. Its success was such that, in 2007, Lilly decided to acquire sole rights to Cialis - by buying ICOS for $2.3 billion.

And then, after a decade each at Amgen and ICOS, the 72-year-old Rathmann started again, as Chairman and CEO of Hyseq, a Silicon Valley genomics company with a unique combination of high-throughput sequencing technology and a vast library of gene sequences with potential applications in cancer and cardiovascular disease.

For Rathmann, the prospects of achieving his boyhood dream of saving human lives were brighter than ever. Speaking at Princeton, his alma mater, in 2002, Rathmann said: "The sequencing of the human genome last year was a positive jolt for the whole field of biotechnology. We've barely scratched the surface of what its impact is going to be".

And added, with his characteristic combination of modesty and enthusiasm: "It's kind of fun to watch it unfold".

CRAIG VENTER

On June 26, 2000, a jubilant President Bill Clinton of the United States and Prime Minister Tony Blair of the United Kingdom jointly announced the outcome of an extraordinary scientific competition.

On one side were a 1,000 or more of the world's best scientists, backed by billions of dollars of government and philanthropic funding. They had been working on the project since 1980. On the other was J Craig Venter, a former Vietnam veteran who had once aspired to be a professional surfer, and who three years earlier had made the remarkable claim that his company, Celera Genomics, could complete the project in a fraction of the time and much more cheaply than the star-studded international team.

From a scientific perspective, the prize was as big as they get: the honour and glory of being first to reveal, almost 50 years after the discovery of the structure of DNA, the entire chemical sequence of the human genome. The outcome, in President Clinton's words, would be even bigger:

> With this profound new knowledge, humankind is on the verge of
> gaining immense, new power to heal. Genome science will have a real

impact on all our lives - and even more, on the lives of our children. It will revolutionize the diagnosis, prevention and treatment of most, if not all, human diseases.

So, what took them so long?

Basically, it was a problem of size. The human genome, like the genome of any other species, is made of DNA, a two-stranded helical ladder in which the only variable is the chemical nature of the rungs. Each of the rungs is formed from a pair of chemicals - adenine and thymine, represented by the letters A and T, or cytosine and guanine, represented by the letters C and G - and it is the precise sequence of those pairs of molecules - the rungs - that ultimately determines the chemical and biological makeup of any individual. Simple enough, one might think, until you learn that in the case of human beings the ladder has no less than 3,000 million rungs. If your genome were to be spelt out in a book with around 3,000 As, Cs, Ts and Gs per page, it would be a million pages long.

The international Human Genome Project, led initially by Nobel Laureate James Watson, one of the co-discoverers of the structure of DNA, began by producing a map of the genome based on the locations of known genes or other markers. They then used the map to break the problem down into smaller chunks, each corresponding to about a million letters of code, or about twice the length of this book. Each chunk of the puzzle was then assigned to a specialist research group, whose role was to use a combination of chemical sequencing and biological information to piece together individual chapters of the code. It was a Herculean task, and when Venter entered the race in 1998 the public consortium had succeeded in sequencing just 3% of the genome.

Venter, never afraid to take on the establishment, argued that the biology-driven approach could not possibly succeed. Rather, he claimed, the solution would lie with random DNA sequencing followed by massive computational analysis of the results. Taking the DNA from five genetically diverse individuals, including himself, Venter and his team shredded it into easily sequenced pieces, roughly equivalent in length to this paragraph. Because of the redundancy inherent in this process, there were multiple overlaps between sequences, just as there are between the last 14 letters of this paragraph and the first 14 of the next. So, all that was then needed was a computer powerful enough to mix and match tens of millions of pieces to produce a consensus sequence of the human genome.

The Human Genome Project, as it turned out, soon adopted many of Venter's techniques, just as Celera in turn used the data determined and published by the public consortium to assist in assembling its sequence. By 1999, both projects were 90% complete, and President Clinton brokered a draw. The two draft sequences were published on consecutive days in February 2001.

But, from Venter's viewpoint, the race had only just begun.

ଝଝଝ

He wasn't always that committed. As a schoolboy, Venter was an outstanding swimmer, but a very poor student. He liked building explosive devices, jumping freight trains and racing his bike alongside DC3s taking off from San Francisco airport. He barely managed to graduate from high school, and then chose to go surfing in Southern California rather than accept a college swimming scholarship, which, had he known it, would have kept him out of the war in Vietnam.

Remarkably enough, Venter credits his drafting into the US army in 1965 with turning his life around. It may have been the revelation that his IQ was the highest among 35,000 fellow draftees, or the discovery of his hands-on medical talents during the two years he spent studying and working as a medical orderly in Californian military hospitals. More likely, it was the six months the 21-year-old spent in charge of the intensive care ward at Da Nang airbase in Vietnam, where the combination of horrific injuries and inadequate medical facilities led him first to the brink of suicide, and then to the opposite conclusion. As he explained to Daniel Morrow:

> The fundamental thing that I learned, and almost anybody else learned that was there, is that the worst thing you had to lose was your life. So I

viewed basically every day since I got back as a gift, and I was determined
not to waste it or have it ruined by other peoples' small thinking. I figured
what's the worst thing that can happen if I take a risk and fail?

ଔଔଔ

Returning from Vietnam with vast practical medical experience but no
academic credentials, Venter studied at San Mateo Junior College before
gaining entry to the premed program at the University of California, San
Diego (UCSD), where his fascination with the fight or flight response
elicited by adrenaline led him to the discovery that its action was
mediated by a "receptor" molecule on the outside surface of cardiac cells.
And the thrill of that discovery led to another change of tack: abandoning
his plans to study medicine, Venter spent the next 15 years pursuing
the elusive adrenaline receptor, firstly as a PhD student at UCSD, then
as a professor at State University of New York, Buffalo, and finally as a
section head at the National Institutes of Health (NIH), where he and his
team taught themselves molecular biology before painstakingly piecing
together the sequence of the adrenaline gene. Never again, said Venter,
of his first experience of sequencing technology: "It was one of the most
ridiculous techniques that I'd ever seen".

Venter's disillusionment with the state of sequencing technology was
well timed. On the other side of the continent, University of Washington
researcher Leroy Hood had come up with a means of automating the
sequencing process, and instrument maker Applied Biosystems had
developed a prototype machine. But it was unproven technology, and no
one at NIH or elsewhere was prepared to risk the investment. No one, that
is, except Venter, who skated around the objections of his employers by
using his own funds, acquired from an earlier US government contract, to
become the proud owner of the world's first automated DNA sequencer.
Nine months later he published the sequences of two more receptor
genes.

Venter was off and running. Over the course of the next ten years he
made a series of dramatic breakthroughs that would revolutionise

sequencing technology and ultimately lead to the spelling out of all 3 billion letters of the human genome.

First, by switching his attention from DNA to RNA, the messenger molecule that dictates which pieces of DNA are translated into proteins, he was able to rapidly produce partial sequences for hundreds of human genes. He called them "expressed sequence tags" because, although they were only partial gene sequences, they provided enough information to enable researchers to go back and complete the sequence of any genes of interest.

It was a revolutionary concept, but not everybody in the scientific world was pleased. For many researchers, Venter's approach provided instant answers to questions that they had been pursuing for their entire careers. As Venter put it to Dan Morrow: "For many of these people, it's more important that they make the discovery than that it gets made". James Watson, now head of the public genome project, contemptuously dismissed Venter's discovery as work that could equally well be done by monkeys. Venter, for his part, saw the opportunity to use his expressed sequence tags to rapidly identify genes linked to the incidence, and ultimately the treatment, of human disease. Accompanied by his then wife and eminent fellow researcher, Claire Fraser, and supported by private investors, he left the NIH to establish the Institute for Genomic Research (TIGR). Within a year, they had sequenced fragments of thousands of human genes, including three previously unknown genes associated with colon cancer.

Second, working with Nobel Laureate Hamilton Smith, Venter came up with the idea that by shredding multiple copies of DNA into thousands of overlapping pieces, the sequencing problem could be converted from a laboriously slow chemical process into an extremely large, but tractable, computing exercise. They called their approach shotgun sequencing and, despite once again being knocked back for funding by NIH, proceeded to demonstrate the power of the technique by sequencing the first complete genome of a living organism, the bacterium *Helicobacter influenzae.*

Third, recognising that the human genome is more than 1,000 times longer than that of *H. influenzae*, and that the computational power required would be even greater again, Venter scaled up the technology. Using 26,000 random sequences from *H. influenzae* as the starting point, he pitted computer companies against each other in a race to assemble the bacterial genome, and then built the world's third largest computer, after those at the US Department of Defense, based on the outcome.

The stage was set. In the nine-month period between September 1999 and June 2000, a private company formed by Venter in association with Applied Biosystems, Celera Genomics, collected random DNA sequences equivalent to a five-fold coverage of the human genome. Those sequences, together with a further three-fold coverage from the Human Genome Project, provided all of the data required for Venter's computers to assemble a consensus sequence for the human genome, and allowed him to join President Clinton and Dr Francis Collins, Director of the National Human Genome Research Institute, in the White House for the announcement of their historic draw.

Again, not everyone was happy. Celera's investors had backed Venter's entry into the genome project in the expectation that the company would have a substantial competitive edge when the time came to commercially develop its outcomes, and the company's market capitalisation had soared to tens of billions of dollars. But the clear messages emanating from the sponsors of the public project gave them pause: as President Clinton and Prime Minister Blair put it in a joint announcement: "Human DNA should be made freely available to scientists everywhere". The Celera share price took a nosedive, and in 2002 Venter was unceremoniously dumped as CEO.

The unexpected dismissal slowed Venter down, but not for long. He went back to TIGR, whose financial stability he had guaranteed with the endowment of half of his Celera stock in happier times, and in May 2007 he announced the sequencing of the first complete genome of an individual human: that of J Craig Venter. The complete genome of a second individual, James Watson, was deposited with the GenBank database by public-sector researchers just two weeks later.

ଧଧଧ

Since then, Venter has moved on to an even larger stage. Sailing his yacht *Sorcerer II* around the globe, he is gathering millions of microorganisms from the world's oceans in an attempt to sequence the collective genome of an entire ecosystem. Based on the massive diversity of those organisms, he proposes to "force the evolution" of new life forms capable of addressing the major environmental issues facing mankind, including the capture of atmospheric carbon dioxide and the production of clean fuels. As he boasted to Roger Highfield of *The Daily Telegraph*: "Nobody knows what the fundamentals of life are or how it works. But I'm closer to answering these questions than science has ever been".

Science fiction? Perhaps not. In 2011, Venter and his colleagues produced the world's first man-made life form - a new bacterial species incorporating a genome synthesised from scratch in the laboratory.

ଧଧଧ

But how many other life forms are already out there that we don't know about yet? And what do they do?

BARRY MARSHALL

When modern humans made their way out of Africa around 60,000 years ago they were accompanied on their journey by a stomach bacterium that we now know as *Helicobacter pylori*. According to the World Health Organization, about half of the world's population (and up to 70% in developing countries) are infected by this bacterium - a common cause of ulcers.

The presence of these spiral-shaped bacteria in association with gastric ulcers was first observed late in the 19th century. Yet their potential involvement in the genesis of gastric disease was widely dismissed, and by the mid-20th century gastric acid was the universally accepted cause of ulcers. Indeed, that belief was so firmly entrenched that the work of the Greek physician John Lykoudis, who claimed to have successfully treated himself and thousands more peptic ulcer patients with a patented cocktail of antibiotics during the 1950s, was not only roundly rejected by his peers, but also ultimately led to his being fined for misconduct by the Athens Medical Association.

It should be no surprise, then, that the ulcer treatments developed during the second half of the 20th century were almost invariably based on efforts to reduce gastric acid levels. Among them were two of the most widely acclaimed developments in the emerging field of drug design.

The first of these developments, led by Dr Robin Ganellin at SmithKlineFrench in the United Kingdom, aimed to prevent histamine-induced gastric acid secretion by designing a drug that selectively blocked the histamine receptor. By systematically modifying the histamine molecule, over a period of 12 years and several hundred chemical iterations, Ganellin and his team produced cimetidine, which was introduced to the market in 1976 and soon became the first drug ever to reach $1 billion per annum in sales.

The second development followed the discovery in the 1970's that the final step in gastric acid secretion, whether induced by histamine or otherwise, was an enzyme known as the "proton pump", named for its capacity to boost hydrogen ion concentration in the stomach. Another team of medicinal chemists, this one led by Dr Per Lindberg at the Swedish pharmaceutical company Astra Hässle, (later AstraZeneca), painstakingly modified a potential lead molecule over a period of several years to produce a highly potent and irreversible inhibitor of the enzyme. The resulting drug, omeprazole, was first marketed in 1988 and by 1996 was the world's largest selling pharmaceutical ever. Its sales peaked in 2000 at $6 billion per annum!

But cimetidine and omeprazole weren't the only booming markets. Although they were both very effective in providing relief from the symptoms of gastric ulcers, they were not cures, and patients commonly returned within a year or two suffering the same symptoms and requiring a fresh diagnosis. The result was a third boom, this time in gastroenterology, and particularly in gastric endoscopy, which was routinely carried out on patients where peptic ulcer was suspected.

And overlaying all of this was the strongly held belief within the medical profession that peptic ulcers were further exacerbated by stress, necessitating changes in patient lifestyle, frequent recourse to antidepressants, and sometimes even psychiatric referrals.

Not to put too fine a point on it, both the pharmaceutical industry and the medical establishment had a lot to lose from some upstart researcher claiming that the real cause of peptic ulcers was a spiral-shaped microorganism that lived happily in stomach acid, and that the majority of patients could be cured with a simple two-week course of inexpensive antibiotics!

ଧଧଧ

Growing up in the outback of Western Australia, Barry Marshall was an experimentalist from the start. Be it building crystal sets, bombs or hot air balloons, his instinct was to try it first and ask questions later. Irrepressibly curious, he learnt early on to trust the evidence before his eyes.

If ever there was someone ready, willing and able to upset the cosy relationship between the pharmaceutical industry and the gastroenterology community, it was the brash young Barry Marshall, fresh out of medical school and ready to make his mark.

ଧଧଧ

When Barry Marshall walked into Doctor Robin Warren's laboratory in 1981, Warren was near his wit's end. He'd spent the past two years investigating the occurrence of tiny curved bacteria in biopsy samples from the stomachs of patients with gastritis. The only problem was that no one believed him. Clinicians at the Royal Perth Hospital, to whom he reported his discoveries, were quick to point out what "everybody knew": nothing whatsoever, let alone Warren's bacteria, could survive in the acidic environment of the stomach. Besides, they asked: "If they are there, why hasn't anyone described them before?"

Marshall, seeking a research project to complete his internship as a physician, had no such doubts. From his point of view, previously unknown bacteria, living in an environment previously supposed to be sterile, represented not an impossibility, but an opportunity, an opportunity to be part of a revolutionary scientific discovery.

Over the course of the next six months, Marshall and Warren collected gastric biopsies from 100 consecutive endoscopy patients, and demonstrated the presence of Warren's curved bacteria in 58% of the cases. They were also successful, somewhat serendipitously, in culturing the new bacterium, subsequently known as *H. pylori*, from a culture plate left sitting on a laboratory bench over the Easter long weekend.

But what was ultimately to prove the truly groundbreaking discovery came when Marshall compared the data from the biopsies with the medical histories of the patients: the biopsies of all 13 patients with duodenal ulcers revealed the presence of the new bacterium. Coincidence, or correlation? And if there were a correlation, did the ulcers attract the bacteria, or the bacteria cause the ulcers?

Marshall, convinced that the evidence supported the latter interpretation, saw his opportunity and ran with it. If all of the patients with duodenal ulcers also harboured *Helicobacter*, then antibiotic treatment, provided it permanently eliminated the bacteria, might also cure ulcers! But first there was the problem of the chicken and the egg. He needed to prove that *Helicobacter* was causative for peptic ulcers, rather than simply associated with them.

Marshall's solution was simple, a tad foolhardy, and highly unlikely to have been approved by his hospital ethics committee. Following an endoscopic examination to establish that his gastrointestinal tract was in good shape - no gastritis, no ulcers, no *Helicobacter* - Marshall swallowed the contents of a vial crawling with cultured *H. pylori*. To the horror of all concerned, he developed a sufficiently impressive case of gastritis to prompt his long-suffering wife, Adrienne, to demand immediate treatment. Not quite an ulcer, but quite enough to encourage Marshall to conduct a series of critical experiments to prove the connection between *Helicobacter* and peptic ulcers.

First, he showed that bismuth, a chemical that had been used historically as an anti-ulcer treatment, but whose mechanism of action had never been understood, inhibited the growth of *Helicobacter* in laboratory cultures. Bismuth, he reasoned, was exerting its effect on ulcers by killing the causative agent, *Helicobacter*.

Second, to test that hypothesis, he began treating peptic ulcer patients in his clinic at Fremantle Hospital with a combination of bismuth and readily available antibiotics to eradicate *H. pylori*. The results were spectacular: the majority of patients were cured in less than two weeks.

Finally, Marshall and his colleagues conducted a placebo-controlled double-blind trial, the gold standard in drug testing, in which they showed that the recurrence of peptic ulcers was dramatically reduced by the eradication of *Helicobacter* as opposed to treatment with conventional drugs used to reduce gastric acid secretion. In other words, while billion-dollar drugs such as cimetidine and omeprazole provided effective relief from ulcers in the short term, it was necessary to remove the underlying cause, *H. pylori*, to prevent their return.

Enough already? Not quite. By the end of 1984, many of the international microbiology community were already persuaded of the connection between *H. pylori* and ulcers, but the medical fraternity, despite - or perhaps because of - Marshall's consummate salesmanship, remained largely unmoved.

From Marshall's perspective, the situation was intolerable: not only were millions of patients being denied improved treatment for ulcers, but billions of dollars were being squandered in unnecessary hospitalisation and lost productivity. With the support of Procter & Gamble, manufacturers of an existing bismuth drug, Marshall decided to move to the United States, where he hoped to rapidly convince medical opinion leaders of the veracity of the *H. pylori* story. But old dogmas die hard: it was ten years before a consensus meeting at the National Institutes of Health finally signalled general acceptance by the medical profession that the essential first step in the treatment of peptic ulcer is the identification and eradication of *H. pylori*.

Marshall, meanwhile, was not sitting on his hands. Working at the University of Virginia, he had spent the intervening period treating patients, developing antibiotic therapies and diagnostics, and generally promoting the *H. pylori* story around the globe, including establishing a foundation for the education of patients and doctors. Now, with *H. pylori* finally accepted as the dominant cause of ulcers, it was time to move on. In 1994, he quit the laboratory to work with a US biotech company on commercialising his *Helicobacter* diagnostic tests, and in the following year returned to Perth, where he has gone on to establish two Australian biotechnology companies and an infectious diseases institute at the University of Western Australia. One of his companies, Ondek Pty Ltd, is developing a genetically modified *H. pylori* bacterium to deliver influenza and AIDS vaccines via the gut. Who else but Marshall would hire a fox to guard the hen house?

ఴఴఴ

In 2005, 24 years after their first observations of the link between *H. pylori* and peptic ulcers, Marshall and Warren were awarded the Nobel Prize in physiology or medicine. As a result of their work, patients who were formerly condemned to expensive gastric acid reducing treatments for the rest of their lives are now routinely cured by general practitioners, and the frequency of gastric cancer in developed societies has declined dramatically.

Marshall, ever the big picture man, concluded his Nobel lecture with the statement that the consequent freeing up of clinical resources for colonoscopic diagnosis and treatment "should have a flow-on effect causing a reduction in colon cancer as well".

REBELS WITH CAUSE

Rathmann, Venter and Marshall are all supremely disruptive innovators, trailblazers whose persistence and courage in the face of relentless criticism, as well as their joy and enthusiasm in the pursuit of new science, have enabled them to change the world of medicine.

When Nobel Laureate James Watson said that Rathmann's ongoing litigation with Genetics Institute was "confusing his anger with good business sense", Rathmann redoubled his efforts and won. When colleagues described Craig Venter as "an asshole" whose results could equally readily have been achieved by monkeys, he staked his job and his reputation on investing in bigger and better monkeys (massive computing power and new sequencing technologies), and then challenged the world's best scientists to take him on. And when a leading Australian gastroenterologist described Marshall as that "crazy guy saying crazy things", he swallowed a Petri dish full of *H. pylori*, and then stared down the medical establishment's derision when he presented the results.

And the outcomes are clear.

Barry Marshall reversed half a century of medical dogma relating to peptic ulcers and other gastric disorders, revolutionising their prevention and treatment for the benefit of mankind. Curing an ulcer with antibiotics now takes less time and costs less than one-tenth as much as treating ulcer symptoms over a lifetime.

George Rathmann created the world's most successful biotechnology company, improving millions of lives and saving billions of dollars by using EPO to delay progression to renal dialysis in patients suffering from chronic kidney disease.

And Craig Venter's groundbreaking work in human genomics is finally delivering on the extraordinary promise of personalised medicine. In

2012 the Western world's first drug to fix a faulty gene, a single-dose treatment that uses a virus to introduce a healthy replacement gene in the potentially lethal hereditary disorder lipoprotein lipase deficiency, was approved by the European Commission.

And yes, if you really want to know, you can now get your personal genome analysed for just $99.

EPILOGUE

In April 2012, George Rathmann died of complications from kidney disease. For the past ten years of his life he had been taking EPO, the genetically engineered drug that Amgen had created under his leadership. Asked, a few years before his death, for his thoughts on the future of biotechnology, he said: "I think we'll see a continuing blossoming of the effects of biotechnology. This is a beautiful, beautiful science".

KEY SOURCES

GEORGE RATHMANN

Argelio R. Dumenigo, "Behind the biotech boom", *Princeton Alumni Weekly*, April 24, 2002.

Rami Grunbaum, "George Rathmann: biotech vet guiding Icos Corp. through hot incubation stage", *Business Journal - Portland*, March 2, 1992.

Arthur Kornberg, *The Golden Helix: inside Biotech Ventures*, Univ Science Books, 2002.

Eric Pfeiffer, "Biotechnology All-Stars", *Forbes ASAP*, May 31, 1999.

Dinesh Ramde, "The birth of biotechnology: harnessing the power of DNA", *Economic Perspectives*, October 2005.

Arnold Thackray, Leo Slater, and David Brock, "George B. Rathmann", Chemical Heritage Foundation, Oral History Transcript # 0187, September 1999.

Luke Timmerman, "George Rathmann, founding CEO of Amgen and Icos, dies at 84", *Xconomy*, April 23, 2012.

CRAIG VENTER

Ross Douthat, "The god of small things", *The Atlantic*, January/February, 2007.

Roger Highfield, "Ripped genes", *The Daily Telegraph*, May 27, 2006.

Jenny Hope, "Drug to fix faulty DNA gets go-ahead in landmark move that may alter medicine forever", *Reuters*, November 2, 2012.

Clyde A Hutchison III, "DNA Sequencing: bench to bedside and beyond", *Nucleic Acids Research*, September, 2007.

Daniel S Morrow, "Dr Craig Venter: oral history", *Computerworld Honors Program*, April 21, 2003.

Susan Okie, "Is Craig Venter going to save the planet? Or is this more hype from one of America's most controversial scientists?", *The Washington Post*, August 12, 2011.

Steven Shapin, "I'm a surfer", *London Review of Books*, March 20, 2008.

The White House, Office of the Press Secretary, "Remarks made by the President, Prime Minister Tony Blair of England (via satellite), Dr. Francis Collins, Director of the National Human Genome Research Institute, and Dr. Craig Venter, President and Chief Scientific Officer, Celera Genomics Corporation, on the completion of the first survey of the entire Human Genome Project", June 26, 2000.

BARRY MARSHALL

Academy of Achievement, "Interview: Barry Marshall, Nobel Prize in Medicine", May 23, 1998.

Mark Kidd and Irvin Modlin, "A century of *Helicobacter pylori*", *Digestion*, 1998.

Barry J. Marshall, "*Helicobacter* connections", *Nobel Lecture*, December 8, 2005.

Stephen Pinnock, "Nobel Prize winners Robin Warren and Barry Marshall", *The Lancet*, Vol. 366, October 22, 2005.

Melissa Sweet, "Snug as a bug", *The Sydney Morning Herald*, August 2, 1997.

Richard A Robbins, "Profiles of medical courage: the courage to experiment and Barry Marshall", *Southwest Journal of Pulmonary and Critical Care*, Vol. 5, 2012.

J. Robin Warren, "*Helicobacter* - the ease and difficulty of a new discovery", *Nobel Lecture*, December 8, 2005.

An individual with an epic ambition to change the world, who ...	George Rathmann	Craig Venter	Barry Marshall
	Born: 1927, Milwaukee, Wisconsin, USA Education: BS, Northwestern University; PhD, Princeton University Organisation: Amgen	Born: 1946, Salt Lake City, Utah, USA Education: BS (Biochemistry), PhD, University of California, San Diego Organisation: J. Craig Venter Institute	Born: 1951, Kalgoorlie, Australia Education: MBBS, University of Western Australia Organisation: University of Western Australia
... sees and seizes opportunities for change ...			
Opportunistic: aggressively seeks and adopts new ideas	Noting that gene splicing from one organism into another was "the most important thing I had ever seen", Rathmann requested sabbatical leave from his senior executive position at Abbott Laboratories, went to California to learn the technology, ...	Learning of the invention of an automated gene sequencing machine, Venter saw an opportunity to become first mover in the emerging field of genomics. Ignoring the decision of the Director of the National Institutes of Health to the contrary, ...	Marshall was the first person to take pathologist Robin Warren's observation of bacteria living in the acidic environment of the stomach seriously.
& Visionary: intuitively grasps the big picture and how it might evolve	... and decided to stay on as founding CEO of Applied Molecular Genetics (Amgen): "The decision was easy for me because the science was so powerful".	... he purchased the very first machine, describing its arrival in his laboratory as "my future in a crate".	Anticipating the potential relevance of Warren's helical bacteria to gastric disease ...
... senses the way forward ..			
Innovative: thinks creatively, ignores boundaries, disrupts the status quo	"I'm almost always viewed by business people as one of the best scientists they know, and I'm almost always viewed by scientists as one of the best business people they know, ...	Realising that successful decoding of the human genome would require massive investments in both sequencing technology and computing power, he came up with a novel investment structure, ...	... he initiated a series of gastric biopsies from endoscopy patients that revealed a possible link between the bacteria and peptic ulcer, ...
but Pragmatic: recognises constraints, devises practical solutions, creates value	... the common denominator is that I'm not much of a scientist or a businessman".	... involving a non-profit research institute that would be free to publish new genome sequences, but be paid for by a commercial venture, Celera Genomics, that would have the rights to further process and market the genomic information.	... but knowing the level of proof required to conclusively demonstrate the connection: "I realised I had to have an animal model and decided to use myself".
... attracts the necessary resources ..			
Persuasive: articulate and convincing communicator, consummate networker	Rathmann raised $19 million, the then largest-ever first round investment in a biotechnology company, earning himself the nickname "Golden Throat", and ...	Having decided that the Drosophila (fruit fly) genome would be an ideal test case for his technology, he convinced the head of the publicly funded Drosophila genome program to join him in a "demonstration project".	In the face of growing personal attacks and a morale-sapping rejection of his results by the Gastroenterological Society of Australia, he found a more supportive audience in Europe ...

& Empowering: attracts talent, inspires loyalty, rewards excellence	...enabling him to attract the best people and create an environment in which they had free rein to pursue their ideas unfettered by the demands of managers and investors.	After successfully completing the 120-million-letter sequence in just four months, he hosted the world's leading Drosophila scientists at Celera for a two-week "annotation jamboree" to interpret the data. "It was like kids in a candy store... it was just an electric atmosphere".	... where there were soon several groups "obtaining results which paralleled those of our group in Perth. We became a closely knit group" and "have shared a remarkable story together".
... and pursues the dream ..			
Focussed: passionate and highly energetic perfectionist, totally committed to an overriding vision	Initially, the scientific program at Amgen was scattered over many projects, but Rathmann knew that he needed not only great science, but also great products, ...	Issuing a public challenge to the international Human Genome Project he claimed that ...	But the medical establishment remained unconvinced. In 1986, Marshall decided that the only way to prove the story to the gastroenterology community was to go to the United States and replicate the research there.
& Confident: driven by unconditional self-belief, assumes absolute authority and accountability	... and bet Amgen's limited capital on a handful of projects, of which two, Epogen and Neupogen, would go on to become multibillion dollar drugs.	... he could sequence the human genome with a "$300 million budget, one-tenth of the public project's budget, and in three years, a fifth of the time of the public project".	"We departed Australia, believing that it shouldn't take more than 2 or 3 years to convince the world that antibiotics would cure most gastric diseases".
... regardless of the odds ..			
Resilient: flexible, thrives on change and uncertainty, learns from mistakes	Ridiculed by investors and the financial press for wasting money on court battles over conflicting EPO patents rather than settling for a share of the action ...	Sacked by Celera, ...	In fact, it took ten years: "My results were disputed and disbelieved, not on the basis of science but because they simply could not be true".
& Courageous: bold, intelligent risk-taker, undaunted by criticism, determined to succeed	... Rathmann gambled on winning it all, and did.	... he raised the stakes, sailing his 95' yacht around the world in a bid to collect and sequence the genome of an entire ecosystem (marine microorganisms) and use it to address the major environmental challenges facing mankind.	Twenty years later, in his Nobel acceptance speech, Marshall quoted the American historian Daniel Boorstin: "The greatest obstacle to knowledge is not ignorance: it is the illusion of knowledge".

Chapter 7

COMING CLEAN

IN MARCH 2011, CHINA ADOPTED its 12th five-year national development plan. Its overriding theme is sustainable growth: how to balance economic growth of at least 7% per annum with the environmental pressures from massive energy use, pollution and resource depletion.

Many of the answers proposed in the plan revolve around cleaner technologies. Of the seven priority industries, slated to grow from 2% of GDP to 8% by 2015, one focuses on new energy sources - notably nuclear, wind and solar - and another on clean energy vehicles. Both are driven by the Chinese government's commitment to reducing greenhouse gas emissions per unit of GDP by 40%, relative to 2005 levels, by 2020.

And underpinning all of this is renewed emphasis on cutting back pollution, particularly of waterways, and tackling the perennial issue of water security in a nation with just 7% of the world's fresh water and 21% of the world's population. The target for this five-year plan is to reduce water consumption by 30% for every new dollar of industrial output, following on the 37% reduction achieved in the preceding five years.

But where will China find the merchants of light capable of delivering on these ambitious environmental targets?

One of its own, Zhengrong Shi, worked on groundbreaking solar cell technology in Australia before bringing it back to China. Visionary Israeli computer scientist Shai Agassi circumnavigated the globe as he gathered support for a revolutionary electric car industry. And Olivia Lum, orphaned in Malaysia, began by tackling the water problems of Singapore before taking her technology to China.

OLIVIA LUM

When the Parliament of Malaysia accepted Prime Minister Tunku Abdul Rahman's recommendation to expel Singapore from the Federation of Malaysia in August 1965, the new country's new Prime Minister, Lee Kuan Yew, faced a daunting prospect: how to sustain a population of 2 million people, increasing at 2.5% per annum, on a 580-km^2 island with virtually no natural resources?

Most of all, he worried about water. Despite the agreement, signed three years earlier, giving Singapore the right to draw up to 250 million gallons of water from Malaysia's Johore River every day for the following 100 years, Lee was deeply concerned by the potential security threat of Singapore's dependence on Malaysia. He vowed to do everything within his power to wean his nation off imported water supplies.

And unbeknown to Lee, the person who would ultimately do more than any other toward achieving his goal was already tackling her own issues with water. Her name was Olivia Lum Ooi Lin, she was four years old and, as she recently recalled in an interview with David Schner of *Leaders* magazine: "I grew up in a hut with no proper sanitation and no running water. From a young age, I learned to value water".

ଷଷଷ

Olivia also learned the value of money. Abandoned at birth, she lived with her adoptive "grandmother" in an attap palm hut in the once wealthy tin-mining town of Kampar, 200 km north of Kuala Lumpur. She was one of five adopted children in the family, and "we all had to learn how to make a living: how to sell products on the street". By the time she was nine, she was the family's principal breadwinner, working before school as a rubber-tapper and supplementing that meagre income by selling fruit and clothing to her classmates, weaving rattan bags and providing musical accompaniment for funeral processions. And along with all that, she found time to excel at school.

Encouraged by her teachers to make more of her life, Olivia Lum left Malaysia for Singapore at the age of 15, and proceeded to door-knock schools until she found one willing to accept her. Then, in a pattern that was to continue for the next ten years, she combined her studies with a series of increasingly sophisticated business activities, ranging from tutoring and waitressing to marketing cosmetics and insurance policies. By the time she began her science degree at the National University of Singapore (NUS) she had established a business partnership delivering meals to workers on construction sites, and earned enough capital to buy her first car.

Graduating from NUS with an honours degree in Chemistry, Lum's first job was every Singaporean student's dream: a secure well-paid position with a major multinational company. But not so for Lum: barely three years after starting as a chemist in the waste water treatment division of Glaxo she quit, informing her gobsmacked boss that "I have no money, no technology to sell, and no customers, but I feel that water is a sunrise business, and that I can do something for the environment". With $16,000 raised from the sale of her apartment and car, she hired two staff and set up Hydrochem (later renamed Hyflux), purveyor of locally produced water treatment services to businesses seeking ways to treat wastewater from industrial processes.

Using all the selling skills and resilience that she had learned in her childhood, Olivia hit the road, working her way up and down the Malay peninsula selling water treatment systems from the back of her motorbike. It was, she said, "a pure leap of faith. I had no business plan, no funding". But she certainly had motivation. On the one hand, she told David Schner: "I was determined to get out of the poverty cycle, to become rich and never to be in want again". On the other hand, "I wanted to save the world. I could see that with so much waste being discharged into natural rivers, one day we would not have clean water to drink".

Within five years she'd made her first million.

But Olivia was not about to rest on her laurels for long. In the early 1990s she made three key strategic moves that would transform her company.

First, recognising the potential of membrane filtration systems to lower the environmental footprint of water purification processes relative to existing chemical technologies, she established an R&D arm focused on developing and manufacturing proprietary customised membranes for use in desalination and wastewater treatment. The resulting ultrafine membrane filters have been the hallmark of Hyflux's operations ever since.

Second, she recognised the effectiveness of in situ demonstration of her products as a direct marketing strategy. Beginning with a recycling plant at Jurong Bird Park, where the penguins - notoriously fussy about their water quality - proclaimed her product a huge success, she went on to demonstrate her membrane technology to multinational engineering conglomerate Siemens, whose resulting contract was her first big commercial break.

And third, recognising the need to bolster her business with markets outside Singapore, and conscious of the likely increase in pressure on China's water supplies resulting from pollution of waterways with industrial waste, she raised $1.2 million from friends and university colleagues to establish a subsidiary company in Shanghai.

It was a brave and prophetic move. In the early 1990s China was still finding its way into the global market, and environmental and water issues were not a priority. For three years, handicapped by her youth, an unfamiliar business and cultural environment, and a lack of sufficient *guanxi* (business relationships), the Chinese subsidiary lost money, virtually bankrupting the entire company. But then, letting her technology and a 60-year-old Chinese associate do the talking, the business began to grow. By 2010 she had built 40 water purification plants, treating waste water from China's booming chemical, pharmaceutical and pulp and paper industries, as well as the biggest desalination plant in China, at Tianjin.

Those successes are now being replicated in India, North Africa and the Middle East. With over 2,000 employees around the globe, she has an order book approaching $2 billion, and dreams of the day that her technology will give access to potable water to everyone on the planet, no matter how poor.

ଧ୧ଧ

But what about Singapore? What of Lee Kuan Yew's issues?

Between 1998 and 2002 a series of acrimonious discussions between Malaysia and Singapore led to Malaysia proposing a 200-fold increase in the price of water supplied to Singapore from the Johore River. Recognising its vulnerability to water warfare, the Singapore government introduced the Four Tap Policy, which aims to dramatically reduce reliance on Malaysian water by increasing the volume of water sourced from seawater desalination, reclaimed water and rainfall.

As usual, Olivia Lum was ahead of the game. When the government announced its plan to build a plant to recycle wastewater into drinking water, she and her staff worked day and night to win the S$16 million contract. Two years later, she won another, as well as the S$200 million contract to build Singapore's first desalination plant. And in 2011, Hyflux was selected as the preferred bidder to design, build, own and operate Singapore's second and largest seawater desalination plant for a concession period of 25 years.

By 2010, Singapore was well on the way toward water independence, with 60% of its water supply coming from wastewater reclamation (30%), desalination (10%) and rainfall (20%). And the technologies and industries spawned in the process, led by the orphan from Malaysia, had prompted the government to announce plans for Singapore "to become a Global Hydrohub through R&D, engineering and manufacturing with the aim of serving three percent of the global water market by 2015".

For Olivia Lum, currently completing construction of a 500,000 cubic metres/day reverse osmosis desalination plant - the world's largest - in Magtaa, Algeria, that won't be a moment too soon.

ৎৎৎ

In 2011, 50 years after being abandoned in the Kampur District Hospital in Perak, Malaysia, Olivia Lum was named Ernst and Young Entrepreneur of the Year, the first woman ever to achieve that distinction.

ZHENGRONG SHI

While the blackest cloud on China's horizon remains the unceasing demand for more and more energy to drive the nation's economic growth, there's also a silver lining: renewable, clean and nuclear energy are projected to supply 52% of increased energy requirements between 2011 and 2015, en route to meeting the nation's target of sourcing 15% of all energy requirements from renewable sources by 2020. And, according to Zhang Xiaoqiang, vice-chairman of China's National Development and Reform Commission, in an interview with *The Guardian* in 2009: "We can be sure we will exceed the 15% target. We will at least reach 18%. Personally I think we could reach the target of having renewables provide 20% of total energy consumption".

A major cause for that optimism is the extraordinary growth in China's solar power industry, driven by a steady stream of expatriate solar engineers returning to seek a slice of China's booming economy. Many of them come from a single laboratory in Australia.

ৎৎৎ

When Martin Green founded the Solar Photovoltaics Group at the University of New South Wales in 1974, a key driver was Telecom Australia's need to provide power sources for microwave repeater stations in outback Australia. But the quality of his research soon attracted international recognition, and when he and his colleague Stuart Wenham developed an efficiency-boosting new technology known as the "buried contact solar cell" smart young scientists from around the world beat a path to their door.

Shi Zhengrong wasn't one of them. He was already at the University of New South Wales, on a one-year Chinese government scholarship, when he saw an advertisement for a job in Green's laboratory.

That was Shi Zhengrong's second serious stroke of luck. The first was 26 years earlier, on the day he was born.

ଛଛଛ

By rights, Shi Zhengrong should have had almost as rocky a start in life as Olivia Lum. His peasant farmer parents, already struggling to feed themselves and two older children, were stunned by the arrival on February 10, 1963, of twin boys. Also in shock, but for different reasons, was the neighbouring Shi family, whose stillborn daughter was delivered on the same day.

The simple and practical solution was obvious to both families. The Shi family adopted the younger Chen twin, named him Shi Zhengrong, and he never looked back.

Both Zhengrong and his adoptive parents clearly valued education. According to one of his teachers, Shi was so keen to learn that, while too young to attend school, he would listen to lessons from outside the classroom. And when, after achieving high grades throughout his schooling, the 16-year-old won a scholarship to Changchun University of Science and Technology, his proud parents turned on a banquet to honour his teachers and celebrate his success.

Like universities throughout China, Changchun was still recovering from its enforced hibernation during Chairman Mao's Cultural Revolution, but was rapidly rebuilding its one-time strengths in optics, electronics and material science. Shi too acquired these strengths, completing his bachelor's degree in 1983 and going on to a master's degree in laser physics at the Shanghai Institute of Optics and Fine Mechanics before winning a coveted spot in China's emerging overseas study program. By 1988, he was enrolled in the Physics Department at the University of New South Wales, Australia, happily married, and supplementing his Chinese government scholarship with a job grilling hamburgers in a local restaurant.

But back in China, things weren't going so well. The crushing of the Tiananmen Square protests by the People's Liberation Army had cast its pall over China's economic reemergence, and Zhengrong Shi soon became less concerned with his studies than with events at home. By the time he knocked on Martin Green's door in December 1989, his motives were simple. He wanted to stay in Australia, and he wanted a job.

That meeting with Green changed the course of Shi's life. Until that point, as he explained to Andrew Batson of *The Wall Street Journal*, all of his academic choices had been made by others: "In our generation, we didn't have the freedom to choose. We just accept what we are given. So it's hard to plan". But now he saw an opportunity to translate his science into outcomes, and he went for it. Accepting Green's offer of a PhD scholarship to do solar research, he worked day and night: "There was so much fun in doing research! And I could be a good scientist! I never thought of it when I was in China". After completing a PhD in record time, he stayed on as a senior research scientist, working with Green and his colleague Stuart Wenham on next-generation "crystalline silicon on glass (CSG)" technology.

The partnership blossomed further in 1995, when Green and Wenham, seeking to further develop CSG and other thin film technologies, raised capital from a state-owned electricity utility to establish Pacific Solar Pty Ltd, with Shi as deputy director of R&D.

It was a fulfilling time. On the one hand, Shi and his research team were able to progress the development of CSG and other technologies needed to scale up and improve the efficiency of solar panels. On the other, he and his family - now including two sons - settled happily into an affluent Australian way of life, including taking up Australian citizenship and investing much of his newfound salary in real estate.

But Shi became impatient with the start-up's focus on research. In his view, it was time to stop researching new technologies and start commercialising some of the old ones. And he began to hear whispers of the investments being made by Chinese provincial governments in attracting smart scientists back to China. He decided to pay a visit to China to see for himself. What he found there drove the next big change in Shi's life.

Back in Australia, Shi wrote a business plan for a company that would fast-track the development of cheaper, more efficient solar cells by exploiting a combination of existing solar cell technologies and the ready availability of inexpensive Chinese labour. With more bravado than detail, it proclaimed that Shi would lower the cost of solar panels from $5 per watt of output to $3, thus developing a major export industry targetting heavily subsidised European and Japanese solar cell markets.

But when he bounced the plan off his colleagues, Shi got a less than enthusiastic response. According to Wenham: "I didn't think it was a good idea, and I told him so". Undeterred, Shi went ahead and put his proposal to the governments of several Chinese provincial cities. The response was rapid, with a delegation from the city of Wuxi arriving in Sydney to make Shi an offer he found hard to refuse - Wuxi would provide cheap land and labour, and identify investors willing to contribute $6 million in return for 75% of the company. Shi, for his part, would contribute his technology, plus the $400,000 he had accumulated from his real estate investments, for the other 25%. Shi would be managing director, and a local government official, Li Yanren, would be chairman of the board.

Shi took the bait and returned to China. And within two years, capitalising on the combination of cheap Chinese labour and the expertise of his colleagues in Australia, he had delivered on his business plan, producing solar panels at just over $2 per watt of output.

But the public/private partnership underpinning the venture was less successful. The Wuxi government and their local investors, seeing the company's success, sought more involvement. Shi, for his part, saw their presence as a constraint. Li Yanren, caught in the middle, became increasingly frustrated. As one of the founding shareholders put it: "I have helped you through so many difficulties, and now that you are starting to make money you push me out?"

Ultimately, in April 2005, Shi prevailed, organising US venture capitalists to buy out the Chinese investors for $80 million: a handy profit, but miniscule compared to what they would have made six months later, when Suntech became the first privately owned Chinese company to list on the New York Stock Exchange - at a valuation of $5.5 billion!

By 2012, Suntech was the world's largest manufacturer of solar panels, with many of its 14,000 employees layering silicon by hand in its four Chinese production facilities. Many more of its employees were engaged in research and development in laboratories in Australia, Germany and Japan, reporting to Chief Technical Officer Stuart Wenham and advised by Shi's former teacher, Professor Martin Green. Shi continued to make regular visits to Australia, funding PhD scholarships, recruiting research scientists and further developing joint technology programs. And six more former students from Green's laboratory had followed in his footsteps to establish successful solar businesses in China.

As Martin Green puts it: "A worthy legacy for a farmer's son from Yangzhong".

But Shi's ambitions remain far from satisfied. He sees the future of his company as an energy company on the same scale as BP or Shell, but as "a solar energy company, not an oil energy company". If he's right, and if the Chinese government has its way, one of his biggest customers will be the auto industry.

SHAI AGASSI

When the Chinese government announced its plans to put 5 million all-electric cars on the road by 2020, some of China's most dynamic entrepreneurs sat up and took notice. Leading the charge was Wang Chuanfu.

Much like Olivia Lum and Zhengrong Shi, Wang had come from a poor rural family, raised by his older brother and sister after the death of his parents. But by 2009 he had made it all the way to the number one spot on the Hurun Rich List, with a personal fortune estimated at $5 billion.

Wang's BYD Company, already the largest producer of mobile phone batteries on the planet, bought into the car business in 2003, with plans to become the world's biggest car maker by 2025. But despite a $250 million investment from Warren Buffet, and strong support from the Chinese government, consumer preferences intervened. Of the 18 million cars produced by Chinese-based car companies in 2011, only 8,000 were electric. Cost was a major factor, as was the preference, among the small proportion of the Chinese population who could afford to buy cars, for luxury Western models.

Wang met the challenge head-on, announcing a joint venture with Daimler that would combine BYD's battery and electric drive technology with the German manufacturer's safety and quality. Their sleek new all-electric vehicle, the DENZA EV, was unveiled at the 2012 Beijing Motor show, with a projected launch date of 2013. But ongoing delays in recharging infrastructure, exacerbated by so-called "range anxiety", continue to put Wang's targets in doubt.

What chance of the Chinese, let alone the Western world, being weaned off gasoline if they need to stop every 150 km for a two-hour recharge?

A very disruptive Israeli thinks he knows.

ଧଧଧ

Born with an entrepreneurial spoon in his mouth, Shai Agassi was seven years old when he began writing computer programs in Fortran. As he explained to Steve Hamm of *BusinessWeek*, "Programming was the ultimate sandbox. You could control things and build things". His first business proposition, made to his father at the age of 14, was: "If you buy me an Apple IIe, I'll give you 10 percent of my lifetime profits from writing software".

ଧଧଧ

Shai Agassi's mother and father were still children when their families migrated to Israel from Morocco and Iraq, respectively, following Israel's declaration of independence from Britain in 1948. His father, Reuven, bitterly disappointed by his failure to gain admission to Israel's technical university, worked for the Communications, Electronics and Computer Corps of the Israeli Defence Force before finally being accepted to study electrical engineering and computing at the Technion in 1968, the year that Shai was born. After graduating, he remained in the army, ultimately rising to the rank of Lieutenant Colonel before moving on to executive roles with electronics and telecommunications conglomerate Tadiran and defence electronics manufacturer Elbit.

Shai followed in his father's footsteps, but in reverse order, enrolling for an undergraduate course in computer science at the Technion at the age of 15, and subsequently undertaking military service in the Israeli Defence Force. Along the way, he was hit by the proverbial bus, resulting in 12 months or more of painful surgery and the lasting legacy of one short leg.

The repayments on the Apple IIe began in earnest after Shai finished his military service. Between 1990 and 1993, he and his father founded a string of four business software companies, all of which they ran as 50:50 partnerships. As Shai told the *San Francisco Chronicle*: "I was the visionary, he anchored me in reality". But in 1995, Shai slipped his moorings, taking one of the companies, TopTier, to the United States while Reuven remained in Israel managing the other three.

Incorporated in the United States in 1996, TopTier Software Inc specialised in the development of enterprise portals - software frameworks that enabled businesses and their customers to integrate and manage information from multiple sources inside and outside the company. And Shai was a master of the art, crisscrossing the globe as he built the company into one of the world's leading providers of portal software. And then, in 2001, he sold it to SAP, Europe's largest software company, for $400 million. He was 33 years old.

Following the sale, Agassi became CEO of SAP Portals, rising rapidly through the ranks to become the first non-German member of the Executive Board, with sole responsibility for all technological development within the company. And by 2006 there was a general expectation - shared by Shai - that he would be the next CEO of SAP, doing battle with Microsoft and Oracle as the world's leading producer of business software.

ಬಬಬ

There had been no shortage of accolades for Agassi during his five years at SAP. Most extraordinary, perhaps, was his anointment, at the tender age of 34, by TIME/CNN as the most influential person in global business. But much more interesting, from Agassi's perspective, was an invitation to join the World Economic Forum's Young Global Leaders group, where he and fellow Israeli entrepreneur, biotechnologist Andrey Zarur, became members of a group addressing the challenge of "how to make the world a better place".

For Agassi and Zarur, the answer was simple: replace every gasoline-powered car on the planet with an electricity-powered equivalent. But the economics were more complicated. For two months following their joint presentation to a Young Global Leaders meeting in Iceland in 2006 they spent every spare moment refining their ideas, ultimately producing a paper titled "Scenarios: The End of Oil", which Agassi presented to a gathering of American and Israeli leaders at the Saban Center for Middle East Policy in Washington in December 2006.

And then came two phone calls that would change the course of Agassi's life.

The first was from Shimon Peres, President of Israel, who had been in the audience at his talk in Washington. Enthralled by the prospect of ending Israel's dependence on foreign oil, Peres exhorted Agassi to give up his job with SAP and establish a private company to convert his dream into reality.

The second was from the chairman of SAP, to tell him that the company's supervisory board had extended the contract of the incumbent CEO, Henning Kagermann, for a further two years.

Agassi quit, and stepped out of the software business into an extraordinary new career. And President Peres, as he himself put it, "helped him break through".

On December 31, Peres organised a meeting with Israel's Prime Minister, Ehud Olmert, who told Agassi: "You go find the money and find a major automaker who will commit to this, and I'll give you the policy backing you need".

Less than a month later, at the World Economic Forum meeting in Davos, Peres brokered meetings with a series of senior auto executives. One of them, Renault CEO Carlos Ghosn, inspired by the combination of Agassi's vision and Peres' assurance of favourable tax treatment from the Israeli government, committed his company to producing all-electric cars for the Israeli market.

And then, in June, he met with Idan Ofer, chairman of Israel Corp, who agreed, despite his company's substantial interests in oil refineries, to contribute $100 million to Agassi's initial venture capital round.

Within a year of his presentation in Washington, Agassi had a company, a country, a car manufacturer, and $200 million in the bank, all set to pursue the end of oil. It was time to figure out the details.

෪෪෪

Agassi named his company Better Place. His mission was to end oil by replacing the world's gasoline-powered cars. But first, there were two major obstacles that needed to be overcome in order to convert his plan from a pipedream to a reality.

One was price: with batteries costing as much as $10,000 each, the upfront outlay for a new car and battery would be prohibitive for most buyers of conventional automobiles.

The other was range: while most daily trips fall well within the capacity of current batteries, what happens when you need to travel 500 km in a day?

Agassi's solution was simple.

First, separate the batteries from the cars. By renting batteries to customers rather than selling them, Better Place could not only bill "electric miles" in much the same way that mobile phone companies bill "minutes", but also reduce the initial cost of the car to below that of a gasoline-driven equivalent.

Second, use the capacity of the battery-charging networks to store excess energy from solar arrays and wind farms. By buying electricity when supply is high but demand low, and selling it back to the grid when demand is high, Better Place could not only deliver electric miles at lower cost, but also become a key player in the clean energy marketplace.

Third, extend the Better Place network to include not only recharging stations, but also battery replacement stations, where a fully charged replacement battery could be installed in the same time that it takes to refuel a gasoline-driven car.

ప్రప్రప్ర

In early 2012, Agassi's dream began to come to fruition with the delivery in Israel of the first 100 Renault Fluence vehicles, supported by hundreds of public recharging sites and the first 4 of 40 proposed battery switching stations. A further 100,000 cars were scheduled for delivery later in the year.

China, too, was on the move. In the new energy vehicle plan released by China's State Council in April 2012 the target for "all-electric" vehicles and plug-in hybrids, backed by generous government subsidies for private buyers, was confirmed as 500,000 cars by 2015.

And for its part, Better Place signed agreements with both Chery, a Chinese car manufacturer, and China Southern Power Grid. With China's rapidly expanding middle class driving car ownership up by as much as 50% per annum, Shai Agassi was determined to be part of the action.

OLD BOY NETWORKS

The Chinese have a word for them: *guanxi* - the network of personal relationships that facilitate business activity in China and, to a greater or lesser degree, anywhere else in the world.

When Olivia Lum decided to open her business in China she was decidedly short on *guanxi*. No one would do business with her for three years. Then she hired an old boy, a 60-year-old in fact, and with the aid of his "good *guanxi*" turned the business around.

No doubt, Shi Zhengrong also benefited from good *guanxi* in China, but in his case access to the international research network built by Martin Green and Stuart Wenham was the key factor in building and maintaining technological leadership in solar panel manufacturing.

But the consummate worker of old boy networks has to be Shai Agassi. First, he used his father's connections in the Israeli Defence Force and the telecommunications industry to access capital and help establish four successful software businesses in his early 20s. And then his master stroke, albeit a serendipitous one, came with access to the ultimate network - that of Shimon Peres, President of Israel, who effectively brought Agassi all of the politicians, the CEOs, and the investors that he needed to start his voyage toward making the world a better place.

ཨ ཨ ཨ

But not everything has gone well on the *guanxi* front. In the latter part of 2012, in the wake of plummeting solar cell prices and slower than expected rollout of electric vehicles, both Zhengrong Shi and Shai Agassi were replaced as CEOs of their companies.

In Israel, the government's promised policy incentives have failed to materialise, leaving thousands of unsold Renault Fluence electric vehicles, the only ones equipped to use Better Place's countrywide battery-swapping network, in car yards across the nation.

And in China, Suntech's global sales have halved as more and more players take advantage of falling silicon prices and improved technology to produce ever-cheaper solar panels.

The final body blows came in mid-2013, when both Suntech's main Wuxi subsidiary and Better Place filed for bankruptcy.

ಜಜಜ

In hindsight, both Shai Agassi and Zhengrong Shi grew too big, too fast. Both relied too heavily on the environmentally friendly incentives envisaged by governments in the halcyon days before the global financial crisis. And both have paid the price.

But, nonetheless, there seems little doubt that their legacies will continue to drive the revolution in clean and renewable technologies required to meet not only China's, but the world's, insatiable appetite for energy. As former Better Place policy director Yariv Nornberg told Ben Sales of the *Jewish Telegraphic Agency*: "The dream is not over. It's only the beginning".

Like Olivia Lum, Shai Agassi and Zhengrong Shi have not only sourced the world's best R&D, but used it to create remarkable "things of use and practice for man's life and knowledge".

Francis Bacon would be proud.

KEY SOURCES

CHINA

Julian Borger and Jonathan Watts, "China launches green power revolution to catch up on West", *The Guardian*, June 10, 2009.

Jonathon Porritt, "China's eco-entrepreneurs", *BBC World Service*, December 7, 2009.

OLIVIA LUM

Liz Bolshaw, "Ambition and optimism: Lum wins entrepreneurship award", *Financial Times*, June 6, 2011.

Neel Chowdhury, "Singapore's all wet", *Time*, September 21, 2009.

Jody Clarke, "Olivia Lum: how I sold my car to jump-start a £231m company", *Money Week*, June 12, 2009.

Rebecca Lim, "Olivia Lum of Hyflux named World Entrepreneur of the Year 2011", *Asian Scientist*, June 13, 2011.

David W Schner, "The boldness to dream: an interview with Olivia Lum", *Leaders Magazine*, 2012.

"Success story: Malaysian Olivia Lum of Hyflux Group". Produced by Ochre Pictures for Discovery Networks International, 2004.

"Women at the top", "The top 50 women in world business 2011". Special report. *Financial Times*, November 15, 2011.

Wong Wei Kong, "Grace under pressure", *The Business Times*, August 2, 2003.

ZHENGRONG SHI

ABC Radio National, "The Sun King", February 23, 2008.

Andrew Baston, "For Chinese tycoon, solar power fuels overnight wealth", *The Wall Street Journal*, October 12, 2006.

Pilita Clarke, "Pinstripe greens", *Financial Times*, November 4, 2011.

Martin Green, "Shi Zhengrong", *Time Magazine*, October 17, 2007.

Eric Knight, "The Sun King: Shi Zhengrong", *The Monthly*, June, 2011.

Wayne Ma, "The man at the center of solar-panel maker Suntech's fall", *The Wall Street Journal*, May 3, 2013.

"Power surge. Are we finally on the brink of a clean energy revolution?", PBS, April 20, 2011.

SBS Dateline, "The Sun King", March 21, 2007.

Zhengrong Shi, "The next chapter", Suntech Power, August 23, 2012.

SHAI AGASSI

Guy Grimland, "Taking high tech to new heights", Haaretz.com, October 23, 2008.

Steve Hamm, "The electric car acid test", *BusinessWeek*, January 23, 2008.

Steve Hamm, "The youngster who's out to energise SAP", *BusinessWeek*, June 26, 2002.

Ben Sales, "Why did Israel's promising electric car maker fail?", *Jewish Telegraphic Agency*, June 3, 2013.

"SAP AG / On the Record: Shai Agassi. He's looking to find genius - all over the world", *San Francisco Chronicle*, June 11, 2006.

"Shai Agassi", *The Clean Revolution*, January 24, 2012.

Clive Thompson, "Batteries not included", *The New York Times*, April 19, 2009.

Gaiya Yemini, "Time/CNN names Shai Agassi as most influential individual in global business", Haaretz.com, November 27, 2003.

An individual with an epic ambition to change the world, who ...	Olivia Lum Born: 1961, Kampur, Perak, Malaysia Education: BSc (Hons), National University of Singapore Organisation: Hyflux	Shi Zhengrong Born: 1963, Yangzhong, Jiangsu, China Education: BSc, Changchun; MSc, Shanghai Institute of Optics and Fine Mechanics; PhD, University of NSW Organisation: Suntech	Shai Agassi Born: 1968, Ramat-Gan, Israel Education: BA, Technion Organisation: Better Place
.. sees and seizes opportunities for change ..			
Opportunistic: aggressively seeks and adopts new ideas	"While working at Glaxo, I saw how companies faced challenges treating the wastewater from their production processes" ...	"I'm a very aggressive personality, so when I saw an opportunity in solar, I just moved very quickly ...	He saw the need of Israel and other nations to reduce their dependence on imported oil ...
& Visionary: intuitively grasps the big picture and how it might evolve	... and "I saw that these problems could only multiply with rising populations, urbanisation, and industrialisation, and there could only be opportunities in this 'sunrise business'".	... to capitalise on the combination of existing technologies, including off-patent US inventions from the time of the space race, and inexpensive Chinese manufacturing capacity".	... and realised that it could be done by switching to electric cars ...
.. senses the way forward ..			
Innovative: thinks creatively, ignores boundaries, disrupts the status quo	Recognising the need for more environmentally friendly water purification technology, she hired her former university teachers to develop membrane-based filtration systems ...	"Suntech's roots are in innovation, and technology differentiation remains the blueprint for our long-term success", ...	... fuelled by a network of recharging stations selling electricity by the mile ...
but Pragmatic: recognises constraints, devises practical solutions, creates value	... and demonstrated their efficacy by installing pilot plants in the factories of her customers.	... but the greatest potential efficiency for the company lies in replacing automated manufacturing processes with manual workers.	... and supplemented by the capacity to replace batteries in less time than it takes to refuel a conventional car.

	Column 1	Column 2	Column 3
.. attracts the necessary resources ..			
Persuasive: articulate and convincing communicator, consummate networker	"From my youth, I cultivated the ability to persuade and to sell, out of necessity in order to earn some money for my family's upkeep".	He raised $6 million from Chinese investors on the back of his business plan, and then another $80 million from US venture capitalists to buy them out ...	He raised $400 million from private investors, convinced Renault to spend $600 million re-engineering their cars, induced the leaders of Israel and Denmark to offer generous tax breaks ....
& Empowering: attracts talent, inspires loyalty, rewards excellence	"I tell my people, I'm trying to expose your best performance. If you can't go beyond that, then let's stop there. But before that, let's explore the limits".	... and hired his former professors to lead the company's R&D, providing them with the opportunity to put their theories into practice.	... and attracted the best and bravest of his former SAP colleagues to join the cause.
... and pursues the dream ...			
Focused: passionate and highly energetic perfectionist, totally committed to an overriding vision	"I've been described as a tyrant and a pressure cooker. But opportunities don't wait for you: you have to seize them".	"This is our R&D lab. I think this is the best lab in China. The whole lab is basically designed by myself".	He told them "Our mission is to end oil".
& Confident: driven by unconditional self-belief, assumes absolute authority and accountability	"There are no difficulties you can't overcome when you have faced the challenges of hunger and poverty".	"So I realised if I come back to China, I can really do something because I have so much more advanced experience and knowledge than people here do. So I think my country needs me".	"When someone tells you something won't work, but they don't have a good reason, ignore them".
.. regardless of the odds ..			
Resilient: flexible, thrives on change and uncertainty, learns from mistakes	Certain that China represented a vast future water market, Lum set up the Shanghai arm of her business in the early 1990s. Despite three years without a single contract ...	When the rights to a patent over work that Shi had undertaken in Australia were sold to a German company in 2005, he could no longer access the technology. Five years later, he bought the German company.	"I was afraid of taking risks. But then I realised that if I don't take risks, my whole value goes away".
& Courageous: bold, intelligent risk-taker, undaunted by criticism, determined to succeed	... she persevered, gaining a vital first-mover advantage over her much bigger international competitors. By 2010, she had built 40 water purification plants in China, accounting for 20% of her business.	"We had to accomplish in a decade what many told me would take a century. Some believe that we grew too fast; and certainly, you can't achieve what Suntech has achieved without some growing pains. But the world couldn't afford to wait a hundred years to solve our planet's energy and environmental crisis".	"If what I'm saying is right, this would be the largest economic dislocation in the history of capitalism".

Part III

HAPPY PEOPLE

We hold these truths to be self-evident, that all men are created equal, that they are endowed by their Creator with certain unalienable Rights, that among these are Life, Liberty and the pursuit of Happiness.
The US Declaration of Independence, July 4, 1776.

IN 2010, FOR THE FIRST time in our history, more than half of the world's population lived in cities. And of these, around 10% lived in megacities - the 23 cities whose inhabitants number more than 10 million.

Rampant urban sprawl, loss of intergenerational family structures, and a decline in religiosity all pose enormous challenges for maintaining connectivity, either between individuals or between them and the natural environment. Yet, as humans, our social networks and relationships are critical not only to our personal sense of happiness and well-being but also to the overall health of our communities.

Who will weave the social fabric needed to give us back our sense of belonging in this increasingly fragmented world?

ଢଢଢ

Two French intellectuals, writing in the late 19th and early 20th century, provided many salient observations on, and some visionary solutions to, this very 21st-century question.

The first was Émile Durkheim, the father of modern social science, who coined the term "anomie" to describe the loss of family and religious connections, and an apparently associated increase in suicide risk, that he observed among young men living in urban environments in late 19th-century France.

In particular, Durkheim predicted the need for new networks of social interactions capable of compensating for the problems that he saw as characterising the descent of modern society into anomie: the dearth of supportive relationships with friends and family; the loss of self-esteem and sense of purpose resulting from a lack of productive employment; and the absence of the moral sanctions provided by church and community.

The second was the famous philosopher, palaeontologist and Jesuit priest, Pierre Teilhard de Chardin, who saw social isolation and marginalisation as inhibitors of the evolution of mankind. From Chardin's viewpoint, isolation was a recipe for our demise, connectivity a prerequisite for our future.

In his ideal future world, Chardin foresaw all humankind as being connected through a vast noosphere, the mental and spiritual equivalent of the biosphere, encompassing the planet and containing the sum total of all human culture, love and knowledge. Often characterised today as predictive of the Internet, Chardin saw his noosphere as being accessible to, and potentially influenced by, every human being on the planet.

Both Durkheim and Chardin saw the need to provide isolated and vulnerable individuals with a new sense of belonging through the creation of networks of personal relationships. Both visualised the renewal of social capital and cohesion by reconnecting people to their communities and environments. And both are turning out to be right.

ཝཝཝ

In the following four chapters we introduce nine extraordinary "bond-builders", überpreneurs whose anomie-battling ventures range from a small fertility clinic in rural India to massive IT empires encircling the planet. Interestingly, none of them have professional backgrounds in religion or social science, but all have employed a remarkable variety of sociological skills and strategies to combat the impact of social isolation among individuals moving from once close-knit communities to the anonymity of modern urban environments.

The deeply personal philosophies of Martha Tilaar and Luiz Seabra have driven the creation of cosmetic and beauty empires that employ thousands of urban women and rural villagers in both Indonesia and Brazil. With products designed to reveal the beauty of women of all ages and ethnicity, they have not only raised the self-esteem of millions of Latin American and Indonesian women, but also conserved and capitalised on the cultural and environmental heritage of their nations.

Jamie Oliver and Oprah Winfrey are evangelists, modern-day elders whose cultural leadership and advice have a remarkable impact on the self-esteem and aspirations of marginalised groups within our society. Both use their media networks to communicate with millions of people at a time, but give each and every one of them the feeling that they are interacting one on one.

Mark Zuckerberg and Pony Ma are empire builders, but the empires they seek are no longer defined by geographic or cultural boundaries, but by social networks. Their companies, Facebook and Tencent, permeate every corner of the globe, helping us maintain the connectivity we need as we transition to a more digitally connected but physically fragmented world.

Gilad Japhet, too, is building a social network, but one focused on rebuilding extended families lost in the diaspora of global migration, while Nayana Patel and Doron Mamet seek to bring the joy of parenthood to those otherwise restricted by medical conditions or sexual orientation to a life without children of their own.

KEY SOURCES

Pierre Teilhard de Chardin, *The Phenomenon of Man*, Wm. Collins Sons & Co., Ltd., London (1955) 1959.

Emile Durkheim, *The Division of Labor in Society* (1893), Translated by George Simpson. New York: Macmillan, 1933.

United Nations Department of Economic and Social Affairs/Population Division, *World Urbanization Prospects. The 2011 Revision*, New York, 2012.

Chapter 8

LOOKING GOOD

WHAT MAKES A COMMUNITY?

According to evolutionary psychologist and social network guru Robin Dunbar, the average size of social groups in monkeys and other primates is directly proportional to the size of the neocortex - the thoughtful bit - relative to the rest of the brain. The reason, Dunbar argues, is that the maintenance of larger numbers of stable interpersonal relationships - of which mutual grooming is the most obvious manifestation - requires correspondingly more neocortical processing capacity.

Extrapolating these data to humans, Dunbar concluded - and subsequently substantiated with a variety of anthropological evidence - that the average cohesive social network in humans comprises approximately 150 members. But, as he points out in his book "Grooming, Gossip, and the Evolution of Language", social grooming in groups this size becomes too expensive to serve as the primary means of maintaining social cohesion. It needs to be supplemented by some cheaper mechanism for keeping up to date with our social networks. That mechanism is gossip.

So, who should we turn to for the appropriate combination of grooming and gossip needed to maintain cohesion in our increasingly disconnected communities?

Enter the beauticians!

ᘒᘒᘒ

Cosmetics based on natural products have been around since the ancient Egyptians used castor oil as a skin balm, juniper berry juice to blacken their hair, and a scalp rub of lettuce leaves for those in danger of losing it. In more recent times, sales of organic and mineral cosmetics have spiralled as consumers, particularly in Europe and the United States, seek more healthy and environmentally friendly alternatives to synthetic products. Of the $300 billion global market in cosmetics, fragrances and toiletries, natural cosmetics now account for 12%, and rising fast.

So, who started it? Ask most Westerners which retail chain first marketed natural cosmetics and chances are they'll name The Body Shop, founded by Anita Roddick in 1976. And they'd be wrong, on at least two counts.

In Brazil, home of more biodiversity than any other country on the planet, Antônio Luiz da Cunha Seabra began supplying what is now the world's third largest cosmetics market with natural cosmetics in 1969. Just over 40 years later, his company holds 24% of the Brazilian market and is an acknowledged world leader in sustainable business practices and corporate governance.

And in Indonesia, another of the planet's most megadiverse nations, Martha Tilaar began marketing cosmetics based on traditional knowledge of Indonesia's biodiversity in 1972. Today, the Martha Tilaar Group has 20% of Indonesia's surging cosmetics market and a chain of spas and salons that is rapidly expanding throughout the region.

Both of them built new social networks at multiple levels: linking women young and old; building mutually rewarding relationships between employees and customers; and reconnecting the lives of women living in modern urban environments with their ancestral communities in the Brazilian rainforests and the tropical islands of Indonesia.

LUIZ SEABRA

According to Luiz Seabra, the guiding principle of his life and his company can be traced back to his reading, as a teenager, of the Roman philosopher Plotinus. Seabra summarises Plotinus' 3rd-century AD writings on the relationships between the transcendent One, the Intellect, and the Soul, with the phrase "the one is in the whole, the whole is in the one".

In simpler, 21st-century terms, Seabra believes that a healthy company cannot exist without healthy workers and healthy customers living in a healthy society on a healthy planet.

After 40 years at the helm of Natura, a company whose mantra is "bem estar bem" (well-being/being well), there's no doubt that he has put his principles into practice. As proudly proclaimed in Natura's 2009 Annual Report: "Our reason for being is to create and sell products and services that promote well-being/being well. Well-being is the harmonious, pleasant relationship of a person with oneself, with one's body. Being well is the empathetic, successful, and gratifying relationship of a person with others, with nature and with the whole".

Harmonious relationships at all levels, Seabra declares, are the non-negotiable key to building a successful business.

ৡৡৡ

Leaving school at the age of 14, Luiz Seabra began work in the Brazilian branch of the multinational equipment manufacturing company Remington Rand, where he rose rapidly through the ranks into senior management positions. But, despite those early career advances, he found the anonymity of working for a large multinational organisation oppressive. When offered the chance, at the age of 27, to manage the small cosmetics laboratory of the well-known beautician Pierre Berjeaut, he jumped at the opportunity. In an economy dominated by high inflation and unemployment, and controlled by a harsh military dictatorship, it was a risky move, but it was also the move that underwrote all of his future success.

Natura was established in 1969 in a small shop in Rua Oscar Freire, Sao Paulo, Brazil, where Luiz Seabra coached his customers in the use of the natural product-based creams and lotions formulated by Berjeaut's son, Jean-Pierre, and began "to appreciate the meaning of cosmetics and fragrances in their lives". No doubt it felt good, but as a business model it was a dismal failure. After five years, they could scarcely pay their bills.

But the principle of one-on-one relationships with the customer was right, and in 1974 Seabra began to implement it at a new level. He and his partners used direct sales consultants, many of whom had no history of paid work, to take Natura's products to customers in their homes. And, mirroring the harmonious relationships between the consultants and the customers, there were equally amicable arrangements between the company and its consultants, who were paid not just commission on sales but also bonuses based on the loyalty of their customers.

It was an inspired model. By 1986, Natura had 16,000 consultants and was growing by 40% per annum. And all this despite the combination of an external debt crisis, continuing high inflation, and the mass exodus of international companies that Brazilians still refer to as the "lost decade" of the 1980s.

Bravely, in an industry dominated by images of teenage beauties, Seabra's next move was to extend harmonious relationships to the "older" woman. To Seabra, the exploitation and manipulation of the anxieties and fears of women by the international cosmetics industry was a crime. He was adamant that women should be confident in themselves at any age, ceasing to aspire to narrow and unattainable notions of what it is to be beautiful, and rejecting vain attempts to halt the march of time.

The Chronos range of facial skin-care treatments, introduced in 1986, celebrated the beauty and vitality of more mature women, with none of the models appearing in the company's advertising campaign being under the age of 30. And, in 1992, Natura created the Truly Beautiful Woman concept, linking beauty not to age, but to self-esteem.

Chronos sold like hot cakes, and by 1994, when the Mamãe e Bebê (Mummy and Baby) line was launched, the company had 105,000 sales consultants and revenues of $350 million. This time, the advertising campaign was built around Shantala massage, and extended the concept of harmonious relationships to the role of Natura's products in building loving bonds between mother and child. The increased sales also allowed Natura to build a $100 million factory and boost its investment in R&D, including forging alliances with universities and research centres around the globe.

Then came Ekos. Launched in 2000, the Ekos range was built entirely around natural products sourced from Amazonian communities, who were not only compensated for their traditional knowledge and intellectual property rights, but also trained in the use of their rainforests' genetic resources to sustainably extract the oils and essences required for Natura's products.

"Well-being/being well" now stretched all the way from the Brazilian rainforest to Brasília, linking Amazonian Indians via several hundred thousand part-time sales consultants to millions of urban consumers, and helping to protect Brazil's fragile ecosystems from the depredations of the nation's expanding timber and cattle industries along the way. And in 2001, Natura was the first company in Latin America to publish an annual report following the Global Reporting Initiative model for reporting on company social and environmental impacts.

In 2004 Natura listed its shares on the Sao Paulo Stock Exchange's Novo Mercado, a market committed to providing investors with higher than average level of transparency and disclosure. It was excellent timing, with the Brazilian cosmetics and toiletries market growing 34%, to become the world's third largest, in the space of 12 months, and Natura's stock price soaring 200% within two years.

But what of harmonious relationships outside Brazil?

Exploring other markets in Latin America, Natura established operations in Chile in 1982, and extended these a decade later to Argentina, Peru and then Mexico. In 2005, the company took its first tentative steps outside Latin America, offering biodiversity-conscious French consumers the Ekos range from its boutique store, Casa Natura, in the upmarket Parisienne neighbourhood of Saint Germain des Près.

So far, Seabra's grand plans for becoming a fully fledged multinational player have proceeded no further than Paris. But with the South American cosmetics, fragrances and toiletries industries representing 15% of the global market, and growing at double the world average, Brazil is still clearly the place to be!

And in truly South American manner, on Valentine's Day 2011, Natura launched its new VôVó range of perfumes, moisturisers and massage creams, pioneering the celebration of relationships between the generations. According to Seabra, this range is designed to promote physical and emotional closeness between grandparents and grandchildren, facilitate the passing of family stories between generations, and symbolise reverence for our ancestors and the knowledge they convey.

But for Luiz Seabra, Natura is not just a business. It is an agent of social change.

In the Amazonian rainforests and other rural communities, the number of native Brazilians earning their livelihoods by gathering the fruits, nuts, grains and other natural products that make up the essential ingredients for the Ekos range of perfumes and oils had by 2010 grown to 2,500 families.

In the slums of Rio de Janeiro, in the aftermath of the combined military operation known as the "pacification of favelas" in late 2010, Natura was there to help. Until the pacification, the Complexo do Alemao was one of Rio's most dangerous and violent shanty towns, accounting for the majority of the drug trade in the Brazilian capital and notorious for drug lords incinerating their opponents in bonfires of used tires. Then Natura came to the rescue with Projeto Commuidade, a microcredit scheme modelled on that of Grameen Bank, helping women with debts become sales consultants and creating new livelihoods for them, their families and their communities.

Likewise in the laboratory. Around 3% of Natura's annual net revenues are invested in research, development and innovation activities, and open sourcing of ideas is undertaken both within the company and globally, with a Natura Campus portal being established to encourage interaction between Natura and the scientific community. And despite a regulatory environment that substantially hinders Brazilian innovation, Natura is ranked by *Forbes* as one of the world's ten most innovative companies.

Socially, environmentally and scientifically, Luiz Seabra is clearly determined to ensure that "the one is in the whole, the whole is in the one". And economically he's not doing too badly either. In March 2012, *Forbes* estimated his net worth at $2.9 billion. Not bad for a dreamy 15-year-old who read philosophy on his way to work.

MARTHA TILAAR

When Martha Tilaar was told she was too old, at 42, to start a family, she sought the assistance of her grandmother, a long-time practitioner of traditional Indonesian medicine, or *jamu*. Based predominantly on herbal remedies, refreshing *jamu* tonics have been sold for centuries by hawkers in Indonesian markets. It's not clear if Grandma prescribed *jamu penyubur*, a mix of medicinal herbs, turmeric and wild ginger commonly used to treat infertility, or one of her own secret recipes, but whatever her potion was, Martha went on to have four children. And one way or another, *jamu* has been a key part of her life ever since.

ༀༀༀ

Martha Tilaar was an entrepreneur from a very young age. Told by her mother that "if you want money, you have to work for it", she repackaged wholesale peanuts into small bags and sold them at school, along with necklaces and bracelets that she made from the hard beads of jali-jali fruit (Job's tears). And she loved it. As she recalled to Chrysanti

Hasibuan-Sedyono of the PPM Institute of Management: "It felt good to earn my own money. Looking back, I realize that the lessons learnt during those times had indeed prepared me to be self-reliant, independent and brave in facing the world, and had been very meaningful later in my life".

And she continued in the same vein. After marrying her professor at the Jakarta Teachers' Training Institute, she supplemented the family income by buying and reselling batik garments from the local market. Then, while her husband studied for a PhD at Indiana University, she used her teacher-training qualifications as the hook for a babysitting business that earned her enough to undertake a three-year course at the Academy of Beauty Culture in Bloomington, Indiana, as well as acquiring an Indiana State licence to practice as a beautician.

Back in Jakarta in 1970, Tilaar used her US qualifications to attract wealthy Indonesian and foreign customers to her first beauty salon, established in the garage of her parents' Jakarta home. Despite its humble beginnings, the business was such a success that within two years she had opened a second salon, and begun to think about the possibility of producing her own cosmetics using modern European technology. But a trip to Europe, where ideas of "back to nature" were just beginning to penetrate the cosmetics industry, opened her eyes to another possibility: why not build on the rich cultural traditions of Indonesian beauty, and particularly those of Indonesia's royal families?

Exploiting the idea of beauty secrets previously known only to royalty, she and a princess from the royal family of Solo, in central Java, developed a brand of cosmetics named Mustika Ratu (Royal Heritage), which they whimsically promoted as capable of transforming a commoner into a princess. It was a magic recipe, and their cosmetics sold as fast as they could supply them. Too fast, perhaps: the princess decided to go it alone, taking the royal brand name with her, leaving Martha to start again.

And then, in 1979, Martha had her first baby, and got seriously interested in *jamu*.

ଷଷଷ

She began by crisscrossing Indonesia in search of traditional herbal remedies and beauty treatments. The result was Sari Ayu (Essence of Beauty), a low-cost brand that incorporated a complete range of skin, hair and body care products, as well as decorative makeup and *jamu* health supplements, targeting middle-class, mainly Muslim, women. And it was followed by a whole series of brands, each offering a similar range of products, but targeting different market segments: with Belia for teenagers and Biokos for more mature, wealthier women, Tilaar's cosmetics were soon being bought by millions of Indonesians.

And feeding off that success came three more areas of activity that would in turn drive the growth of the Martha Tilaar empire.

First, Tilaar entered into an agreement with the Kalbe Group, exchanging a share in the business for a jointly owned manufacturing facility acquired in 1981, and another factory in 1986.

Second, she expanded the teaching activities of her Puspita Martha International Beauty School, initially founded in 1970, and ultimately to train over 300,000 alumni. For some, it is a finishing school, but for many more Puspita Martha offers vocational training in a range of entrepreneurial activities from hairdressing through to managing and owning Martha Tilaar-accredited cosmetic businesses.

And third, she established an R&D facility, the Martha Tilaar Innovation Centre, where Western technological expertise is systematically brought to bear on the identification of new herbal remedies and beauty treatments from Indonesia's natural and cultural resources. And along the way, she established gardens of medicinal, aromatic and cosmetic plants in three Indonesian universities, as well as joint degrees in ethnobotany, medical anthropology and integrated microfinance management between Leiden University in the Netherlands and various universities in Indonesia.

For Martha Tilaar, the R&D program is all about "promise and proof". But even more importantly, from her point of view, its success signals a renewal of national and regional pride in traditional beauty treatments.

ৎৎৎ

In the mid-1990s, the empire came under threat with the appearance in Indonesia of Western-style shopping malls and their international department stores, followed closely by the 1997/8 Asian financial crisis.

Tilaar's characteristically straightforward and effective response to both threats relied heavily on her existing market segmentation philosophy.

At the upper end, she took the newcomers on at their own game, paying premium prices to ensure that her products were displayed alongside those of her foreign competitors in the new shopping malls, and opening her own independent stores. The Biokos brand, in particular, aimed at more mature, wealthier women, was hugely successful in stealing market share from foreign cosmetic companies. As she told Chrysanti Hasibuan-Sedyono:

> That was due to my vision that the Indonesian brand of cosmetics should be proud of the Indonesian identity and should never feel inferior to foreign brands which have strong images. What happened during the economic crisis was that women who used to patronise or favour foreign brands but were affected by the crisis were switching to my brands, which they could not miss because these had always been there, close to the counters they used to visit.

And for those on lower incomes she introduced new premium economy products, including a two-in-one lipstick that predated the Leonard Lauder concept of the "lipstick index" - the tendency for lipstick sales to rise during bad economic times as women seek small luxury purchases - by several years, and increased her sales by 400% as rival manufacturers were laying off staff.

By 1999, she was sufficiently cashed up to buy back the shares in her company acquired 20 years earlier by the Kalbe Group, and begin planning a new venture.

ଓଓଓ

The Martha Tilaar Salon and Spa in Nusa Dua, Bali, opened in October 1999, offering its customers "endless paradise" with "head-to-toe" treatment previously reserved for royalty. Based on the ancient Javanese philosophy of Rupasampat Wahyabyantara, its "balance of inner and outer beauty" exemplifies Tilaar's personal commitment to helping others while making every woman feel beautiful.

By January 2011, when the Martha Tilaar Group subsidiary listed on the Indonesia Stock Exchange, the group comprised 48 spas, 40 retail stores, 9 brands and 5,000 products, with annual sales on the order of $100 million. Building on its 20% share of the local cosmetics industry, the company's new strategy - "Local Wisdom Go Global" - is aimed at using the knowledge gained in Indonesia to access more global markets.

And Martha Tilaar has moved on to new challenges. Working with her Martha Tilaar Foundation on environmental and cultural stewardship, women's empowerment and poverty alleviation, as well as taking up an appointment as an Indonesian Government Ambassador of Education and Human Rights Training, she is intent on creating financially and emotionally rewarding careers for disadvantaged women from both urban and rural communities.

BUILDING CARING COMMUNITIES

Both Luiz Seabra and Martha Tilaar have built pipelines of close and caring relationships stretching all the way from forest-dwelling plant collectors to big city consumers. Building their empires on a combination of ethics, transparency and trust, they share three remarkably similar philosophical beliefs.

First, they both believe in the absolute sanctity of the environment.

And they translate that belief into an unswerving commitment to protect and restore the biodiversity of their nations, working closely with R&D organisations and their indigenous suppliers - Amazonian tribesmen and Indonesian farmers - on ways to sustainably harvest the natural ingredients that form the basis of their cosmetics.

Second, they both believe in their duty to look after others.

Seabra extends Plotinus' "one is in the whole, the whole is in the one" dictum to encompass the view that a healthy company cannot exist without healthy customers and healthy workers. Tilaar uses Rupasampat Wahyabyantara's philosophy to argue that outer beauty cannot exist without its inner counterpart: caring for others. Both treat their employees as family whose welfare they wish to protect, and their customers as friends whose beauty they seek to enhance.

Third, they both believe that beauty is the province of all women, of all races, all creeds, all shapes and all ages.

Seabra wants women everywhere to cease chasing after the artificial, unhealthy and unattainable notion of beauty represented by Western supermodels, and begin rejoicing in the bodies that life has given them. Tilaar designs cosmetics for Muslim women, including those swathed in veils. Both have built entire product ranges that celebrate the beauty of mature women. And the embracing of their products by women of all ages is a testament to their success in bringing heart and soul to the beauty industry.

KEY SOURCES

Robin Dunbar, *Grooming, Gossip, and the Evolution of Language*, Harvard University Press, 1998.

LUIZ SEABRA

Fernanda Bonifacio, "A lesson in sustainability: Natura's Marcos Vaz", *GCI Magazine*, September 2010.

Ian Fraser, "Natura's back-to-nature success", *World Business Magazine*, July - August 2006.

Luciana Hashiba, "Innovation in well-being - the creation of sustainable value at Natura", *Management Innovation Exchange*, June 3, 2012.

Paul Lima, "Perfume do sucesso", *Trip Magazine*, April 2007.

Chris Meyer and Julia Kirby, "Where capitalism is a thing of beauty", *Harvard Business Review Blog Network*, August 13, 2010.

Louise Sherwood, "Rio reborn: The favela where cosmetics reps have replaced drug gangs", Povertymattersblog, *The Guardian*, June 27, 2011.

Ricardo Ubiraci Sennes and Antonio Britto Filho (eds), "Technological innovations in Brazil", *Cultura Acadêmica Editora*, 2012.

MARTHA TILAAR

Chrysanti Hasibuan-Sedyono, *Martha Tilaar: the business of making women beautiful*, Asia-Pacific Economic Cooperation, 2003.

Safrita Ayu Hermawan, "Martha Tilaar: Beauty icon: Moving dynamically at the stock exchange", *The Jakarta Post*, January 8, 2011.

"My mother told me never to depend on anyone else", *The Jakarta Post*, March 25, 2011.

Sarah Lacy, *Brilliant, Crazy, Cocky: how the top 1% of Entrepreneurs profit from global chaos*, John Wiley and Sons, 2011.

Putri Prameshwari and Ronna Nirmala, "Cosmetics queen turns eye on human rights", *Jakarta Globe*, June 8, 2010.

Michael Vatikiotis, "The beauty of business", *Far Eastern Economic Review*, July 25, 2002.

Ahmad Zamroni, "Queen of beauty", *Forbes Indonesia Magazine*, February 2011.

	Antônio Luiz da Cunha Seabra	Martha Tilaar
An individual with an epic ambition to change the world, who ...	Born: 1942, São Paulo, Brazil Education: Ensino Fundamental Organisation: Natura Cosmetics	Born: 1937, Kebumen, Jawa Tengah, Indonesia Education: B. History Studies, IKIP Jakarta; B. Beauty Culture, Academy of Beauty Culture, Bloomington Organisation: The Martha Tilaar Group
.. sees and seizes opportunities for change ..		
Opportunistic: aggressively seeks and adopts new ideas	Recognising the potential of cosmetics and fragrances to give women and men of all ages a sense of "well-being and being well", ...	"So many women in Indonesia, 100 million of them, ...
& Visionary: intuitively grasps the big picture and how it might evolve	... he foresaw that this sense would be greatly enhanced if the products were seen by the customer to be produced in a socially and environmentally responsible manner, ...	... and I have to beautify them" using Indonesia's immense cultural wealth of traditional herbal medicines and cosmetics (*jamu*).
.. senses the way forward ..		
Innovative: thinks creatively, ignores boundaries, disrupts the status quo	... by working with indigenous tribes ...	"We started with local branding of cosmetic products in different provinces ...
but Pragmatic: recognises constraints, devises practical solutions, creates value	... to sustainably harvest ingredients from Amazonian rain forests.	... and combined Western technological expertise with our rich Eastern natural and cultural resources".

.. attracts the necessary resources ..		
Persuasive: articulate and convincing communicator, consummate networker	He recruited and trained an army of mainly female sales consultants, most of whom had never worked outside the home before.	She treats her employees as partners in the business, and they respond in kind. During the Asian financial crisis, they helped keep the company alive by foregoing salary increases …
& Empowering: attracts talent, inspires loyalty, rewards excellence	Inspired by his vision and the opportunity to acquire marketable skills, they now number more than 1.4 million, spread over seven countries, and remain fiercely loyal to the company.	… while she helped women laid off at other factories by organising courses to enable them to find jobs: "I don't give handouts. I provide skills, which are far more important".
.. and pursues the dream ..		
Focussed: passionate and highly energetic perfectionist, totally committed to an overriding vision	Forty years after founding the company, Seabra continued to develop new brand concepts, often inspired by his respect for oriental cultures and religions, as well as his interest in mythology. …	"As an Indonesian, we must preserve our culture, and push local wisdom. If not, …..
& Confident: driven by unconditional self-belief, assumes absolute authority and accountability	… which led him to introduce the highly successful Mamãe & Bebê collection despite market forecasts that the market would be too small.	… there is no uniqueness, everything would be flat, everything would be Estee Lauder".
.. regardless of the odds ..		
Resilient: flexible, thrives on change and uncertainty, learns from mistakes	Using downturns in the Brazilian economy at the end of the 1980s and 1990s as an opportunity to buy out shareholders who did not support his vision, …	At the start of the Asian financial crisis, Tilaar owed her Singapore bankers IDR1 billion, rising to IDR6 billion with subsequent inflation. Swearing to pay it back, …
& Courageous: bold, intelligent risk-taker, undaunted by criticism, determined to succeed	… he took the company back to its core values of promoting "harmonious relationships" and "truth in cosmetics".	… she went head-to-head with foreign-branded cosmetics: "People were amazed - they found my products very cheap but also very effective. So sales went up. We had to be very proactive and innovative".

Chapter 9

FEELING GOOD

THE DECLINE IN RELIGIOSITY OBSERVED by Émile Durkheim over a century ago has gathered pace in more recent times, with mainstream religions frequently being seen, particularly by young city-dwellers, as narrow and disconnected from their daily lives.

But while the baby-boomers and their X and Y generation offspring may not miss the hierarchy and dogmatism of traditional religion, many do miss its guidance, both morally and spiritually. There is a vacuum emerging in Durkheim's "moral sanctions" space, and that vacuum is rapidly being filled, at least among the wealthier citizens of the Western world, by a new priesthood: the lifestyle gurus.

For those who can afford it, there are now not just parenting coaches, fashion advisors and other makeover experts: you can even hire a "wantologist" who will help you identify and tackle your unrealised goals. But what of those who can't afford the one-on-one guidance of a handful of personal gurus?

The answer awaits you on daytime TV.

&&&

In Britain, and elsewhere in the Western world, Jamie Oliver is empowering millions of fast-food addicts and couch potatoes, often for the first time in their lives, to cook simple meals, thus reducing their susceptibility to obesity and life-threatening noncommunicable diseases.

And in the United States, Oprah Winfrey's role in building literacy, social participation and hence self-esteem is bringing a new sense of belonging to underprivileged black women and other marginalised groups in American society.

JAMIE OLIVER

Worldwide, three of every ten adults are overweight, and one of every ten is obese. Their children are hot on their tails. For the Director General of WHO, Margaret Chan, the prevalence of obesity is "a tell-tale signal that something terrible has gone wrong in the social environment in which people make their personal choices".

So how did we get so fat?

Some point to the perfect storm of ever richer and more powerful multinational food corporations pushing ever saltier, sweeter, fattier, cheaper and more profitable, but deadly, foods, and fewer and fewer people with the time and the talent to prepare a healthy, nutritious meal.

Others point to deeper social issues, and particularly poor self-esteem. But while the links between obesity and low self-esteem are widely recognised, it is far from clear which is the chicken and which is the egg. One major study, based on 6,500 British children, found that low self-esteem in childhood leads to a higher probability of obesity 20 years later. Another used data from 2,800 Canadian children to show that early childhood obesity resulted in lower self-esteem in teenage years.

Either way, obesity is reaching epidemic proportions, and afflicting rich and poor nations, children and adults, alike. Jamie Oliver is determined to reverse the trend.

ౘౘౘ

Jamie Oliver didn't lack for early childhood cooking classes. He began helping out in the kitchen of his parents' pub at the age of five, and by the time he turned eight he was expert at many aspects of food preparation. He was also pretty good at getting his message across: sleeping in a room above the bar, he learnt to communicate directly with the patrons in their own forthright language. By the age of 13, he had his first job in a restaurant.

School, however, was a different question. On the one hand, he was a dyslexic and disinterested member of a special needs class that he referred to as "the village idiots"; on the other, he was already showing signs of entrepreneurial talent, establishing a profitable sideline buying sweets wholesale through his father's business and reselling them at school.

It was only after moving to a catering college at the age of 16 that Jamie really came into his own. He was a first-class student, picking up prizes and later jobs in leading restaurants, including a three-year stint as sous chef at London's famous River Cafe. And that's where the 22-year-old Jamie happened to be, standing in for a sick workmate, on the day the BBC came to film a documentary.

It was a classic case of fortune favouring the bold. When the BBC program went to air, Jamie's unscripted but charismatic interventions stole the show. On the day following its first screening, he was contacted by no less than five television production companies, all seeking to discuss ideas for a new series.

The one he chose was Optomen, run by Pat Llewellyn, who had previously produced the very successful foodies program "Two Fat Ladies", and who claimed she was attracted to Jamie by "the contrast between his baby face and bashed-up hands". She is said to have named the new series *The Naked Chef* on the grounds that it would allow viewers to see good cooking - but not the cook - stripped down to the bare essentials.

Despite this inspired title, it was a year before the BBC was finally persuaded to take on the program, but both the television series and the accompanying books were ultimately hugely successful, establishing Pat Llewellyn as the star maker of British food and drink broadcasting, and reinvigorating the entrepreneurial flair that Jamie Oliver had displayed since childhood.

Beginning in 2000, he struck out on his own, making a dozen or more TV series, most of which were accompanied by glossy publications that were timed to appear in bookstores just before Christmas, often smashing previous records for nonfiction book sales in the process. His many television series have now been broadcast in over 100 countries, and the books translated into more than 30 languages.

But while Oliver's television and publishing activities stuck closely to the original Naked Chef formula, more and more new business ventures emerged around them as Jamie recognised the opportunity to convert his celebrity into products and services.

Over the course of the next decade, he earned more than £1 million per annum as the face of the British supermarket giant Sainsbury's, maintaining a close working relationship with the chain despite differences with management over animal welfare issues such as intensive poultry farming and his reported observation that he personally would never shop in a supermarket. He also diversified his business empire to include deals promoting signature tableware and cookware products, set up a retail division marketing foods and gifts, developed cooking games and iPhone apps, and established a multilevel marketing operation called Jamie at Home. And on top of all that he opened restaurants, including the popular Jamie's Italian chain, which offers cheap Italian fare built around fresh ingredients and homemade pasta in a dozen or more British cities.

But even more importantly, he used his celebrity to pursue some of the social causes that had preoccupied him since childhood.

First, he established London's award-winning Fifteen Restaurant, where groups of unemployed young people from disadvantaged backgrounds are offered the opportunity to learn, and become key players in, the catering and restaurant trade. Each year, 18 apprentices are selected from 200 or more applicants on the basis of their passion for food and cooking and ability to work in a team. Since opening in 2002, Fifteen has served as a model for similar restaurants, with associated training programs, in Amsterdam and Melbourne and at Watergate Bay in Cornwall.

Second, he launched a campaign called "Feed me Better", aimed at putting pressure on government and local authorities to provide more nutritious meals for British schoolchildren. Not everyone agreed, with some parents showing up at lunchtime to smuggle junk food to their children through the school fence. But Jamie's persistence and influence, including regular appearances as a guest chef at 10 Downing Street, ultimately won the day. In 2005, the Blair government introduced direct government subsidies for training canteen staff as well as new standards for school meals. But not for long: in 2011, despite demonstrable improvements in school attendance and academic performance following the introduction of the new menus, the Cameron government removed the subsidy. Jamie Oliver isn't happy, but he's not holding his breath. He has launched the Kitchen Garden Project, with the aim of providing food growing and cooking classes for every child in Britain by 2022.

Third, he established the Ministry of Food, aimed at teaching people who had never learned to cook how to prepare and serve simple nutritious meals to their family and friends. As Jamie put it: "We can save people money, we can save them time, we can make parents feel like parents again, to nourish themselves and their kids, and we can help people live longer". Focused on cities with obvious obesity problems, not all of whose citizens greeted their city's selection with unqualified delight, the program now offers practical hands-on cooking classes in six regional centres in the United Kingdom and two in Australia. And in 2010, in a seriously brave move, he launched his Food Revolution in the United States, challenging schools, government and the public to address the tsunami of non-communicable diseases that is threatening the very viability of the US health system.

All three of these ventures have had substantial impact on the health and well-being of the communities in which they operate. And yes, just in case you're wondering, all three of them have also been the basis for high rating TV shows and bestselling books. And those TV shows and books, in turn, are enabling millions more families to rediscover the joy of preparing and consuming nutritious meals together, in less time than it takes to visit the nearest fast-food outlet.

ଓଓଓ

None of this is lost on WHO Director General, Margaret Chan. As she points out, the population-wide measures needed to stem the diabetes and cardiovascular disease fuelled by obesity are largely beyond either the power of the health sector or the appetite of government.

Fortunately, no one told Jamie. In Britain and Australia, kitchen gardens and cooking classes are now appearing in many schools, and in 2012 the US Department of Agriculture, ridiculed during the Reagan years for classifying ketchup and other condiments used in school lunches as vegetables, introduced new meal standards for national school lunch and breakfast programs.

OPRAH WINFREY

In August 2008, Craig Garthwaite and Tim Moore, both graduate students at the University of Maryland, wrote a paper on the role of celebrity endorsements in politics. In a county-by-county study of the results of the 2008 US Democratic Party presidential primary, they found a striking relationship between high levels of subscriptions to *O, the Oprah Magazine* and the numbers of voters favouring Barack Obama over Hillary Clinton. By contrast, in a similar analysis of the data from Obama's 2004 Democratic Party primary bid for the US Senate, there was no such correlation between magazine subscriptions and voter preferences. The difference, they concluded, was the result of Oprah Winfrey's very public endorsement of Barack Obama as a presidential candidate in the lead-up to the 2008 race. According to Garthwaite and Moore, she delivered Obama approximately 1 million additional votes.

Not too surprising, perhaps. In 2008, *the Oprah Magazine* had a monthly circulation of 2.4 million copies and the weekly audience for the Oprah

Winfrey Show in the United States was a staggering 46 million. She was the world's first black female billionaire and had been described by *USA Today* as the most influential woman and most influential black person of the preceding quarter century.

She'd come a long way in 54 years.

ଓଓଓ

The first 14 of those years were seriously tough. Born in 1954 to an unmarried and dirt-poor teenage housemaid in Kosciusko, Mississippi, she was shipped north and south between her grandmother in Mississippi, mother in Wisconsin and, finally, her mother's boyfriend, Vernon Winfrey, in Nashville, Tennessee. By the time she was 15 years old she had suffered both physical and sexual abuse, run away from home, and borne and lost a baby son.

But she was also extremely smart, and an extraordinarily gifted communicator. Taught to read by her grandmother, she was reciting Bible verses in church at the age of three, and revelling in the praise of the congregation. At high school in Nashville, her speaking skills won her a part-time job as a radio newsreader, and a full scholarship to study communication at Tennessee State University.

The same pattern of public success and private despair continued into her 20s. Starting as a TV news anchor in Nashville, she was soon co-anchoring the 6 p.m. news and co-hosting a talk show in Baltimore. But at the same time she had a series of relationships that left her feeling worthless: "I'd end up with these cruel self-absorbed guys who'd tell me how selfish I was, and I'd say 'Oh thank you, you're so right' and be grateful to them. Because I had no sense that I deserved anything else".

It was time to start building her self-esteem.

ଓଓଓ

In her 30th year, Oprah moved to Chicago to go head-to-head with Phil Donahue, the reigning king of tabloid talk shows. In reality, head-to-toe

was probably more accurate. Donahue was after all the creator of the
tabloid talk genre - where people that viewers would otherwise never
have heard from discussed topics that they would otherwise never have
confronted - and was already widely syndicated.

Winfrey took Donahue's format and raised it a notch. She joined in,
matching her guests' stories with revelations from her own tumultuous
life, sharing their hopes and fears as well as their tears. Within months she
was out-rating Donahue, and two years later she launched the nationally
syndicated Oprah Winfrey Show, which almost immediately became the
top-rating daytime talk show in the United States. And she owned it.

So, what was the secret of her success? At its core, it was all about empathy
and trust. She cared: by displaying her understanding and sympathy for
the issues faced by her guests, she encouraged similar understanding and
sympathy in her audience. And she shared: by revealing her own secrets
she encouraged her guests to share theirs, striking another chord with
studio and home audiences alike. The result was what the *Wall Street
Journal* called "Oprahfication": public confession as a form of therapy.
And the public loved it: by the mid-1990s more than 10 million people
were tuning in to the Oprah Winfrey Show every day.

And she was very smart. Rather than focusing on a specific demographic,
Oprah shrewdly targeted women of all ages and backgrounds. And when
she sensed that the market was becoming saturated with tabloid "freak"
shows, she moved upmarket, focusing on three areas of direct relevance to
her audience.

First, she addressed the issue of self-esteem. With self-improvement
programs devoted to health, spirituality and social issues, she exhorted
her viewers to do as she had done, to pull themselves up by their
bootstraps and live their best lives: "Every day brings a chance for you to
draw in a breath, kick off your shoes, and step out and dance".

Second, harking back to her teenage years, when Vernon Winfrey
required her to read, and review, a book every week, she sought to build
the literacy of her audience with regular discussions of both new books

and classics. Driven by the massive audience of the Oprah Winfrey Show, and the significantly wealthier readership of *O, the Oprah Magazine*, it was not uncommon for the selection of a book by the Oprah Book Club to deliver its author a million or more additional book sales.

Third, she took up the cudgels for causes she cared about, including those of minority groups. She provided a welcoming platform for gays and lesbians, mounted a ferocious and successful attack on the sexual predators of young children, and founded a leadership academy for disadvantaged girls in South Africa.

And, along the way, she produced movies, wrote books and published magazines. She founded a radio station and co-founded a women's cable television network. And she identified, endorsed and gave away hundreds of products that she referred to as her "favorite things", with predictable but unprecedented impacts on their sales.

And then, in 2007, she did something she'd never done before: she chose a favourite politician, Barack Obama, and used her brand to endorse his candidacy over that of Hillary Clinton in the 2008 Democratic primary race. And while the million votes she delivered to Obama may well have been the tipping point for Obama, her failure to support the woman who might have become the nation's first female president was certainly a tipping point for Oprah. Fans who had been happy to follow her advice on everything from what book to read to which health guru to follow rose up in protest at her betrayal of what they had perceived as a shared cause. With her constituency split down the middle, both her ratings and her personal popularity sank like stones.

By 2011, the richest self-made woman in American history could see the writing on the wall. After 25 years at the very top of US daytime television, she went to air with the 4,561st and last Oprah Winfrey Show, and transferred her attention to her new cable channel, the Oprah Winfrey Network. Will it work? Will an Oprah Winfrey Network with Oprah at the helm bring back the disciples that flocked to the Oprah Winfrey Show with Oprah in the flesh? For a while, it looked as if the ratings were saying no, but less than two years later, following interviews with celebrities and sinners ranging all the way from Whitney Houston's mother to disgraced cyclist Lance Armstrong, Oprah had not only doubled OWN's ratings but also reasserted her position as America's leading TV interviewer.

ଧଧଧ

In a commencement address to the class of 2012 at Spelman College - an historically black liberal arts college for women located in Atlanta, Georgia - Oprah offered her spellbound audience three pieces of advice, each of which points unmistakably to key decision points in her own life.

First, know who you are, and what you want: "Be in the driver's seat of your own life, because if you're not, life will drive you".

Second, find a way to serve. In 1993, "I made a decision that I was no longer going to just be on TV, but I was going to use TV as a platform, as a force for good. And that decision ... changed my career exponentially".

Third, always do the right thing: "Be excellent. Let excellence be your brand ... when you are excellent you become unforgettable. People remember you. You stand out. Regardless of what it is, you become an unforgettable woman. And that is what we all want".

She ended with a warning, and a last piece of advice:

> All of you have the potential for enormous success. There's a price that comes with that: people don't always like you, and they're not always happy for you ... They're going to say "who does she think she is?" That only happens when you are around people who do not ... want ... the best for you. People who want the best for you want you to be your best. So, my greatest advice to you is to surround yourself with people who are going to fill your cup until your cup runneth over.

Reading between the lines, it seems Oprah may still be that 3-year-old seeking the love and praise of her grandmother, or the 25-year-old craving the approval of an abusive man. But she's not going to let that stop her doing what she does best: talking to women with needs and wants just like hers, and making them feel special.

FROM EMPATHY TO EVANGELISM

What is it about Jamie Oliver and Oprah Winfrey that enables them to play the role of village elders, using the most public of media, television, to offer seemingly private and personal advice to tribes numbering hundreds of millions?

First, they are quintessentially human, sharing an instinctive empathy with their viewers, and a genuine understanding of the everyday issues that they face. When Jamie goes vegetable shopping we are so closely involved in the process that we might as well be pillion passengers on his Vespa. And when Oprah regales us with her own struggles with obesity, confessing that she uses "food for the same reasons an addict uses drugs: to comfort, to soothe, to ease stress", we are with her, sharing her joy and despair with every pound lost or gained.

Second, they are both fearless advocates for what they believe is right. Jamie Oliver has no hesitation in taking on supermarkets, food producers, governments or anyone else he regards as promoting obesity with sweet, salty and fatty foods, including picking a fight with soccer hero David Beckham over his endorsement of Pepsi on the eve of the 2012 London Olympics. And Oprah Winfrey took no prisoners in her efforts to portray Islam as a religion of peace in the months following the September 11 attack, or in her staunchly anti-war stance on Iraq.

And, third, they care. Jamie has devoted much of his fame and fortune to selling the public and governments alike on the importance of good food, including establishing multiple organisations to promote nutritious diets and culinary skills among socially disadvantaged populations, while Oprah has been no less evangelical in her efforts to raise the perspicacity and self-esteem of her constituency, most notably women and blacks.

For hundreds of millions of their fans around the globe, Jamie Oliver and Oprah Winfrey are the tribal elders of the 21st century, the good shepherds whose advice and example they seek in confronting many of the most important issues of their everyday lives.

KEY SOURCES

JAMIE OLIVER

Margaret Chan, "Obesity: bad trouble is on its way", Lecture delivered to the Women's International Forum, New York, September 21, 2012.

Antonin Leonard and Mark Barraud, "How corporate social consciousness changes business: the Jamie Oliver case", *Scribd*, December, 2010.

Jamie Oliver, "Jamie Oliver's TED Prize wish: teach every child about food", *TEDTalks*, February 2010.

Jay Rayner, "Jamie Oliver: You might want to hate him, but you can't help cheering", *The Guardian*, July 5, 2012.

Miranda Sawyer, "Dish of the day", *The Observer*, April 14, 2002.

Andrew Ternouth, David Collier and Barbara Maughan, "Childhood emotional problems and self-perceptions predict weight gain in a longitudinal regression model", *BMC Medicine*, September 2009.

F Wang, T C Wild, W Kipp, S Kuhle and P J Veugelers, "The influence of childhood obesity on the development of self-esteem", *Statistics Canada, Health Reports*, June 2009.

OPRAH WINFREY

Susan Chandler, "Oprah Winfrey and OWN on the ropes", *Chicago Magazine*, June 2012.

Craig Garthwaite and Tim Moore, "The role of celebrity endorsements in politics: Oprah, Obama, and the 2008 Democratic primary", Department of Economics, University of Maryland, 2008.

Pat Hartman, "Oprah Winfrey's very public food addiction struggle", *Childhood Obesity News*, August 24, 2010.

Edmund Lee and Andy Fixmer, "Discovery's Oprah problem", *Business Week*, May 3, 2012.

George Mair, *Oprah Winfrey: the real story*, Carol Publishing Group, New York, 1994.

Oprah Winfrey, Spelman College commencement address, May 20, 2012.

An individual with an epic ambition to change the world, who ...	**Jamie Oliver** Born: 1975, Clavering, Essex, UK Education: Catering, Westminster Kingsway College Organisation: Jamie Oliver Group	**Oprah Winfrey** Born: 1954, Mississippi, USA Education: BA (Speech and Performing Arts), Tennessee State University Organisation: Harpo Productions
.. sees and seizes opportunities for change ..		
Opportunistic: aggressively seeks and adopts new ideas	Initially drawing media attention for his unscripted interruptions to a documentary that he wasn't supposed to be in, he saw the opportunity ...	Observing the dominance of white males in the emerging genre of TV tabloid talk shows, she recognised the opportunity ...
& Visionary: intuitively grasps the big picture and how it might evolve	... to use television to bring his passion for simple home-cooked food into the lives of millions of working-class Britons, ...	... for a woman to capture their predominantly female audience ...
... senses the way forward ..		
Innovative: thinks creatively, ignores boundaries, disrupts the status quo	... replacing the formality of existing programs with a cocky and appealing conversational style, ...	... by moving from the role of passive interviewer to being part of the action, identifying with the issues faced by her viewers, ...
but Pragmatic: recognises constraints, devises practical solutions, creates value	... and parleying his personal popularity into more and more TV series, new lines of food and cooking ware, and a dozen or more best-selling cookbooks.	... and working with her guests to find ways to address them.

.. attracts the necessary resources ..

Persuasive: articulate and convincing communicator, consummate networker	He applied all his charisma, as well as his entire media empire, to addressing the worldwide obesity epidemic, ...	"The thing you fear most has no power. Your fear of it is what has the power. Facing the truth really will set you free".
& Empowering: attracts talent, inspires loyalty, rewards excellence	... teaching people who had never learnt to cook how to prepare affordable, nutritious meals in less than 30 minutes, ...	"The biggest adventure you can ever take is to live the life of your dreams".

.. and pursues the dream ..

Focussed: passionate and highly energetic perfectionist, totally committed to an overriding vision	... and bringing relentless pressure to bear on governments, supermarkets, food producers and the general public to ...	And she did. Within two years of her Chicago debut at the age of 30 she had syndicated the Oprah Winfrey Show nationally, ...
& Confident: driven by unconditional self-belief, assumes absolute authority and accountability	"create a strong, sustainable movement to educate every child about food, inspire families to cook again and empower people everywhere".	... and proceeded to use it as a launching pad for a series of best-selling books and magazines, all built around the theme of "live your best life".

.. regardless of the odds ..

Resilient: flexible, thrives on change and uncertainty, learns from mistakes	Despite his disillusionment about working with politicians: "I am turning into a grumpy old man where the Government is concerned", ...	As tabloid talk show ratings shrank during the first decade of the 21st century, Winfrey took the decision to wind up the Oprah Winfrey Show ...
& Courageous: bold, intelligent risk-taker, undaunted by criticism, determined to succeed	... he decided to tackle the obesity problem on its home turf, establishing Jamie Oliver's Food Revolution to agitate for political and corporate reform in the United States.	... and began all over again with a new venture, the Oprah Winfrey Network: "I am in the climb of my life. I am climbing Kilimanjaro".

Chapter 10

FINDING FRIENDS ...

HOW DO PEOPLE WHO ONCE lived their lives in close-knit communities keep up with former schoolmates scattered around the globe? How should they meet new people with whom to share their interests and concerns, or even find romance, in the megacities of the world? And how do the lonely "little emperors" of China's one-child generation identify, let alone keep in touch with, friends?

Enter the noosphere!

ʔʔʔ

In the year 2000, 26.4% of the world's Internet users lived in the United States, and just 6.2% in China. By 2012, the numbers were almost completely reversed, with 22.5% in China and 10.8% in the United States. It wasn't that there were fewer people in the United States using the Internet. In fact, there were 150% more. But in China, the numbers were up by more than 2,000%.

What were they up to?

In the United States, where the Internet reaches out to 78.3% of the population, more than 60% of users are over the age of 30. Most of them, most of the time, are seeking information through services such as Google. But things are changing. On a site-by-site basis, Google lost its position at the top of the ladder in 2010. Since then, the largest number of active US users on any one site has been on Facebook, checking out their friends. And if Facebook founder Mark Zuckerberg has his way, that's how the pecking order will stay.

In China, with 38.4% of the population (more than half a billion) connected to the Web, the bulk of Internet users are between 10 and 39 years old. Not surprisingly, their number one priority is also keeping in touch with friends. And Pony Ma, the founder of Tencent, the third largest Internet business by market capitalisation in the world, is making sure that they can do just that. In 2012, over 750 million active users were on Tencent, chatting via QQ, its instant messaging service, or linking up with friends online via QZone.

MA "PONY" HUATENG

Speaking in Shenzhen in September 2010, China's President Hu Jintao wasn't kidding when he described the southern Chinese city as an economic miracle. In the 30 years since Deng Xiaoping designated the fishing village across the border from Hong Kong as China's first Special Economic Zone, it had ballooned to a city of 9 million people, with an economic growth rate of 25.8% per year. Powered by the ability to accept foreign investment, as well as other free-market-oriented policies aimed at promoting and integrating science, trade and industry, Shenzhen had become, as Hong Kong tycoon, Li Ka-shing, put it: "the driving force of China's reform and opening up".

And one of the most powerful forces behind Shenzhen's explosive growth has been Ma Huateng, commonly known as Pony Ma, whose parents moved to Shenzhen from the tropical island of Hainan, in the South China Sea, in 1984, when Ma was 13 and the Special Economic Zone was just getting off the ground.

ଧଧଧ

Pony Ma's first serious exposure to the Internet was in 1996, when the 25-year-old telecom software developer was sent by his company on a training programme in the United States. He was blown away, not just by the Internet, but by the vast array of new online communication technologies that it was incubating. One of them was ICQ, an instant messaging technology created by Israeli start-up company Mirabilis.

Two years later, in a shabby building in the backstreets of Shenzhen, Pony Ma and a group of fellow graduates from Shenzhen University founded an Internet services company. They named the company Tengxun (galloping messenger), and in February 1999 they created a Chinese-language equivalent of ICQ, which they called OICQ. Both names soon changed: Tengxun to Tencent to accommodate Western ears, and OICQ to QQ to avoid litigation from America Online, which had just paid a startling $400 million for ICQ.

Pony Ma didn't have $400 million, or anything like it, but he had had some limited success playing the stock market, and he put up most of Tencent's initial half million yuan ($75,000) capital himself. But with QQ rapidly becoming a more and more popular free download, the company soon ran out of both server capacity and cash.

Ma needed money fast, but Chinese investors weren't interested in a company whose only assets were the enthusiasm of its founders and the intangible benefits of its tens of thousands of customers. Fortunately for Ma, international venture capitalists took a different view. Two of them, Hugo Strong of International Data Group, the so-called godfather of Chinese venture capital, and Richard Li of Hong Kong-based Pacific Century CyberWorks, came to the party, investing a total of $2.2 million for almost 50% of the company.

It was an astute investment. Eighteen months later a South African media company, Naspers, acquired 46.5% of Tencent, including most of the stake of the earlier investors, for $34 million. And Naspers didn't do too badly either: ten years later their holding in Tencent was valued at almost $3 billion.

ଝଝଝ

Tencent's transition from rags, relatively speaking, to riches was the result of five very smart strategic moves, each of which was calculated to address the idiosyncrasies of a market dominated by young Chinese-speaking users in search of social networks and entertainment.

First, linking Internet messaging to mobile phones. Tencent adapted ICQ to forward messages to mobiles, the primary means of communication for young Chinese, and then did a deal with the state-owned mobile operator to split the resulting revenues 50/50. "That", said Ma, "was our first bucket of gold".

Second, making it cute. Tencent's instant messaging service is hosted by a fat little penguin named QQ, who wears a bright red scarf and winks at his customers as he bounces round the screen. Curiously, perhaps, to Western eyes, QQ is a huge hit in Asia, where in 2012 there were more than 750 million active users of Tencent's instant messaging service.

Third, making it personal. As Pony Ma told David Barboza of *The New York Times*: "Every internet user (in Asia) likes personalization". Taking on board the virtual world pioneered by Korean social networking sites, Tencent provided for personal avatars, and then set up a virtual banking system, QQ Coins, to sell users clothes, pets and other virtual goods with which to personalise them.

Fourth, having fun. With the interactive gaming market worth more than $60 billion, and its elite "athletes" commanding similar fame to the soccer stars of Europe, there was even more fun to be had from Internet marketing. By searching the world for the most popular online games, licencing and adapting them to the tastes of Chinese consumers, and then linking them to the QQ software, Ma opened up another avenue for selling users virtual goods.

Fifth, making it focused. Tencent has social networking sites specifically oriented to the youth market (Qzone) and others specifically for adults. Weixin (meaning "tiny messages", but remarkably similar to wei xing, meaning "for sex"), for example, is a free online dating service that offers users the ability to chat to, and view fetching photographs of, any other user within a 1-km radius.

The common theme of all this, to paraphrase Deng Xiaoping, is "instant messaging with Chinese characteristics". By tailoring his "one-stop online lifestyle services" to the interests and culture of his customers,

Ma has laughed off competition from international messaging services such as Microsoft's MSN, as well as other local imitators of the original ICQ technology. And unlike Western Internet companies, which depend largely on advertising revenue, almost all of Tencent's profits are derived from selling billions of small, usually virtual, items to users.

In 2004, Tencent listed on the Hong Kong Stock Exchange, raising $200 million at a market capitalisation of $800 million. And by mid-2012 the market cap had multiplied by a factor of nearly 100 to a whopping $70 billion.

ᘔᘔᘔ

But it hasn't all been plain sailing.

The flip side of what Ma calls "microinnovation" - taking ideas and technologies from other sources and adapting them to the Chinese market, often with a range of functions and services as well as Chinese-language capability - is what some of his milder-mannered competitors call copying. Others use stronger terms.

The front cover of the July 26, 2010 issue of *China Computerworld* probably summarised their views reasonably accurately. Under the headline "Fucking Tencent" it depicted Tencent's penguin mascot bleeding from multiple knife wounds, and went on to quote competitors who claimed that Tencent is never the first to "eat crab" - try something new - but waits to move in as soon as someone else has built the market.

Sour grapes, says Ma, who maintains that imitation is the most reliable form of innovation. And certainly, Tencent's research capacity implies more emphasis on innovation than Ma's competitors suggest. Roughly half of the firm's 20,000 employees work in R&D, and the company has also funded a research institute with laboratories on three Chinese university campuses. And *Forbes* agrees, listing Tencent as number 4 on its 2011 list of the world's most innovative companies.

But some of the criticism has struck home. Following a 2011 forum at which other industry leaders were invited to comment on Tencent's performance, Ma has committed to establishing a 10 billion yuan ($1.5

billion) fund to invest in new gaming and social networking technologies in collaboration with local and international companies. "Our mission", he told Joe Havely of the National University of Singapore: "is to enlarge the cake and then share it".

ೞೞೞ

Where next? Although Ma failed in his first attempt, in 2006, to penetrate the US and Japanese markets, he remains determined to take Tencent onto the global scene. To that end, he has acquired a series of smaller software development companies in the United States and Asia, including Los Angeles-based Riot Games, the creator of Tencent's hugely popular League of Legends. And in a clear signal that he doesn't intend to make the same mistakes that Western firms made in China, Ma emphasised to Joe Havely: "Investing in local teams is a sound strategy, because they are familiar with the local culture".

His major shareholder certainly thinks he's on the right track. With classic understatement, the 2012 Annual Report of Naspers, the company whose $34 million investment Ma has multiplied almost 100-fold, notes: "Tencent continues to record excellent results".

MARK ZUCKERBERG

When a photograph of the mutilated face of Khaled Saeed, who had been bashed to death by Egyptian security police on June 6, 2010, was posted on the Internet by his outraged brother, the world's first online revolution began. Choreographed by a Facebook page called "We are all Khaled Saeed", hundreds of silent protestors, clad in black, lined the banks of the Nile in Alexandria. Over the following months more Internet-orchestrated events followed, culminating in the acceptance by 80,000 Egyptians of an anonymous Facebook invitation to attend "the day of the revolution against torture, poverty, corruption and unemployment" in Cairo's Tahrir Square on January 25, 2011. Eighteen days after that, Hosni Mubarak, the fourth president of Egypt, resigned from office after 30 years. In the words of Internet activist and author Wael Ghonim, "the power of the people is greater than the people in power".

At the heart of that power was another revolution, a social networking revolution, led by a young man who ten years earlier was still in high school. His name was Mark Zuckerberg.

ৼৼৼ

Building an IT empire was on Mark Zuckerberg's cards from the start.

On the one hand, the schoolboy Mark was into the classics. He loved to read and quote from Homer's Iliad ("Let there be one ruler, one king", perhaps?) and Virgil's Aeneid ("An empire without bound"). And his choice of sporting activity matched his taste in literature: he captained his school at fencing, the most classical of the martial arts.

On the other, he was a prodigious computing talent, who loved to use his programming skills to address real-world problems. In 1997, while Pony Ma was still contemplating building a company around Israeli instant messaging technology, the 13-year-old Mark Zuckerberg was creating his own, albeit primitive, instant messaging service, Zucknet, between the computers in the family home and his father's dental surgery.

But the first real sign of things to come was the Synapse Media Player, a program he and a classmate created to statistically analyse their friends' musical preferences and construct play lists in which they would be interested. And his schoolmates weren't the only ones interested. Microsoft and others offered a million dollars and more in the hope of acquiring both Zuckerberg and his software. But Zuckerberg wasn't interested. He wanted his own empire.

ৼৼৼ

In a foretaste of things to come, Zuckerberg turned down the million-dollar offers and went to Harvard, where he proposed to major in psychology and computer science. In many respects he was much like any other undergraduate student: studying, partying and staying up all night discussing the future of mankind. In others, he was already marching to the beat of a different drum, the same one that had led him to create Zucknet and Synapse. In his words, he "liked building things": when faced with a social or academic question, Mark Zuckerberg's first instinct was to convert it to an algorithm, and then program it.

And so it was, in his first week as a Harvard sophomore, that he built Coursematch, enabling a highly appreciative Harvard student body to choose courses and create study groups that maximised social benefits.

And then came Facemash, the product of a few days of intense coding, hacking and more hacking during the last week of October 2003. Like the publicly available "hotornot" site, it took the discussion of potential sexual partners out of the locker room and onto the Internet, giving Harvard students the opportunity to rank their classmates, based on their photographs, as more or less "hot" than others.

Facemash went viral, registering over 20,000 votes in a single day, before closing down in a storm of administrative and student indignation: in the administration's view, Zuckerberg had illegally hacked into Harvard's computers to acquire the photographs; in the students' view, he had invaded their privacy. Reprimanded by Harvard, Zuckerberg stepped back, but not far. Three months later, in another burst of all-night programming, he created theFacebook, which provided all of the same photographs and contact details as Facemash, as well as student profiles and social interests, but without the inflammatory physical comparisons. It was a service that the University had promised, but failed to deliver, for two years. Zuckerberg, as he proudly proclaimed, created it in a week.

Like Facemash, theFacebook went viral. By June 2004, four months after going online, there were 160,000 active users, and Zuckerberg and his roommate Dustin Moskovitz decided to spend the summer vacation in California, building theFacebook and discovering what made Silicon Valley tick. They rented a house, hired intern programmers, and set to work. And they never went back.

And theFacebook's extraordinary growth never stopped.

As the site, now renamed simply Facebook, spread from universities to high schools to the workplace, and from the United States to the world, the number of active users increased exponentially, from 1 million at the end of 2004 to over 900 million in mid-2012. And as the numbers grew, so did the interest of investors. From its late-2004 valuation of less than $10 million, based on a $500,000 angel investment from PayPal co-founder Peter Thiel, the notional value jumped to $100 million in 2005 when venture capital firm Accel Partners invested $12.7 million for 11% of the company, and was multiplied tenfold in 2006 when Zuckerberg knocked back Yahoo's offer of a billion dollars. In 2007, Microsoft's purchase of 1.6% of the company for $240 million raised the valuation to $15 billion, and when the long-awaited IPO came in 2012 the market valued Facebook, briefly, at $104 billion.

So, how did that happen?

Basically Zuckerberg did three very smart things.

First, he learnt from the masters. Within weeks of his arrival in Silicon Valley, at the age of 20, he teamed up with Sean Parker, the elderly (25-year-old) and battle-scarred veteran of two previous technology start-ups, who brought Zuckerberg his knowledge and bitter experience of the Silicon Valley venture capital scene. And before long, he was sharing visions with Steve Jobs as they strolled together in Palo Alto, and attracting the likes of David Graham, former CEO of the *Washington Post*, to sit on his board.

Second, he hired the best - and fired the rest. On the one hand, he hired stars like Sheryl Sandberg, who had built and run Google's online sales organisation, as COO, and gave her total authority over distractions like human resources, settling lawsuits and making money out of advertising, leaving him free to focus on his strengths - product design and overall strategy. On the other hand, the ones that didn't work out were dispensed with, rapidly and dispassionately. Their ranks included his Harvard co-founder Eduardo Saverin, who had put up the initial working capital and much of the initial enthusiasm for the business, but whose return to Harvard rather than moving to California represented, at least in Zuckerberg's eyes, a serious lack of commitment.

Third, he never ceded control. From the first VC round in 2005, where Parker's advice ensured that Mark Zuckerberg controlled two of the five board seats, to the IPO, from which he emerged with 57% of voting stock, he has retained total dominance over the direction of the company.

And he made mistakes, lots of them, most of which resulted directly from his absolute confidence in the infallibility of his vision for the kind of social network that Facebook users really wanted, or should want: an open, interconnected world where all personal information was shared.

But were they mistakes, or simply mistimings?

In 2006, for example, he introduced News Feed, collecting information on the activities of his users, and converting it into a living, breathing newspaper, chronicling their lives and sharing them with their friends. Amid howls of protest, Zuckerberg apologised, but News Feed survived and prospered, to become an integral and immensely popular part of Facebook.

Then, in 2007, he introduced Beacon, telling all and sundry just what their friends and lovers were purchasing on the net. Again there were howls of protest, and again Zuckerberg apologised. But it wasn't long before a slightly scaled-back version of Beacon became a key, and valued, component of Facebook. The resulting personal endorsements of products offered Facebook advertisers opportunity to surgically focus their messages, while at the same time allowing Facebook users to interrogate the likes and dislikes of their friends as the basis for choosing anything from a new handbag to a holiday.

And throughout it all, he kept his sights on the empire. Whether by expanding beyond the constraints of individual institutions and borders, by introducing game-changing innovations such as photo tagging, by opening up Facebook as a platform for millions of application writers, or by converting it to a portal to access the most popular websites, he has relentlessly pursued his goal of building the biggest Internet site in the world.

ཛཛཛ

So, where next?

Married to his long-term half-Chinese girlfriend Priscilla Chan, and spending an hour a day learning Mandarin, the next big step has to be

China. But China is not so sure. Wary of the prospect of Facebook-fuelled events like those in Egypt and elsewhere, China banned Facebook in 2009.

And at home, the 2012 IPO left the 28-year-old Zuckerberg with the onerous task of reporting to the market for the first time. How will he fare? So far, the market is not too sure. As the number of monthly active members passed the 1 billion mark on September 14, 2012, making Facebook's "population" three times that of the United States and three-quarters that of China, the stock price was stumbling along at between 50% and 60% of its valuation at the IPO.

But, like his famous predecessor in the social media space, Rupert Murdoch, Zuckerberg has sufficient voting stock to maintain control. And, like Rupert Murdoch, he has no doubt about what to do with it: "We don't build services to make money; we make money to build better services". For Mark, it was never about the money.

BEG, BORROW OR STEAL

At first glance, the differences between Pony Ma and Mark Zuckerberg are more obvious than the similarities. Pony Ma, for example, met his potential investors in a suit, anxious to win their approval, while Zuckerberg rocked up in his sweatshirt and hoodie, and on one famous occasion in his pyjamas.

But when it comes to serious business, they are both the same.

Pony Ma borrows new ideas wherever he can find them, and defends his actions with the mantra that the heart of innovation lies not in the original idea, but in its implementation. Zuckerberg shares that view, defending his empire to the death in both the technology marketplace and in the courts. To a long-standing case brought by fellow Harvard undergraduates Cameron Winklevoss, Tyler Winklevoss and Divya Narendra, that "he stole the moment, he stole the idea, and he stole the execution", Zuckerberg responds that the idea of social networking was everywhere in 2004, and that he was simply the most successful in implementing it. And when photo-sharing company Instagram emerged in 2012 with technology that might conceivably benefit his competitors, Zuckerberg pre-empted them by purchasing the company.

Likewise, in the battle for market share. Pony Ma has focused on mobile phone networks and instant messaging as the core of a business catering mainly to Chinese-speaking users. Zuckerberg has focused on online social networking and English-language offerings. Now they both want to steal the other's space: Pony Ma wants to move into the West and social networking, Mark Zuckerberg into the East and smartphone networks.

 କକକ

The ultimate prize, for both Pony Ma and Mark Zuckerberg, is to run the world's biggest Internet site. But will the noosphere they create be the global village of Chardin's dreams?

Some, like MIT professor Sherry Turkle, think not: "We live in a technological universe in which we are always communicating. And yet we have sacrificed conversation for mere connection".

Almost 2 billion others - young Chinese seeking new friends, outraged Egyptians seeking social justice, people everywhere seeking closer contacts with their far-off loved ones - beg to differ.

KEY SOURCES

China Internet Network Information Center, "30th Statistical report on Internet development in China", September 2012.

Internet World Stats, "Usage and population statistics", 2012.

Sherry Turkle, "The flight from conversation", *The New York Times*, April 21, 2012.

MA "PONY" HUATENG

David Barboza, "Internet boom in China built on virtual fun", *The New York Times*, February 5, 2007.

David Barboza, "China's Internet giants may be stuck there", *The New York Times*, March 24, 2010.

Bruce Einhorn and Brad Stone, "Tencent: March of the penguins", *Bloomberg Businessweek*, August 4, 2011.

Joe Havely, "Turning Tencent into billions", *Think Business*, National University of Singapore, June 25, 2012.

Chen Hong, "President hails Shenzhen SEZ a world 'miracle'", *China Daily*, September 7, 2010.

"Interview with Tencent CEO", *The Economic Observer*, February 6, 2012.

Mark Lee, "Tencent revamps businesses to expand in mobile, grow overseas", *Bloomberg*, May 17, 2012.

"Talking dirty. Looking for love? Try Tencent's Weixin", *Week in China*, issue 145, April 13, 2012.

MARK ZUCKERBERG

Facebook Inc, "S-1 Registration Statement, United States Securities and Exchange Commission", February 1, 2012.

Lev Grossman, "Person of the Year 2010. Mark Zuckerberg", *Time Magazine*, December 15, 2010.

Evelyn M. Rusli, Nicole Perlroth and Nick Bilton, "Facebook's Mark Zuckerberg, at a turning point", *The New York Times*, May 12, 2012.

E. Benjamin Samuels, "A look at Mark Zuckerberg through the years", *The Harvard Crimson*, October 7, 2010.

John D. Sutter, "The faces of Egypt's 'Revolution 2.0'", *CNN*, February 21, 2011.

Jose Antonio Vargas, "The face of Facebook", *The New Yorker Magazine*, September 20, 2010.

An individual with an epic ambition to change the world, who	Ma "Pony" Huateng	Mark Zuckerberg
	Born: 1971, Hainan, China Education: BA, BSc, Shenzhen University Organisation: Tencent Holdings Ltd	Born: 1984, White Plains, New York, USA Education: Harvard University Organisation: Facebook
.. sees and seizes opportunities for change ..		
Opportunistic: aggressively seeks and adopts new ideas	On a training trip to the United States he was impressed by Israeli instant messaging technology ...	Recognised that the focus of the Internet would move from networks of computers ...
& Visionary: intuitively grasps the big picture and how it might evolve	... and recognised its potential as a communication tool in China.	... to networks of people, thus creating a more open and connected world ...
.. senses the way forward ..		
Innovative: thinks creatively, ignores boundaries, disrupts the status quo	He and his colleagues developed a Chinese-language version of the Israeli software, adapted it for pagers and mobile phones, ...	... in which people could construct virtual social networks that maintained and built on a lifetime of friendships ...
but Pragmatic: recognises constraints, devises practical solutions, creates value	... and used it to provide young Chinese users with "one-stop on-line lifestyle services", including a mind-boggling array of social networks and online games.	... while offering advertisers an immensely powerful and targeted marketing tool.

.. attracts the necessary resources ..

Persuasive:
articulate and convincing communicator, consummate networker

Although he provided most of Tencent's initial capital (ca $75,000), he kept less than half the stock, splitting the rest between his four co-founders (and fellow Shenzhen graduates), ...

On a flight to Davos on Google 1, he persuaded Sheryl Sandberg to leave her senior management role at Google, the biggest company in the space, to join its fledgling competitor, where ...

& Empowering:
attracts talent, inspires loyalty, rewards excellence

... who all retain senior administrative and advisory roles with the company.

... he gave her total control of day-to-day operations ...

.. and pursues the dream ..

Focused:
passionate and highly energetic perfectionist, totally committed to an overriding vision

By 2012, although less than 40% of China's population were connected to the Internet, Tencent had over 750 million active users, and growing fast.

... while he focussed on product design ...

& Confident:
driven by unconditional self-belief, assumes absolute authority and accountability

"China will lead the world in terms of the number of internet users. This means that China's Internet companies will have the opportunity to create world-leading business models and applications, and that from having been 'students' they will become 'teachers'".

... and strategy: "We're trying to map out what exists in the world ... through the people and relationships around us".

.. regardless of the odds ..

Resilient:
flexible, thrives on change and uncertainty, learns from mistakes

Threatened by international Internet providers, he relied on his understanding of the cultural complexities of the Chinese market to provide services that Western companies couldn't or wouldn't deliver ...

"Move fast and break things. The idea is that if you never break anything, you're probably not moving fast enough".

& Courageous:
bold, intelligent risk-taker, undaunted by criticism, determined to succeed

... and then set out to do the same thing in Western markets by acquiring smaller foreign companies capable of providing similar understanding of their local cultures.

"At Facebook we're less afraid of making mistakes than we are of losing opportunities".

Chapter 11

... AND FAMILY

AS THE POPULATION OF THE planet grows ever greater, so does our desire to find our place in the scheme of things. Who were my ancestors? Where was my ancestral homeland? Do I still have relatives there? Will I too have an opportunity to bring a child into the world? To raise a family?

ଚଚଚ

Many of us are familiar with the names attributed to our famous ancestral relatives: Lucy (Australopithecus, 3.2 million years ago), Peking Man (*Homo erectus*, 700,000 years ago), and even Mitochondrial Eve, the most recent matrilineal ancestor of all humans alive today, who is thought to have lived in East Africa around 200,000 years ago.

Fewer will realise that our most recent common ancestors, common to most humans alive today, almost certainly lived less than 5,000 years ago. And while most of us may know the identities of our parents and grandparents, as well as our siblings and cousins, when it comes to our fourth cousins and great-great grandparents, we are pretty much in the dark. Or, at least, we were until the advent of companies like MyHeritage, founded by passionate Israeli genealogist Gilad Japhet, that enable us to trace and expand our family trees.

And what about the future? Our families are defined as much by our children as by our parents, but as many as 10 - 15% of people of childbearing age suffer from infertility, and perhaps another 5% are gay or lesbian. Prior to the advent of *in vitro* fertilisation (IVF), both groups were denied biological families of their own, but surrogacy pioneers like Nayana Patel and Doron Mamet are rapidly putting paid to that.

We have a need to identify our ancestors and indemnify our succession. And where there's a need, there are überpreneurs.

GILAD JAPHET

The concept of kinship is fundamental to both Judaism and Israel. In orthodox Judaism, the child of a Jewish woman is by definition Jewish, and the "children of Israel", although drawn from a vast range of different cultures and languages, can thus be seen as a single kinship network going back to one or a small number of women.

But where are they? The Jewish Diaspora, first exiled from the Kingdom of Judah by Babylonian King Nebuchadnezzar in the 6th-century BC, now number approximately 13 million. About 40% live in Israel, another 40% in the United States and the remainder are scattered throughout the world. For most, tracing the family tree is no simple task.

ცცც

Gilad Japhet is one very smart nerd. Studying full time at Israel's prestigious Technion Institute of Technology, Japhet also had a night job as a senior software engineer at BRM Technologies, a start-up company specialising in computer security, where he led a group responsible for designing and coding algorithms for the intelligent detection and removal of computer viruses. Then, soon after graduating in the top 1% of his class in computer science, he moved to Silicon Valley, where he played a key role in taking another Israeli firm, BackWeb Technologies, from a small start-up to a NASDAQ-listed company.

Back in Israel, married, but having difficulty settling into life as director of product management for two other Israeli technology start-ups, he took six months off to pursue the hobby that had fascinated him since he was 13 years old: genealogy. But he was soon frustrated by the lack of quality software available to help make sense of the wealth of family relationships that he was unearthing. Early in 2003, he decided it was time to write his own.

The next three years were tough for Japhet. He mortgaged his house, hired good people, wrote great software, and founded MyHeritage. But the investment community had little interest in genealogy, and even less in an entrepreneur who had never run his own company. Worse still, they observed, he allowed all and sundry to download his software for free!

But what Japhet lacked in business acumen, he made up for in chutzpah. By 2005, he had persuaded two Israeli angel investors, technology guru Yukul Rakavy and foreign exchange specialist Aviv Raiz, to invest $2 million. In the following year they were joined by Simon Levene, of venture capital firm Accel Partners, in a further $3 million capital raising.

Their investment was just in time. Early in 2007, Silicon Valley's PayPal mafia discovered genealogy, pouring money and, more importantly, user-friendly Internet technology into Geni, a new competitor that hit the ground running with a market capitalisation of $100 million. As one of Japhet's investors noted, the situation was reminiscent of MetaCafe, the Israeli company that was first into the YouTube space, but was virtually wiped out by the financial and networking power of its me-too competitor from Silicon Valley.

Japhet was shocked, but all the more determined to win. He went back to the market, raising two more rounds of venture capital by convincing investors that he could take on the Silicon Valley titans and beat them at their own game. His strategy was threefold.

First, he focused on the family as a social network. Recognising that Facebook had captured social networking among friends, and that LinkedIn would soon do the same for professionals, he noted that there was a huge opportunity for a social network that enabled users to identify and make contact with living family members. MyHeritage, he said: "will become the de facto social network for families".

Second, he recognised that the family members of his potential customers in the global melting pots of Israel, the United States and elsewhere were scattered all over the world, and it was therefore essential that "support for multiple languages and cultures was built into the DNA of the company from day one". By 2011 MyHeritage was available in 38 languages.

Third, he saw the need to offer the best technology not only for the technical work of identifying family members and ancestors, but also to provide the best and friendliest user interface. With that in mind, Japhet embarked on a carefully premeditated series of mergers and acquisitions. As he explained to Sarah Lacy of *Techcrunch*, following the acquisition of a major European competitor in 2010: "It was founded by two very talented individuals, and I knew from their track records they were serial entrepreneurs. I thought from the start they wouldn't have the patience to run this for 10 years, maybe they'd be willing to merge their vision with ours. Eventually that theory proved correct".

This careful assembly of skills and technologies via strategic mergers and acquisitions has proved extraordinarily effective in enabling MyHeritage to remain at the cutting edge. Its Smart Matching™ technology, for example, facilitates automatic and accurate searching across family trees in multiple languages, while the 2011 acquisition of World Vital Records, with its billions of birth, marriage, death and census records, enables ancestors to be automatically connected to historical records.

Similarly, by partnering with a global genetic genealogy company, MyHeritage has been able to provide a range of affordable DNA testing that allows users to explore a common genetic heritage as well as discovering their ethnic roots. For Japhet: "While DNA tests can break through brick walls in family history research by revealing biological relations, … Smart Matching technology then steps in to help piece together the paper trail by uncovering how the family trees of related people actually connect".

By mid-2012 MyHeritage had over 63 million members worldwide, with 1 billion profiles, nearly 23 million family trees and over 150 million photographs. It has indeed become the de facto social network for families. And yes, just in case you wondered, it has even begun to make money. MyHeritage will not only remind you of your sister's birthday, it will also suggest a suitable present, and take a commission on the way by. The service may be free, it's the add-ons that make the profits.

ଧଧଧ

In November 2012, in a stunning reversal of the MetaCafe/YouTube story, Japhet raised a further $25 million in venture capital and acquired Geni, the "PayPal mafia"-backed competitor that had been expected to blow MyHeritage away. As Japhet told Matthew Lynley of *The Wall Street Journal*: "MyHeritage is a forest of private hyperlinked family trees, and Geni is building a family tree of the whole world. If you combine the two, you end up with a reference of the world, everyone is on there".

Not content with simply reconnecting the Jewish Diaspora, Japhet is now on the brink of connecting all of humanity through a single family tree.

NAYANA PATEL

The world's first test-tube baby, Louise Brown, was delivered by Caesarean section in the Oldham and District General Hospital, near Manchester, on 25 July, 1978. Just 10 weeks later, on October 3, 1978, a second test-tube baby girl, Kanupriya Agarwal, was born in Calcutta.

The doctors responsible for these momentous events were not universally acclaimed.

In Britain, Robert Edwards and Patrick Steptoe were, in the words of the biochemist Joseph Goldstein, "immediately attacked by an unlikely trinity - the press, the Pope, and prominent Nobel laureates". Both before and after the birth of Louise, their applications to the Medical Research Council for grants to pursue IVF research were rejected.

In India, the claims of Doctor Subhash Mukherjee, now recognised as having pioneered several key elements of modern IVF technology, were met with deep suspicion. The government of West Bengal established an enquiry to investigate his claims and subsequently concluded that they were entirely bogus. Denied the opportunity to continue his groundbreaking work, he committed suicide in his Calcutta apartment in June 1981.

How times have changed.

In 2010, Bob Edwards - then aged 85, suffering from short-term memory loss and no longer in a position to appreciate the honour - was awarded the Nobel Prize for physiology or medicine. By that time, 32 years after the birth of Louise Brown, some 4 million babies had been conceived by IVF, representing up to 5% of live births in some developed countries. And in India, IVF and related technologies, collectively known as "assisted reproductive technologies" (ARTs), were at the forefront of the nation's booming medical tourism industry, offering Westerners first world medical care at third world prices.

ৼৼৼ

The keys to India's ARTs business are surrogate mothers, a small army of women who seek to pay off debts, build homes, educate their children or simply buy food for their families by renting out their wombs. And the woman who opened the door was Dr Nayana Patel, Director of the Akanksha Fertility Clinic in Anand, the administrative centre of the dairy farming industry in the Indian state of Gujarat.

Nayana Patel made her debut on the world stage in 2003, announcing that a 43-year-old Anand woman had successfully given birth to her own twin grandchildren! A newsworthy and, at first glance, somewhat disturbing thought, but logical enough in the world of IVF. As it turned out, the woman had simply loaned her womb to a daughter whose genetic disorder had rendered her physically unable to bear a child. Patel and her team extracted eggs from the daughter, fertilised them with sperm from her husband, and implanted them in the womb of the young woman's mother. All perfectly above board, though complicated by the fact that the young couple were British, the grandmother/surrogate Indian, and the twins temporarily stranded betwixt and between.

That story opened the floodgates. Before long there were waiting lists of couples from India and overseas seeking Patel's assistance to produce longed-for children, and increasing numbers of young women seeking to join her clinic as surrogates.

But Patel is notoriously fussy about who she takes on from either group. She insists that she will only arrange surrogacies for heterosexual couples with a genuine infertility problem, and she only accepts surrogates who are young, free of vices like alcohol, smoking and drugs, clinically healthy, and with at least one living child of their own. Appearing in 2006 on the Oprah Winfrey show, she noted that the latter condition was necessary to ensure that the surrogate was able to handle the pregnancy and delivery, and to minimise the chances of too close an emotional attachment developing between the surrogate and the newborn baby.

She is also fiercely protective of the welfare of her surrogates. Before acceptance into the program, potential surrogates are visited in their homes by counsellors who seek to ensure their husbands and families are supportive, and they are subsequently housed in the clinic or adjacent hostels throughout their pregnancies. Apart from ensuring the quality of their food and housing, Patel notes that this arrangement provides surrogates with the opportunity to take classes in English and computing, and to learn the financial skills needed to put their surrogacy fees - often ten or more times their household's annual income - to effective use.

There is, of course, plenty of talk of exploitation of impoverished Indian women by wealthy Western couples, but Patel insists that every deal is a win-win. As one young American client put it to Oprah Winfrey: "We were able to come together, (the surrogate) and I, and give each other a life that neither of us could achieve on our own. And I just don't see what's wrong with that".

The business model is certainly simple - the perfect one-stop shop. Couples come to the clinic for a three-week visit during which ovulation is stimulated, eggs harvested and fertilised with the partner's sperm, and embryos implanted in the surrogate's womb. Some come back to observe progress during the course of the pregnancy, and all return for the birth of the child, usually by Caesarean section.

And the win-win formula clearly works: since 2002 hundreds of babies have been delivered at Patel's clinic, with 50 or more surrogates living in the clinic and adjacent hostels at any one time. And the waiting lists of ready buyers and willing sellers just continue to grow. Patel's surrogate list now numbers more than 350, and the overall commercial surrogacy market has been estimated as representing around $400 - $500 million per annum of the multibillion-dollar Indian medical tourism industry.

But it hasn't all been plain sailing. One Japanese couple divorced during their surrogate's pregnancy, leaving Patel literally holding India's first stateless surrogate baby. In other cases, although current Indian law precludes surrogates from making custodial claims, authorities in the genetic parents' home countries have denied infants citizenship on the grounds that they belong with the gestational mother.

A draft bill intended to strengthen the surrogacy guidelines developed by the Indian Council of Medical Research is slowly working its way through the bureaucracy toward the Indian parliament. Among other things, the new law will require foreign nationals to obtain written acknowledgement of their infant's future citizenship rights before they are permitted to enter into a surrogacy agreement. But according to Dr Patel, as reported by *PBS Newshour*: "Until medicine perfects a uterus transplant, the business of surrogacy is certain to be ... a legal and ethical work in progress".

And for one person at least, a key conclusion of that legal and ethical work in progress should be clear-cut: if surrogacy can deliver healthy babies to infertile women, why not provide the same service to gay men?

DORON MAMET

The importance of family continuity in Israeli society goes way beyond the linkages to living relatives and ancestors facilitated by MyHeritage. There is also tremendous pressure, from state and family, to follow the biblical injunction to be fruitful and multiply. Backed by a range of child allowances and other financial incentives, the pressure to reproduce extends to substantial support for assisted reproductive technologies. IVF treatment, for example, is available completely free, not only for infertile heterosexual couples, but also for single and lesbian women, including entitlements to sick leave where necessary. As a result, Israel now has more IVF clinics per capita, and a higher fertility rate, than any other country in the Western world.

But not for gays. Adoption by same-sex couples was legalised in 2008, and gestational surrogacy has been permitted since 1996, but only infertile heterosexual couples are allowed to hire surrogates. Stymied by the rules, gay Israeli partners Doron Mamet and Doron Godony paid a total of US$140,000 to procure the conception, gestation and delivery of their daughter, Talia, in the United States, where commercial egg donation and surrogacy are legal for all comers in a number of states.

Although delighted with this outcome, coming home with the baby wasn't quite so simple. Mamet and his partner had taken great pains to ensure that no one, including themselves, knew who was the biological father of their child. As Mamet told April Hovav, who interviewed him as part of her postgraduate research at Budapest's Central European University: "We both donated the sperm ... whatever stuck, stuck". But the Israeli government required a paternity test before their daughter could be granted Israeli citizenship. Mamet decided that there had to be a better way.

Based on his experience in international outsourcing of technology programs, Doron Mamet saw an opportunity to establish a surrogacy service that was not only more affordable, but also provided more guidance through the medical, legal and emotional complexities of the surrogacy process. And within a few months of his daughter's birth, he seized that opportunity, leaving his position as a senior project manager at a global high-tech company to establish Tammuz International Surrogacy.

ଔଔଔ

At its heart, Mamet's business is the same as Nayana Patel's: bringing comparatively wealthy childless couples, predominantly from the Western world, together with generally poor surrogate mothers, mainly in India.

But there are some key differences.

First, the clientele. Mamet's customers are mostly gay, whereas Patel limits her activities to couples whose infertility arises from what she describes as genuine medical reasons. With respect to same-sex couples, as she commented to Abigail Haworth of *marie claire*: "I get e-mails from gays and lesbians, some of them very well written, but I don't feel right about helping them".

And second, the business model. Patel conducts the entire business, from fertilisation through gestation to delivery, in her clinic in the small Indian agricultural town of Anand, accommodating prospective parents in local hotels and surrogate mothers in hostels associated with the clinic. Mamet, on the other hand, conducts a global outsourcing exercise spanning four continents, as depicted graphically in Israeli filmmaker Zippi Brand Frank's 2009 documentary, *Google Baby*.

Briefly, the Tammuz process is as follows. Sperm, from either or both of the prospective parents, is flown to a specialist IVF centre in either the United States or India, where it is used to fertilise one or more eggs sourced from donors in India, the United States or other Western nations. Eggs sourced from the United States are the most expensive, but also offer the prospective parents the opportunity to choose from a range of donors, mostly students in their early 20s, on the basis of detailed profiles and photographs. In India, parents may choose eggs provided by local donors, the least expensive option, or those supplied by young women from South Africa who are paid to travel to India for the procedure.

Similar options are available following fertilisation. For eggs fertilised in the United States, the embryos are either implanted in a US surrogate (the most expensive option), or frozen and couriered to a clinic in India, where they are implanted in surrogates from the Mumbai region, as are the embryos from the Indian clinic. Specialists are involved at every stage of the process, from transporting embryos to delivering the babies, and the prospective parents need never leave home until it's time to collect the baby. All up, they'll pay between $32,000 and $115,000 (depending on the choice of surrogacy plan) to buy their legacy on demand.

Or, to put it more simply, as April Hovav records Doron Mamet's explanation to his daughter Talia:

> Dad and dad wanted children very much. To have a child we needed a woman to help us. There is one woman in the United States who agreed to help us. She gave us some material, we mixed it with dads' material and then we put it into the belly of another woman who took care of you for nine months.

Is Tammuz an example of superbly efficient global outsourcing, or third world exploitation gone mad?

According to sociologist Anne Kerr, commenting on coverage of the Tammuz story in the film *Google Baby*: "What this film shows us is that wealthy consumers and entrepreneurs are creating the conditions for poor and vulnerable women to turn their reproductive potential into tradable commodities so that they too might join the consumer classes. It is a lesson in global capitalism we can ill afford to ignore".

Sharadaben Solanki, one of the first of Nayana Patel's surrogate mothers, concurs. As she told Anupama Katakam of *Frontline*: "I would never have made this kind of money even if I worked 24 hours every day for the rest of my life. I built a house, bought three acres of land, two cows and two buffaloes in my village, Waghpura, near Anand. I don't have to worry now".

ଓଓଓ

In December 2012, the Indian Home Ministry introduced a new ruling that required couples seeking children through an Indian surrogate to obtain a "medical visa", and further specified that such visas would only be available to heterosexual couples that had been married for at least two years.

The reaction from the key protagonists was swift and dismissive. According to Nayana Patel: "While we need regulation, creating bureaucratic hurdles through such regulations contradicts India's claims of promoting medical tourism". And, as Doron Mamet explained to Yanir Dekel of *A Wider Bridge*:

> There are two facts that work in our favour: one is that the instruction comes from the department that's responsible for granting visas to foreigners coming to India, not by the authority who decides who may undergo a process of surrogacy in the country. Secondly, the surrogacy industry in India is based primarily on same-sex couples' surrogacy and single parents. Clinics, which make millions from the procedure and the large number of same-sex couples requesting it, do not accept the provisions easily.

Meanwhile, the Assisted Reproductive Technology (ART) Regulation Bill 2010 is still awaiting tabling in parliament.

FOR LOVE OR MONEY?

For these three it's plainly about love.

Gilad Japhet may one day be seriously rich, but only because his venture capital investors will demand it. If it weren't for them, he'd still be giving his software away. His motivation, and that of his team, is genealogy for the love of it. For the love of linking people to family members that they would otherwise never find.

Nayana Patel's first surrogacy case only ever happened because a local Anand woman wished to volunteer her womb to enable her daughter to mother a child. Inspired by the joy that her intervention brought to both parties, Patel's initial foray into surrogacy was nevertheless at a very low-key level. But demand from both sides soon led her to establish her specialist fertility clinic.

Doron Mamet wanted to share the joy of his newfound fatherhood with his gay friends, but recognised that few of them could afford the price that he and his partner had paid to hire a surrogate in the United States, or stomach the legal hassles that followed. He resolved to find a more economical and less stressful alternative.

All three are very obvious examples of people whose initial goal in life was to change the world for someone they knew personally, and whose ultimate goal remains to change the world for people at a personal level. For Japhet, it's about finding the family that they didn't know they had; for Patel and Mamet, it's about creating the family they never thought they'd find.

જ્ઞજ્ઞજ્ઞ

And at another level, their love for what they do is evident in the way that they put together the disparate pieces of their businesses.

Japhet the multilingual chess player patiently links together the software and databases he needs to enable others to find family regardless of where they may be or what language they may speak. Japhet the photographer matches faces across generations as he chronicles and connects their lives.

Patel the doctor grills her customers and her surrogates alike to be certain that they understand and are likely to benefit from the process they are undertaking. Patel the social worker counsels prospective parents and surrogates alike to ensure that they do so.

Mamet the gay activist fights for the right of his gay colleagues to enjoy the pleasure of fathering a child and raising a family. Mamet the project manager carefully coordinates the many players, professional and otherwise, needed to achieve their dream.

Ultimately, all three are builders - lovingly putting together the disparate facilities, technologies, people and resources needed to do the job. Like builders, they assemble the pieces you need to make a home.

The rest is up to you.

KEY SOURCES

GILAD JAPHET

Lisa Louise Cooke, "Interview: MyHeritage CEO Gilad Japhet on Joining the US Genealogy Records Scene", *RootsTech* 2012 Salt Lake City, Utah, February 11, 2012.

Pascal-Emmanuel Gobry, "How a startup no one would touch crushed Silicon Valley moguls and became a giant", *Business Insider,* July 18, 2011.

Sarah Lacy, *Brilliant, Crazy, Cocky: how the top 1% of Entrepreneurs profit from global chaos*, John Wiley and Sons, 2011.

Sarah Lacy, "MyHeritage buys Germany's OSN", *Techcrunch*, February 2, 2010.

Matthew Lynley, "MyHeritage raises $25 million, acquires Geni", *The Wall Street Journal*, November 28, 2012.

NAYANA PATEL AND DORON MAMET

Yanir Dekel, "The end of gay surrogacy in India", *A Wider Bridge*, January 2, 2013.

Anindita Ghose "The forgotten hero of IVF", *livemint.com*, October 14, 2010.

Abigail Haworth, "Surrogate mothers: womb for rent", *marie claire*, July 29, 2007.

April Hovav, "(Re)conceiving Kinship: Gay Parenthood through Assisted Reproductive Technologies in Israel", thesis submitted in partial fulfillment of the requirements for the degree of Masters of Arts, Central European University, Budapest, 2011.

"Journey to Parenthood", *Oprah Winfrey Show*, January 1, 2006.

Anupama Katakam, "Wombs for rent", *Frontline*, August 27, 2011.

Anne Kerr, "Google Baby: A lesson in global capitalism", *BioNews*, July 4, 2011.

Fred de Sam Lazaro, "Reporter's notebook: India's new baby boom", *PBS Newshour*, August 4, 2011.

David Lee, Tan Wei Xin and Muhd Nurluqman Suratman, "Wombs for rent", *Straits Times*, June 13, 2009.

Madhavi Rajadhyaksha, "New surrogacy norms will hit 'genuine couples'", *The Times of India*, January 19, 2013.

Rotem Sela, "Proud parents", *Creative Family Connections*, June 8, 2010.

Radha Sharma, "A womb to let", *The Times of India*, May 15, 2010.

Poonam Taneja, "India's surrogate mother industry", *BBC News*, October 12, 2008.

Nicholas Wade, "Pioneer of in vitro fertilization wins Nobel Prize", *The New York Times*, October 4, 2010.

An individual with an epic ambition to change the world, who ...	Gilad Japhet	Nayana Patel	Doron Mamet
	Born: 1969, Israel Education: BSc, Technion Organisation: MyHeritage	Born: ca 1960, Rajkot, Gujarat, India Education: MD, MP Shah Medical College Organisation: Akanksha Infertility Clinic	Born: Israel Education: BA, Ha'Universita Ha'Petuha Organisation: Tammuz International Surrogacy
.. sees and seizes opportunities for change ..			
Opportunistic: aggressively seeks and adopts new ideas	While gathering photographs and historical information on his family heritage, Japhet noted a lack of quality software suitable for processing the data. Realising that	In 2002, when India legalised surrogacy to further boost its global share of the booming medical tourism business, she saw the opportunity to use her medical training ...	Faced with Israeli law that prevents gay couples from entering into commercial surrogacy agreements, global high-tech manager Doron Mamet wondered ...
& Visionary: intuitively grasps the big picture and how it might evolve	... the "world did not recognize the power of genealogy and family history as the bond that connects all people worldwide", ...	... to not only provide childless couples from around the world with much-wanted babies, but also offer a way out of chronic poverty for many rural Indian women.	... if IT can be outsourced to India, why not surrogacy?
.. senses the way forward ..			
Innovative: thinks creatively, ignores boundaries, disrupts the status quo	... Japhet used his savings to hire a team of genealogy enthusiasts with strong IT skills, founded MyHeritage and, ...	She recruited surrogates from the local community and housed them in dormitories in her clinic, thus enabling her to meticulously monitor their health and well-being	He created a global business that connects sperm in one country with eggs in another, and wombs in a third, ...
but Pragmatic: recognises constraints, devises practical solutions, creates value	... despite offering his software for free, ...	... while protecting them from potential religious or community backlash.	... using frozen embryos, Fedex, and credit cards.

.. attracts the necessary resources ..			
Persuasive: articulate and convincing communicator, consummate networker	... persuaded members of the Israeli technology investment community that he could build a competitive genealogy site by ...	Counselling prospective surrogates to think of the pregnancy as "someone's child comes to stay at your place for nine months"...	"Fulfilment awaits you. We are here to help by facilitating the safest, simplest and most economical process by which to bring your baby into the world".
& Empowering: attracts talent, inspires loyalty, rewards excellence	... offering users the opportunity to identify previously unknown relatives regardless of borders, languages, and cultures.	... she ensured that the surrogates themselves were the primary beneficiaries of their earnings. "I personally make sure they use the money judiciously. It's not just a conceive-deliver relationship, it is also about empowerment".	Prospective parents can choose exactly the egg donor they want: matching race, religion, physique and personal interests.
.. and pursues the dream..			
Focused: passionate and highly energetic perfectionist, totally committed to an overriding vision	He supplemented his considerable IT skills and passion for genealogy ...	Recognising that risks are inescapable: "We have to be very careful. We overdo all the health investigations. We do not take any chances",...	He used his extensive experience developing and administering large-scale, international projects in the high-tech world to guide prospective parents through the medical, legal and emotional complexities of the surrogacy process ...
& Confident: driven by unconditional self-belief, assumes absolute authority and accountability	... with user interface software and genealogical databases acquired through strategic mergers and acquisitions, and ...	... and relying on her impressively high success rate to attract couples with infertility problems from Western nations as well as increasing numbers from the intensely religious and conservative Indian community, ...	... and to champion the rights of openly gay Israeli men to raise their own biological children via surrogacy: "I for one believe that there is a big moral issue with those who seek to decide for me or to interfere with my chances to be a father and with the chances of a surrogate to help her family".
.. regardless of the odds..			
Resilient: flexible, thrives on change and uncertainty, learns from mistakes	... undeterred by emerging competition from Silicon Valley, he proclaimed that he would never sell, ...	... she used a combination of medical expertise and entrepreneurship, guided by a transparent set of ethical principles, to operate in an unregulated commercial surrogacy market ...	Forced to comply with an Israeli court order requiring him to conduct a paternity test before bringing his daughter from the United States to Israel, he decided that next time ...
& Courageous: bold, intelligent risk-taker, undaunted by criticism, determined to succeed	... and went head-to-head with his glitzier but less global US competitors.	... while waiting for the draft Assisted Reproductive Technologies Regulation bill to make its tortuous way through Parliament.	...he would fight. As he told April Hovav: "With the second child, we didn't agree to check. We filed a lawsuit against the state".

Part IV

BETTER WORLD

*In September 2000, building upon a decade of major
United Nations conferences and summits, world leaders
came together at United Nations Headquarters in New
York to adopt the United Nations Millennium Declaration,
committing their nations to a new global partnership to
reduce extreme poverty and setting out a series of
time-bound targets - with a deadline of 2015 - that have
become known as the Millennium Development Goals*

THE GLOBAL TRANSFORMATIONS TARGETED BY the UN
Millennium Development Goals (MDGs) are hugely ambitious. Among other
things, they require halving the proportion of people who live in extreme
poverty, suffer from hunger, or lack sustainable access to safe drinking
water; achieving universal primary education for boys and girls everywhere;
and halting the spread of HIV/AIDS and the incidence of malaria. When
achieved, they will have transformed the lives of billions of human beings.

Who should be tackling them? For most of us, the scale of the MDGs places
them firmly in the province of governments, aid agencies and philanthropic
organisations. But many of the most spectacular gains achieved over the
past 20 years have quite clearly been the work of individuals.

ৰৰৰ

One of those inspiring individuals is Bill Drayton, founder of Ashoka: Innovators for the Public, who was himself inspired by the 3rd-century BC Indian leader King Ashoka. According to Buddhist legend, as well as the inscriptions on ancient stone pillars found throughout his empire, Ashoka spent the first eight years of his reign indiscriminately slaughtering the populations of neighbouring countries as he set about unifying the Indian subcontinent. But then he saw the light, became a fervent Buddhist, and spent his remaining 30 years engaged in vast social welfare programs, including planting medicinal herbs to treat sick humans and animals, digging wells to provide water for thirsty travellers, and encouraging respect for other nations, religions, and individuals. As Drayton notes: "For his creativity, global mindedness and tolerance, Ashoka is renowned as the earliest example of a social innovator".

Drayton founded Ashoka in 1980 with an annual budget of $50,000. By 2012, with a budget of $30 million per annum, the organisation was supporting the work of 3,000 Ashoka Fellows in 70 countries. Dubbed social entrepreneurs, most of them tackle issues such as the MDGs by establishing enterprises that are largely based on business principles, but whose purpose is to achieve social change rather than create economic gains. Others take a more commercial approach, using the promise of a combination of social improvement and financial profit to attract substantial investment in their enterprises.

All of them are single-minded in the pursuit of their goals. As Bill Drayton puts it: "Having decided that the world must change in some important way, they simply find and build highways that lead inexorably to that result. Where others see barriers, they delight in finding solutions". He calls them "change-makers".

 క్ష క్ష క్ష

In the next four chapters, we introduce nine such change-makers: überpreneurs whose transformative activities cover the entire spectrum from nonprofit enterprises, supported by aid agencies and philanthropic foundations, through to unashamedly profit-driven business ventures that nevertheless impact directly on social issues such as the MDGs.

Striking at the heart of social disadvantage are Bangladeshi "Banker to the Poor", Muhammad Yunus, and Claus-Peter Zeitinger, a one-time student radical who builds "banks for ordinary people" throughout the developing world. Their very different approaches to the provision of loans and other banking services have helped millions of people in the world's most disadvantaged communities to escape from poverty.

With over 30 million people worldwide living with HIV/AIDS, and almost 2 million new infections per annum in sub-Saharan Africa alone, halting the spread of HIV/AIDS is a prodigious task. But those numbers are just a fraction of what they would have been without the visionary interventions of two men, US obstetrician and gynaecologist Dr Mitch Besser and Thailand's "Mr Condom", Mechai Veravaidya.

In similar vein, the critical numbers of homeless and unemployed youth in India and the Middle East inspired two extraordinary women, Jeroo Billimoria and Soraya Salti, to create new sources of educational and employment opportunities for the street kids of Calcutta and the disenfranchised youth of the Middle East. Increasingly, their ideas are being adopted around the globe.

And in sub-Saharan Africa, where 27% of people remain undernourished (marginally improved from 31% in 1990), the challenge of feeding the planet juxtaposes the vast commercial farming interests of Sheik Mohammed Al-Amoudi and Sai Ram Karuturi with the microfarming approach of Roy Prosterman, who is working with governments around the world to deliver ownership of small land-holdings to hundreds of millions of families.

KEY SOURCES

David Bornstein, *How to Change the World: Social Entrepreneurs and the Power of New Ideas*, Oxford University Press, 2007.

Ven. S. Dhammika, *The Edicts of King Ashoka*, Buddhist Publication Society, Kandy Sri Lanka, 1993.

Bill Drayton, *Everyone is a Change-Maker*, Innovations MIT Press, Winter 2006.

John Elkington and Pamela Hartigan, *The Power of Unreasonable People: How Social Entrepreneurs Create Markets that Change the World*, Harvard Business Press, 2008.

United Nations, "We can End Poverty: 2015 Millennium Development Goals".

Chapter 12

MONEY MATTERS

IN 2012 THE UN ANNOUNCED that "for the first time since poverty trends began to be monitored, ... poverty rates fell in every developing region" of the world. In Southern Asia, the proportion of people living on less than $1.25 a day fell from 51% in 1990 to 34% in 2008, and in Latin America and the Caribbean the corresponding decrease was from 12% to 6%.

In less than two decades the number of people living in extreme poverty in the developing regions of the world fell by 600 million. For many of those individuals, escape from abject poverty was a direct result of the remarkable economic progress of China. For others, the seeds of change had been planted 40 years before.

ଝଝଝ

In 1968, the year of the Prague Spring and the founding of the Club of Rome, a Mexican wave of social upheaval rolled around the globe. Campuses became battlegrounds for social change as students demanded university reforms, civil rights, the overthrow of repressive governments and an end to the Vietnam War.

In Tennessee, a youthful Muhammad Yunus was studying on a research and teaching fellowship at Vanderbilt University when, on April 4, 1968, Martin Luther King was assassinated a day after delivering his famous "Mountaintop" address. Riots broke out in over 100 cities as blacks took to the streets, paradoxically determined to avenge the death of the 20th century's icon of peace and nonviolence.

In Germany, Claus-Peter Zeitinger and his future wife, Gabriele Heber, were at the heart of the German student movement, whose revolt against the government reached its climax in April 1968 following the attempted assassination of student leader Rudi Dutschke, who had been labelled a public enemy by the government and the tabloid press.

And in Bengal, resentment over military dictatorship from West Pakistan was already building toward its culmination in the March 1971 Bangladesh Declaration of Independence and subsequent civil war. Muhammad Yunus, by then an assistant professor at Middle Tennessee State University, became actively involved, publishing the Bangladesh Newsletter from his home in Nashville and working with the Washington-based Bangladesh Information Center to lobby for an end to US military aid for Pakistan.

ట్టట్ట

Both Muhammad Yunus and Claus-Peter Zeitinger would go on to complete PhDs in economics.

Both would become increasingly concerned by the poverty and financial disenfranchisement of much of the world's population, of whom one-third were living on less than $1 per day, and two-thirds lacked access to bank accounts or other financial services.

One would become known as the "banker to the poor", the prophet who eschews profits. The other, less well known, would become the builder of "banks for ordinary people", the hard-headed businessman who believes that the extension of effective financial services to the poorest nations of the globe must ultimately be based on commerce rather than charity.

MUHAMMAD YUNUS

Muhammad Yunus' childhood exposed him to both sides of life in the Third World. On the one hand, he came from a family of 14 children, of whom 5 died in infancy. On the other hand, the family was sufficiently well off to allow Yunus to attend a string of Boy Scout jamborees in India, Canada, Japan and the Philippines during the 1950s, and to graduate from the University of Dhaka with an MA in economics in 1961. His first job was as a lecturer in economics at Chittagong University, where he supplemented his academic income with the profits from a packaging company that he set up on the side.

In 1965 he was awarded a Fulbright fellowship to study in the United States, where he completed his PhD in economics at Vanderbilt University, and stayed on as an academic teacher and researcher at Middle Tennessee State University. Then, with the end of the Bangladesh Liberation War in 1971, Muhammad Yunus returned to play his part in the building of the new nation, working briefly with the Bangladesh Planning Commission before rejoining Chittagong University as head of the Department of Economics.

No one was prepared for what happened next. Throughout 1974, Bangladesh was hit by a devastating famine, exacerbated by severe floods, which led to over a million people dying of starvation. Most were poor labourers and artisans, without land of their own, and utterly unable to afford sky-rocketing rice prices.

Muhammad Yunus took to the streets and fields of Jobra, an impoverished village alongside Chittagong University. Initially he worked with farmers, loaning them money to buy irrigation equipment as well as sufficient seed to plant a winter dry season crop. But, although the experiment was successful, he soon realised that it did nothing to protect those hardest hit by the ravages of famine - those without any land at all.

The solution emerged as Yunus and his students delved more deeply into the finances of a group of 42 village artisans - stool-makers and basket-weavers - women who were trapped in a cycle of borrowing tiny sums of money for their raw materials in return for interest rates as high as 10% per week and agreement to sell their products back to the moneylenders at rock-bottom prices. Incredibly, and famously, Yunus found that for just

$27 he could free all 42 women from the clutches of the moneylenders. He gave them the money, they repaid the loans, and the idea of the Grameen ("village" in Bengali) Bank was born.

Bringing the idea to fruition was another matter. Established banks regarded Yunus' plan for providing start-up funds to enable poor artisans to buy raw materials for their businesses as ludicrous. As he recalls in "Banker to the Poor", one bank manager told him that the size of the tiny loans he envisaged would not even cover the cost of the loan documents. "They don't have any collateral. They can't fill out our forms. This plan will never take off".

But ultimately it did.

Beginning by guaranteeing loans from his own pocket, Muhammad Yunus gradually built up a portfolio of small and effective start-up loans to village artisans. And along the way he created a set of three cardinal rules that would form the basis for the Grameen organisation in Bangladesh, and its progeny in Africa, India and elsewhere.

First, loans were primarily directed toward women borrowers, initially to compensate for the fact that the established banks in the patriarchal Bangladeshi society would only lend to men, and later because of Yunus' realisation that "lending to women in the poor villages of Bangladesh was a powerful way to combat poverty for the entire society".

Second, loans were usually made to small groups rather than individuals, thus ensuring that they were collectively guaranteed.

Third, and most importantly, they were made without collateral, driven by Yunus' belief that a person's ability to repay a loan should be assessed not according to their material possessions, but on the basis of their potential. And, after all, in Yunus' view, "all human beings, including the poorest, are endowed with endless potential".

ৰৰৰ

In fact, despite frequent assertions to the contrary, Muhammad Yunus did not invent the concept of microcredit. That distinction belongs to

ACCION, which began offering microloans in Brazil in 1973. But it was Yunus that put it on the map.

From its inception in 1983, the Grameen Bank has grown to over 2,500 branches with more than 20,000 staff serving 8 million borrowers in 80,000 villages. It lends $100 million per month with an average loan size of $200 and a repayment rate of 98%. According to the Grameen Bank Web site:

> The average household income of Grameen Bank members is about 25 percent higher than non-members in Grameen Bank villages. The landless have benefited most, followed by marginal landowners. This has resulted in a sharp reduction in the number of Grameen Bank members living below the poverty line, 20 percent compared to 56 percent for comparable non-Grameen Bank members.

Not surprisingly, the Grameen model has now been applied to projects in more than 50 countries around the globe.

And it has not stopped there. Driven by Muhammad Yunus' abiding faith in the financial sustainability of social businesses - those which he defines as returning only the initial investment to shareholders, with any surplus being ploughed back into the business - Grameen has established social businesses using innovative technologies such as cell phones and solar energy systems to provide better communication, healthcare and agricultural services. They have also formed social business partnerships offering affordable shoes (Adidas), mosquito nets (BASF), drinking water (Veolia) and vitamin-fortified food (Danone). The goal is to make social business an integral part of economies around the globe.

ಜಜಜ

In 2006, Muhammad Yunus' stunning achievements were recognised with the award of the Nobel Prize for Peace to him and the Grameen Bank. He was feted around the globe, acclaimed by presidents and prime ministers, religious leaders and philanthropists.

But then things began to come unstuck.

The first catastrophe was one that everyone, including Yunus, agreed he had brought upon himself.

In February, 2007, with Bangladeshi politics in turmoil, the leaders of both major political parties under house arrest and a caretaker military backed government in charge, Muhammad Yunus decided to establish a political party, the "Citizens' Power" party, which he proclaimed would introduce honest governance and accountability to politics. In an open letter to the people of Bangladesh he outlined the philosophy and organisation of the party. Like the Grameen Bank, it was to be village-based, lead in the fight for female empowerment, and put an end to poverty and corruption.

Needless to say, Bangladesh's political leaders were far from happy, and although Yunus abandoned the idea less than three months later, he has never been forgiven. In December 2010, Prime Minister Sheikh Hasina accused him of "sucking blood from the poor in the name of poverty alleviation", and in March 2011 the central bank announced his removal from his post at the Grameen Bank on the grounds that he was past the statutory retirement age of 60. His appeal to the Supreme Court was dismissed shortly thereafter.

The second, and probably much more traumatic issue for Muhammad Yunus, was the emergence around the globe of a groundswell of opinion that the Grameen Bank might not be the best model. Critics argued that burdening the poorest of the poor with debt without providing quality health care, education and infrastructure could leave them worse off than before. Others said that the use of group solidarity loans as a form of psychological collateral to help ensure repayment was unreasonable, and the ability of borrowers to take multiple loans from a variety of microcredit suppliers placed them at unconscionable risk. In the worst examples, microcredit was blamed for a series of suicides among poor farmers in the Indian state of Andhra Pradesh.

But, regardless of these criticisms, the industry spawned by Muhammad Yunus and his Grameen Bank continues to grow. Competition has led to the relaxation of rules such as formal group liability as well as the introduction of new financial products (e.g. individual savings accounts, insurance) and other development services (e.g. Grameen Phone). Microfinance in its various forms now reaches around 23 million borrowers in Bangladesh alone: that's 23 million people, from a total population of around 150 million, who would not otherwise have had access to a formal banking system.

And Yunus, far from retreating, holds firmly to his view that the right to credit is not only a fundamental human right, but the key to the total eradication of poverty: "Poverty does not belong in civilized human society. Its proper place is in a museum. That's where it will be".

CLAUS-PETER ZEITINGER

"Museum of poverty! It's ridiculous!", snorts CP Zeitinger: "To claim that microfinance is going to solve poverty is a myth. From ancient Greece to today, poverty has been with us and it will occupy us forever". And, as for credit being a fundamental human right, he tells Connie Bruck of *The New Yorker*: "Can we please remember that credit means you owe something and you can get overly indebted?"

On the one hand, CP Zeitinger is still the anti-authoritarian figure of the 1960s, professing complete disregard for what anyone else may think. On the other, he is a man of immense commitment, dedicated to creating financially inclusive societies throughout the developing world. "I only want to be a banker, not a microfinance banker", he says, but "if in doing business, a charitable outcome emerges, so much the better".

How should we reconcile these contrasting personas?

According to his friend and colleague from their days together in the student activist movement, economics professor Reinhardt Schmidt, Zeitinger's anti-authoritarian stance is an act, a publicity stunt to draw attention to the work and the philosophy of his business. But underneath, Schmidt points out, Zeitinger has always been the quintessential

Schumpeterian entrepreneur, who carefully takes on board the lessons of both history and his personal experience in drawing his conclusions on how to change the world.

The story of his work over the past 30 years tends to support Schmidt's views.

During the 1970s, fresh from the student barricades, Zeitinger worked largely inside the "Establishment", initially at the Chase Manhattan bank, where he was fired the day after decorating the hall of the Frankfurt office with a Vietcong flag, and subsequently at various German government development agencies, including a stint in South America working with Schmidt on a project analysing the effectiveness of subsidised development loans. Their conclusion was that the government programs were a dismal failure. "It's obvious what happens when loans are subsidised. Someone puts the difference in their pocket", says Zeitinger. The people at the Ministry, to nobody's surprise, were less than interested in hearing that their development policies had failed, and once again Zeitinger was fired.

In 1981, with DM7000 and an old VW as collateral, Zeitinger and two colleagues founded consulting company Interdizciplinare Projekt Consult (IPC), and throughout the 1980s they worked extensively in South America on the development of new banking laws and financial institutions. One of their major projects, undertaken on behalf of the German Agency for Technical Cooperation (GTZ), was aimed at using the German savings bank model to build a similar structure in Peru. But although successful in establishing the model, Zeitinger regarded it as a failure. As he saw it, the use of financial guarantees from local government, seen as necessary to reassure depositors of the security of their savings, was once again a recipe for corruption at the local level.

The answer, from Zeitinger's perspective, was clear. For banks to operate successfully in the developing world, they had to be private, funded by socially responsible investors looking for sustainable long-term returns, and offer their services not just to the poorest of the poor but to the

entire financial sector, including both small and medium enterprises.
In a further substantial departure from the Grameen model, Zeitinger
argued that loans should be offered to individuals rather than solidarity
groups, on the grounds that borrowers should be judged on their own
merits rather than being held responsible for defaults by others. Finally,
and most importantly, every loan had to be based on a careful analysis of
the client's cashflow and business prospects, and backed by some form of
collateral of real value to the client. Zeitinger calls it "information-based
credit".

ଔଔଔ

In 1992, Zeitinger took the opportunity to apply his model to the
establishment of the Bolivian financial NGO, Procrédito, which later
morphed into Caja Los Andes, the first private Bolivian bank to extend
microfinancial services to the rural and agricultural environment.
This was followed in 1997 by the Micro Enterprise Bank of Bosnia and
Herzegovina, the first of a number of joint ventures in Eastern Europe,
Latin America and Africa with the World Bank's International Finance
Corporation (IFC). A key component of this partnership was the use of
IFC and other donor funds in the initial training and establishment phase,
enabling the development of strong management skills and financial
networks prior to the subsequent transition to commercial viability.

And, in 1998, Zeitinger formed the umbrella group ProCredit Holding
(PCH), with the aim of providing banking services in developing
countries based on two core principles:

First, to be "the house bank of choice for the very small, small and
medium-sized enterprises which create jobs and drive economic
development".

Second, to be a trusted neighbourhood bank offering fair and accessible
savings and banking services to "ordinary people", including lower- and
middle-income savers who had previously had limited access to formal
financial services.

Established as a public-private partnership, PCH investors include philanthropic foundations, pension funds and several government-owned banks, including the IFC. As of June 2011, the group owned 21 banks with 751 branches and 15,173 employees in Eastern Europe, Latin America and Africa, and had provided €3.7 billion in loans, averaging €7,580, backed by €3.1 billion in local deposits.

In Zeitinger's words, the ProCredit banks are "profit-oriented, but do not aim for short-term profit maximization. They seek a reasonable balance between social and economic goals".

As is the case for Yunus and the Grameen Bank, Zeitinger's values pervade the organisation. "In order to ensure that they truly share a commitment to the institution's mission", board members are unpaid, and management salaries are capped at a fraction of the levels paid in typical banks: "I believe that very high salaries and performance-related bonuses are completely inappropriate ... they would do nothing less than poison the heart of the organisation".

And as for the heart, so for the soul: "A company only has a soul if the majority of its staff are truly committed to a vision and take a part in achieving that vision. They should be trained in technical areas and, moreover, empowered to do so in a humanistic sense".

To that end, ProCredit Holding has established the ProCredit Academy, where staff from around the globe undertake three-year part-time training programs aimed at building communication skills as well as the detailed understanding of finance and risk management required to manage banks in emerging markets. One of their teachers is Claus-Peter Zeitinger, who instructs them in anthropology, ancient history and the history of religion. What else would you expect from a student activist turned banker?

PRINCIPALS WITH PRINCIPLES

Zeitinger and Yunus have a great deal more in common than their backgrounds in economics. Both share absolute certainty that their chosen paths are the best and only way forward, and unrelenting stubbornness in pursuing their goals. Neither brooks any criticism of their approach, and neither baulks at dishing out a little criticism of their own.

According to Yunus: "Some misguided people have applied the term 'microcredit' to describe companies that are really just loan sharks in disguise".

And according to Zeitinger: "I would strongly argue that the most vulnerable groups in society do not, as a priority, need loans: they need governments to invest in better infrastructure, schools, health and clean water. Very often the 'poorest of the poor' are not running viable enterprises and they are very vulnerable to consumer debt they simply cannot afford".

But are the two really alternatives?

In reality, the two models address qualitatively and quantitatively distinct, if sometimes blurred, markets.

The Grameen Bank's average loan is $200 and its market is the poorest of the poor. As Muhammad Yunus says:

> Grameen Bank even lends money to beggars. They use the loans
> to enter the business of selling goods - toys, household items,
> foodstuffs - from door to door, along with begging … During the four
> years since this program was launched over 18,000 (of the 100,000
> beggars in the program) have quit begging.

His goal is to lift people out of poverty.

ProCredit's average loan is €7,580, about 50 times that of Grameen, and its banks target low- and middle-income earners building very small, small and medium-sized enterprises. As Zeitinger says:

> These are banks for ordinary people. That means everybody who does not
> have access to the financial system. I want to stabilize the middle class in
> these countries as well.

His goal is to help build nations.

Ultimately, the world needs both.

KEY SOURCES

WORLD POVERTY
United Nations, "The Millennium Development Goals Report 2012".

MICROFINANCE
Connie Bruck, "Millions for millions", *The New Yorker*, October 30, 2006.

Tom Easton, "Special Report: Microfinance", *The Economist*, November 3, 2005.

Ian Fraser, "Microfinance comes of age", *Scottish Banker*, August 3, 2007.

MUHAMMAD YUNUS
Alastair Lawson, "How Grameen founder Muhammad Yunus fell from grace", *BBC*, April 5, 2011.

Elisabeth Rhyne, "Microfinance in Bangladesh: It's not what you thought", *The Huffington Post*, February 10, 2012.

Muhammad Yunus, *Banker to the Poor: Micro-Lending and the Battle Against World Poverty*, Public Affairs, New York, 1999.

Muhammad Yunus, *Building Social Business: The new kind of Capitalism that serves Humanity's most pressing Needs*, Public Affairs, New York, 2010.

CLAUS-PETER ZEITINGER
Brigid Janssen, *IFC and Internationale Projekt Consult finance microcredit start-ups in developing countries*, International Finance Corporation Media Hub, June 22, 2000.

Christiane Karweil, "Was bewegt Claus Peter Zeitinger?" *Zeit Online*, December 9, 2004.

David Roodman, *Due diligence: an impertinent inquiry into microfinance*, Center For Global Development, 2012.

Claus-Peter Zeitinger, "How can a MFI manage to have a commercial status and still target 'vulnerable' people as a core client group?" *Proparco's Magazine*, September 3, 2009.

An individual with an epic ambition to change the world, who ...	**Muhammad Yunus** Born: 1940, Bathua, East Bengal Education: BA, MA, Dhaka; PhD, Vanderbilt Organisation: Grameen Bank	**Claus-Peter Zeitinger** Born: 1947, Germany Education: PhD, Goethe University of Frankfurt Organisation: ProCredit Bank
... sees and seizes opportunities for change...		
Opportunistic: aggressively seeks and adopts new ideas	"If you go out into the real world, you cannot miss seeing that the poor are poor not because they are untrained or illiterate but because they cannot retain the returns of their labour. They have no control over capital, and it is the ability to control capital that gives people the power to rise out of poverty".	Visiting Nicaragua to investigate the effectiveness of subsidised development loans on behalf of the German government, Zeitinger recognised that the subsidies finished up in the pockets of the powerful rather than benefitting poor farmers and traders, ...
& Visionary: intuitively grasps the big picture and how it might evolve	"I made a list of people who needed just a little bit of money. And when the list was complete, there were 42 names. The total amount of money they needed was $27. I was shocked. I thought if you can become an angel for $27, it would be fun to do more of it".	... and saw the opportunity to build private banks that served "ordinary people - everybody who does not have access to the financial system", ...
... senses the way forward...		
Innovative: thinks creatively, ignores boundaries, disrupts the status quo	Yunus began by making small loans to poor women rather than their husbands ...	... but were built on commercial principles, with loans balanced against private investment and savings accounts, ...
but Pragmatic: recognises constraints, devises practical solutions, creates value	... because "women have plans for themselves, for their children, about their home, the meals. They have a vision. A man just wants to enjoy himself".	... underpinned by grants from international financial institutions to enable expansion into new rural regions.

..attracts the necessary resources..

Persuasive:
articulate and convincing communicator, consummate networker

& Empowering:
attracts talent, inspires loyalty, rewards excellence

.. and pursues the dream..

Focussed:
passionate and highly energetic perfectionist, totally committed to an overriding vision

& Confident:
driven by unconditional self-belief, assumes absolute authority and accountability

.. regardless of the odds..

Resilient:
flexible, thrives on change and uncertainty, learns from mistakes

& Courageous:
bold, intelligent risk-taker, undaunted by criticism, determined to succeed

---

During the first ten years of the Grameen Bank's existence, Yunus attracted almost $150 million in soft loans and grants from donors, ...

... but today the bank is almost entirely funded from savings deposits, including those of its 8 million borrowers.

"We got rid of colonialism, we got rid of slavery, and we got rid of apartheid - everyone thought each one of them was impossible. Let's take the next impossible ..... and create a world free from poverty".

"Let us create the world of our choice".

Insisting that "a culture that holds people back should and can be changed", Yunus went head-to-head with the Bangladeshi patriarchy by enabling the financial and social empowerment of rural women.

"In the future the question will not be, 'Are people credit-worthy', but rather, 'Are banks people-worthy?'".

Despite being sacked from both traditional banks and government development agencies, he attracted huge investments, not only from the World Bank but also from private sources, ...

... and put together an outstanding management team, none of whose salaries exceed €140,000, and all of whom share Zeitinger's obsession with changing this "god-damned world for the better".

ProCredit has established banks in 21 African, Eastern European, and South American countries, based on a consistent lending methodology ...

... over which the holding company maintains full control: "We are not polite, we know what we want, we have it our way".

Zeitinger operates with absolute lack of respect for established authority, particularly big government and big banks, in markets where traditional bankers fear to tread. "Anarchy is frightening ...

... but it is an opportunity as well, because it allows you to impose your own structure and grow faster and become more important and more profitable".

Chapter 13

AIDS CRUSADES

WHEN THE PUZZLING CASES OF Kaposi's sarcoma and
Pneumocystis carinii pneumonia, characteristic of acquired immune
deficiency syndrome (AIDS), were first detected in San Francisco and
New York in 1980, it seemed that the victims of the syndrome were all
homosexual men from North America. Indeed, by 1982 it was being
referred to as GRID: Gay-Related Immune Deficiency. It was untreatable,
no one knew where it came from, and everybody who contracted it died.

Twenty years later, at the start of a new millennium, AIDS was a
syndrome whose victims were predominantly heterosexual men and
women, as well as their children, most of whom came from Africa and
Asia. It was eminently treatable, almost everybody agreed that it was due
to Human Immunodeficiency Virus (HIV), and hardly anyone died.

At least, not in the developed world. Elsewhere, it was an entirely different
matter.

※※※

In January 2000, when Dr Mitch Besser arrived in Cape Town to establish
an HIV/AIDS clinic for pregnant women, more than 4 million South
Africans, including a staggering 25% of all pregnant women, were
infected with HIV. As if that weren't bad enough, the then President of

the nation, Thabo Mbeki, was an avowed AIDS denialist, and the Health Minister, Dr Manto Tshabalala-Msimang, was given to promoting the benefits of garlic, lemons, African potatoes and beetroot over those of antiretroviral drugs.

In July that year, during the International AIDS Conference held in Durban, 5,000 prominent physicians and scientists issued a declaration describing the evidence that HIV was the cause of AIDS as "clear-cut, exhaustive and unambiguous". But even that categoric statement had no discernible impact on the public health policies of the Mbeki government, which are now said to have been responsible for more than 300,000 unnecessary deaths from AIDS. Dr Mitch Besser had a serious problem on his hands.

On the other side of the globe, in Thailand, the HIV/AIDS issue had been on and off the political agenda for 15 years. Although the first AIDS case in the country had been reported in 1984, Thai politicians, like their South African counterparts, were initially sceptical of the significance of the disease. As one government official put it: "The general public need not be alarmed. Thai-to-Thai transmission is not in evidence". By 1989, that observation had proved dramatically wrong, with HIV incidence soaring, initially among gay men and drug users, and then via sex workers and their clients to the general population.

It was not until the installation of Prime Minister Anand Panyarachun in 1991, by which time the annual number of new infections had climbed to 143,000, that AIDS became a national priority. Anand increased the AIDS prevention and control budget 20-fold, introduced compulsory condom use for sex workers, and launched a massive public education campaign. Twelve years later the annual number of new infections had dropped to just 19,000, and Thailand was being held up as a model for how to conquer HIV/AIDS.

On March 4, 2000, Thailand's first ever Senate elections were held. Among those elected to the new Senate was the man who, almost single-handedly, had inspired and driven Prime Minister Anand's campaign to bring Thailand's HIV/AIDS epidemic under control. His name was Mechai Viravaidya, aka The Condom King.

Between them, Mitch Besser and Mechai Viravaidya have changed the course of millions of lives.

MECHAI VIRAVAIDYA

Everyone assumed that Mechai Viravaidya would follow in the footsteps of his mother and father, and his paternal grandfather, and study medicine. And so did he, until the day his father asked for Mechai's help as he stitched up a partly amputated finger. After that, he recalls: "I felt very faint. I said, I can't be a doctor".

Mechai was 15 years old, and on his first trip home from Geelong Grammar School in rural Victoria, Australia. He had already been living away from home, at boarding school in Bangkok and Geelong, for many years, and would be away for many more before completing his degree in commerce at the University of Melbourne at the age of 24. But, despite his early departure from home, his parents had always maintained a strong influence on the shape of his beliefs and his career.

Mechai's mother was a Scot, his father Thai, and his upbringing in suburban Bangkok was both bilingual and bicultural: fruit, milk and healthy games outdoors in the sun with his Scottish mother; sugar and spice and indoor games, away from the harmful effects of the sun, with his Thai aunt. He departed for Australia at the age of 13 with a note from his father to the school headmaster saying: "My son is a Buddhist. But could he please experience the beauty, the joy, of Christianity in the church. Could he please attend"? His mother, meanwhile, wrote weekly with news from home, thoughts on social issues and advice on Western etiquette.

His social circle was equally wide-ranging. At school, strong friendships built thanks to his outgoing nature and sporting prowess led to holidays in the homes and on the farms of his wealthy schoolmates. At university, summer jobs in factories and driving trucks exposed him to the lives of much poorer, immigrant Australians.

The upshot was truly cosmopolitan. By the time he returned home Mechai was equally at ease with rich and poor, English and Thai, Christianity and Buddhism.

Back in Bangkok, aided by powerful family connections to both royalty and industry, the world was his oyster: but what would he do? He toyed with the idea of government, private industry, even the diplomatic corps. His mother had the last word: "If people like you, with an education, don't work for the poor, who will"? He met with the secretary general of the National Economic and Social Development Board (NESDB), learned of its responsibility for monitoring everything from health and agriculture to education, and "jumped into it immediately". And in his spare time, he wrote a weekly newspaper column, hosted a radio talk show, and starred in a popular TV drama series!

But the things he observed during his travels in rural Thailand with NESDB worried him. As he told Dan Rivers of *talkasia*: "What I saw in the villages was just kids, kids, kids everywhere. And I wondered whether what we were doing would be sufficient for them in the future". His answer was no: none of the development programs that he was monitoring would have a significant long-term impact unless something was done about Thailand's soaring population growth, which in 1974 was running at 3.3%, driven by an horrendous birth rate of seven children per family.

But how? Many rural Thai women knew nothing of family planning, and those that did were reluctant to discuss it with remote, unknown and, almost invariably, male doctors. And the doctors, for their part, numbering less than ten per million of the Thai population, had no time to discuss it anyway.

Mechai's solution was typically straightforward. Why should you need doctors to prescribe contraceptives?

With a five-year grant from the International Planned Parenthood Federation he began recruiting and training respected members of village communities - from shopkeepers to farmers - to dispense condoms and birth control pills. They were also trained to provide practical family planning advice, administer incentive schemes and arrange for vasectomies and sterilisation procedures, all of which they delivered from village family planning depots identified by billboards "much bigger than a Coca-Cola sign".

And in parallel with that, Mechai launched a publicity blitz. He persuaded Buddhist monks to bestow their blessings on bowls of brightly coloured condoms, offered free vasectomies on the King's birthday, organised courses in birth control for teachers and led condom-blowing championships for their students. Eventually, condoms came to be known as "mechais" and Mechai as The Condom King. He was delighted.

But grant funding only went so far: Mechai now needed an ongoing source of cash to feed the non-profit organisation - the Population and Community Development Association (PDA) - that he had established to drive the family planning depots. Again, his solution combined good humour and good sense. He founded a restaurant chain called "Cabbages and Condoms", which offered prophylactics in place of after-dinner mints, and a resort named "Birds and Bees", where condoms could be found nestling in the minibar. The profits from both were ploughed back into PDA.

It was a magic mix. Before five years were up, the family planning program had expanded from 70 to 16,000 villages, and by 1984, with 65% of Thai families practising family planning, the population growth rate had fallen to 1.6%. The World Bank called it "one of the most successful and effective family-planning programs in the world".

And then AIDS arrived.

ଝଝଝ

When Thailand's first AIDS case appeared in 1984, scientists were still searching for the cause of the syndrome. In Asia, in particular, it was seen

as an American import, and there was widespread public concern that
it might be transmitted by casually touching, or even speaking with, a
carrier. Some felt that foreigners should all be tested for HIV before being
allowed into the country.

In this environment, and fearful of the potential impact of publicity on
the nation's sex-fuelled tourism industry, the Thai government remained
silent as the number of AIDS cases grew from one in 1984 to 25 in 1989,
with 31 already dead and 10,000 more, mainly intravenous drug users and
prostitutes, confirmed HIV-positive.

Not so Mechai. With newspaper and TV reporters at his side, he
distributed condoms in restaurants and red light districts, at toll booths
and bus terminals, to soldiers and socialites. Police were co-opted to join
a "cops and rubbers" campaign handing out condoms at traffic lights, and
when the government refused to broadcast his videos on state-controlled
TV channels, he persuaded the supreme commander of the army, which
controlled two TV networks and 126 radio stations, to do so instead.
And through PDA, he issued a steady stream of up-to-date information
on the disease, its transmission, and, most importantly, the need to avoid
stigmatising its victims. To press home the point, he fronted the cameras
sharing a glass of water with a woman infected with AIDS.

But the numbers were still climbing. A survey of 1,000 prostitutes in
Chiang Mai showed that 44% were infected with HIV, and in 1990 a
report appeared suggesting that, if nothing were done, 4 million Thais
would be infected by the year 2000.

It was against this backdrop, and in the wake of a military coup, that
Prime Minister Anand Panyarachun was appointed in 1991. Mechai
seized his opportunity: "The new prime minister was a very enlightened
person. He listened to my reasons, and agreed to 'total war' on HIV/
AIDS". He also agreed to Mechai's request that he should become the
interim AIDS czar in the Prime Minister's Office, with a mandate to
tackle each of the broad behavioural, social and health issues surrounding
HIV/AIDS.

Together, Mechai and Anand introduced extraordinary reforms. Business and government departments were required to supply timely and accurate HIV protection information to all their staff, radio and TV stations were required to broadcast a 30-second AIDS message every hour, and AIDS education was provided to all students in the final two years of primary school. Most importantly, brothels were required to enforce compulsory condom usage and regular health testing of sex workers, with stiff and escalating penalties being imposed on any establishments where a staff member was found to be infected or failed to comply with the condom rule.

The results were remarkable. As noted by Mechai, "by the end of 1993 there was a 77% decline in sexually transmitted disease in Thailand and an accompanying decline in HIV cases". In fact, from the peak in 1991, the annual number of new cases continued to drop throughout the 1990s. And despite the Asian Financial Crisis of 1997/98, which saw the AIDS prevention budget quartered, Thailand was able to introduce a raft of new measures that maintained the momentum. These included the use of antiretroviral drugs to reduce mother-to-child transmission and an official commitment to providing adequate treatment to all people living with HIV, thus prolonging lives and delaying progress of the virus to AIDS.

But with improved treatments came new problems: survivors! By 2000 there were over half a million people living with HIV in Thailand, but few of them were living well. Both families and employers continued to reject even seemingly healthy AIDS victims, many of whom were unceremoniously dumped into overcrowded hospices.

Once again, Mechai came up with a novel solution. Starting in 2002, PDA's Positive Partnerships Program made loans to small businesses started by an HIV-positive individual together with an uninfected business partner. Both partners received a loan, with the HIV-negative individual being tasked with talking up the benefits of the business, and, by implication, the presence of those living with HIV, to the community. The upshot was threefold: increased productivity in the community;

economic empowerment of the HIV-positive individual; and a reduction in the stigma associated with the disease. With a repayment rate above 80%, Mechai described the program "as putting something strong together with something not so strong to build a giant".

By 2011, HIV prevalence among adults in Thailand was 1.3%, down from more than 2% 20 years earlier. But Mechai warns, this is no time for complacency: "The younger generation is having sex earlier these days with no regard to sexually transmitted diseases", while "the government has fallen asleep at the wheel".

Time for more Mechais!

MITCH BESSER

Whether by nature or nurture, Mitch Besser was probably predestined to become a physician in HIV-battered Africa. His father, also a gynaecologist, liked to spend his summer vacations relieving public health physicians on Indian reservations in Arizona and Dakota, and his paternal grandfather was a family doctor with a similar bent for serving the less fortunate members of his community.

Mitch himself was first immersed in public service in 1971, when he spent a year as a 16 - 17-year-old American Field Service exchange student in South Africa, and three years later when he took eight months' leave of absence from his college studies to work as an ambulance driver among the magnificent landscapes and welcoming people of Zululand and Swaziland. But sharing lunch with his black co-workers didn't go down well with South Africa's apartheid policy, and Mitch was soon prematurely obliged to leave both the hospital and the country.

Despite this early setback, his interest in tackling the medical challenges in underserved communities remained undiminished. After completing his medical degree at Harvard and postgraduate training in obstetrics and gynaecology at the University of California, San Diego, Besser spent three years in Micronesia, where he helped initiate family planning programs and comprehensive maternal health care, before returning to the United States as head of a midwifery program for underprivileged, mainly Hispanic, women in San Diego.

And, as was the case for Mechai Viravaidya, Besser's work in family planning and maternal health care led him inexorably toward the evolving issues with AIDS. In 1992, following the death from AIDS of a friend who was running the maternal HIV Clinic at UCSD Medical Center, Besser added his friend's former role to his midwifery responsibilities. And it was there, over the course of the next five years, that his work played a significant role in demonstrating the value of antiretroviral drugs in preventing the transmission of HIV from mother to child.

By 1997, when Besser returned to South Africa for the first time in over 20 years to present a lecture at the University of Cape Town, the transmission of HIV from infected mothers to their babies in the United States had plummeted, and none of the mothers attending Besser's San Diego clinic had given birth to an HIV-positive baby since 1994. But in South Africa, he was horrified to discover, mother-to-child transmission rates in some areas were as high as 40%.

Both Besser and his hosts saw the need and the opportunity. Nearly a decade later, speaking to Denise Difulco from the alumni magazine of his former school, Williams College, he recalled: "I had an exciting opportunity to do something that I had become more and more interested in doing in San Diego. It was an opportunity for me to give something back to a place that had changed me in very important ways".

And it was an opportunity that he was not slow to take up. In January 2000, he moved with his family to South Africa, joining the staff of the University of Cape Town's Department of Obstetrics and establishing his first clinic for pregnant women with HIV/AIDS at the University's Groote Schuur Hospital.

Then he began to see the real dimensions of South Africa's HIV/AIDS problems.

First, on a population basis, the numbers of doctors and nurses in South Africa were a tiny fraction of those in California. All up, sub-Saharan Africa bears 24% of the global disease burden, but has only 3% of the world's health care providers. Besser needed a model that would allow him to introduce the innovations he had pioneered in San Diego, but without traditional medical personnel.

Second, the fear and stigma associated with HIV/AIDS among South Africa's black population was so profound that many women would not attend a clinic even if one were available. Besser needed to find a way to offer them practical advice and sympathetic counselling from someone they could trust.

His solution was elegant and transformational: mothers caring for mothers.

In September 2001, with a grant of $7000, Besser founded mothers2mothers, m2m. His idea was simple. Rather than relying on a health system driven solely by doctors and nurses, he would train former patients, HIV-positive mothers whom he had already helped to deliver HIV-negative babies, as mentor mothers to bring hope and encouragement to pregnant women and new mothers living with HIV.

Besser's training program was unique. He not only taught his mentor mothers the basics of HIV biology and treatment, upgrading their knowledge annually, but paid them a salary, raising both their status and their self-esteem. Many also acted as ambassadors for the organisation, reaching all the way from remote African communities to US First Lady Laura Bush, who returned their hospitality by inviting a group of mentor mothers to tea and a reception at the White House, followed by meetings with various Senate committees and roundtables at US universities.

The mentor mothers soon became m2m's greatest resource. They not only provide counselling and support to young women terrified by the first diagnosis of HIV/AIDS, but also follow up with hands-on assistance with the ordeal of disclosing their disease to family and friends. They guide the mother-to-be through the use of prenatal antiretroviral medication and postnatal feeding practices to prevent mother-to-child HIV transmission. And, last but not least, they offer ongoing help and advice in how to sustain the health of both mother and child.

At every stage of that process, they can say: "I am HIV-positive, but my child is HIV-negative. You are going to make it, and you will raise a healthy baby. I am proof that there is hope". That's a real win-win for mothers.

And mothers were not the only ones who came to Besser's aid. Whether attracted by his charisma, his cause or a combination of the two, the string of celebrities supporting m2m has been truly remarkable. Within two years of its inception in 2001, megamusicians P. Diddy, Bono and Beyoncé had all beaten a path to Besser's door, followed in subsequent years by politicians Barack Obama and Tony Blair, as well as AIDS activists Elton John and Annie Lennox.

Old mates also came to the party. His college friend Gene Falk, a prominent gay rights activist and Senior Vice President at Showtime Networks, where he was responsible for marketing everything from Mike Tyson fights to Rolling Stones concerts, initially took on the job as New York-based lead fundraiser and chairman of the board. But an extended visit in 2003 inspired him so much that in 2005 he sold up and moved to South Africa to oversee m2m's rollout and expansion as CEO.

That expansion was indeed rapid. In 2010, m2m generated over $20 million in income from government grants, foundations and corporations. The organisation was operating in nine sub-Saharan countries and employing over 1,750 mentor mothers, all living with HIV, across more than 700 programme sites. During the course of that year, over 300,000 new HIV-positive mothers were enrolled in peer-mentoring programmes. That was 20% of the new, HIV-positive mothers on the planet.

In June 2011, a South African study reported that national HIV transmission rates from mother to child had fallen to 3.5%, down from more than ten times that figure when Besser arrived in Cape Town a decade earlier.

POWER OF PERSUASION

While politicians looked the other way, both Mechai Viravaidya and Mitch Besser realised that AIDS had the potential to wipe out entire societies.

Both knew that solutions based on scarce medical resources would never succeed in addressing the family planning and AIDS prevention issues of resource-poor nations such as Thailand and South Africa.

Both saw the opportunity for a win-win-win: an opportunity to create satisfying and high-status jobs for members of economically disadvantaged communities while simultaneously reducing both HIV transmission and the stigma associated with the disease.

Both of them used their charm, and their charisma, to garner personal, political and corporate support for their cause.

And both of them have proved so extraordinarily effective in slowing the progress of HIV/AIDS that people are beginning to ask the question that no one ten years ago would have dared contemplate. Can AIDS be beaten? Is there a chance that AIDS, like smallpox, can be eliminated from the planet?

The short answer may well be yes, but only with the aid of the 3 Ms.

First Mitch. In 2008, 1100 HIV-infected babies were born every day. Of those, Besser said: "Less than one comes from the United States. One comes from Europe. One hundred come from Asia and the Pacific. And a thousand - *a thousand* - babies are born each day with HIV in Africa". By continuing to expand the m2m model throughout Africa, he foresaw the prospect of the total elimination of mother-to-child transmission of HIV. And the United Nations agreed. By 2012, coordinated action in high-burden countries, combined with UNAIDS' global "Countdown to Zero" plan, had succeeded in reducing the number of HIV-infected babies from 1,100 to 800 per day.

Second Mechai. Thailand's population growth rate dropped from 3.3% in 1974 to 0.5% in 2007, and, according to the World Bank, Mechai's

HIV/AIDS prevention measures saved 7.7 million lives. Publicity campaigns of the type launched in Thailand, combined with a similar regime of compulsory condom use and regular screening of sex workers, have the potential to produce equally dramatic drops in infection rates in Africa, India and other emerging HIV/AIDS hotspots. Male circumcision and antiretroviral vaginal gels may further inhibit transmission.

And third, money. Of the 34 million people currently infected with HIV worldwide, at least half are asymptomatic. They have no immediate need of antiretroviral drugs for the treatment of their disease. But they and their sexual partners have an urgent need for those same drugs to help prevent its transmission. A 2011 study published in the *New England Journal of Medicine* showed that when antiretroviral drug treatment is initiated early in the course of infection, the risk of sexual transmission to others is reduced by 96%. But that means more money for screening at risk populations and more money to supply all infected individuals with drugs.

Both Mitch and Mechai are rooting for it.

KEY SOURCES

Myron S. Cohen and others, "Prevention of HIV-1 infection with early antiretroviral therapy", *New England Journal of Medicine*, August 11, 2011.

"HIV and AIDS Information", AVERT.org

MECHAI VIRAVAIDYA

Jon Fernquest, "Mechai warns of new HIV/AIDS crisis", *Bangkok Post*, December 21, 2012.

Ramon Magsaysay Award Foundation, "1994 Ramon Magsaysay Award for Public Service. Biography of Mechai Viravaidya".

Glenn A. Melnick, "From family planning to HIV/AIDS prevention to poverty alleviation: a conversation with Mechai Viravaidya", *Health Affairs*, September 25, 2007.

Dan Rivers, "Interview with Mechai Viravaidya", *talkasia*, July 23, 2007.

Mechai Viravaidya, *How Mr. Condom made Thailand a better place*, TEDxChange, filmed and posted September 2010.

MITCH BESSER

Mitchell Besser, "Mothers helping mothers fight HIV", TEDGlobal, filmed July and posted September 2010.

"Countdown to Zero: Global plan towards the elimination of new HIV Infections among children by 2015 and keeping their mothers alive", Joint United Nations Programme on HIV/AIDS (UNAIDS), 2011.

Denise Difulco, "Saving Africa", *Williams Alumni Review*, January 2006.

Maya Kulycky, "Mitch2Maya", *Forbes Magazine*.

Samuel Loewenberg, "Mitch Besser - helping mothers with HIV become mentors", *The Lancet*, 2 April 2011.

An individual with an epic ambition to change the world, who …	Mechai Viravaidya	Mitch Besser
	Born: 1941, Bangkok, Thailand Education: BCom, University of Melbourne Organisation: Population & Community Development Association	Born: 1954, Princeton, New Jersey, USA Education: BA, Williams; MD, Harvard Organisation: Mothers2mothers
… sees and seizes opportunities for change.		
Opportunistic: aggressively seeks and adopts new ideas	When a satirical newspaper article suggested that condoms should be called "mechais", Mechai saw his chance: "This was a public relations windfall – the opportunity to have condoms become synonymous with my name was too good to be true. I seized the opportunity and have used it to my advantage ever since".	"I started to see the same problems all over the country. Doctors and nurses did not have the time, or the experience, to explain to mothers in this highly charged, highly stigmatised environment, how to handle their illness and how to care for their babies".
& Visionary: intuitively grasps the big picture and how it might evolve	"We realised that people who need family planning are not sick. In fact, they are very healthy. That's why they are having so much sex. Why do you need doctors to prescribe contraceptives?"	Besser realised that tackling mother-to-child transmission of HIV would require rethinking traditional doctor-centred treatment …
… senses the way forward..		
Innovative: thinks creatively, ignores boundaries, disrupts the status quo	"We called the birth-control pill the family welfare vitamin".	… and that mothers who had previously been successfully treated and trained in how to avoid infecting their children with HIV would be the most effective mentors for mothers and mothers-to-be living with HIV.
but Pragmatic: recognises constraints, devises practical solutions, creates value	"Contraceptives have to be as easily found as vegetables".	"A mentor mother can spend an hour with a mother counselling her on the best way to feed her baby. A doctor wouldn't take the time to do that".

.. attracts the necessary resources..

Persuasive:
articulate and convincing communicator, consummate networker

His invitation to "come share my dream" brought everyone from Annie Lennox to Laura Bush onto his fund-raising team ...

& Empowering:
attracts talent, inspires loyalty, rewards excellence

... as well as attracting 1750 HIV-positive mothers of HIV-negative babies to help him tell their peers how it's done.

.. and pursues the dream..

"One day, during a training session for a thousand teachers, I pulled out a condom and started blowing it up. The teachers roared with laughter".

"That was the beginning of the condom blowing championships for teachers. They realised that the condom is not a dirty product. It doesn't kill. It became normal".

Focussed:
passionate and highly energetic perfectionist, totally committed to an overriding vision

"Personal energy applied to problems, even enormous problems, drives change".

"Mechai Viravaidya is the kind of go-getter who can make the workaholics of the world feel bad".

& Confident:
driven by unconditional self-belief, assumes absolute authority and accountability

"No child should be born with HIV".

"It is easier to ask for forgiveness than permission".

.. regardless of the odds..

Resilient:
flexible, thrives on change and uncertainty, learns from mistakes

When one of his medical friends died from AIDS in 1992, Mitch took on his job - running a maternal HIV clinic in San Diego - in parallel with his own. After trialling antiretroviral drug treatments that eliminated mother-to-child HIV transmission from that clinic ...

"I had no money whatsoever, so I had to come up with things that the media found interesting, that they would publicise".

& Courageous:
bold, intelligent risk-taker, undaunted by criticism, determined to succeed

... Mitch moved to South Africa, where mother-to-child transmission was still running at 40%, and the Health Minister believed that AIDS should be treated with garlic and African potatoes.

"We had a special vasectomy day on the Fourth of July to vasectomise American men, to show our appreciation for America's foreign assistance and to signify that Thailand also wanted to give foreign assistance back to America".

Chapter 14

KIDS' BIZ

WHEN THE NUMBER OF PEOPLE on the planet reached 7 billion early in 2012, just over half of them were under the age of 30.

The size of this youthful bulge varies from place to place. In developed economies, where fertility rates have generally fallen to less than two children per woman, the proportion of the population under 30 is just 35%. But in sub-Saharan Africa, where child mortality has decreased while fertility rates remain high, 70% of the population is under 30. All up, of the 3.5 billion people on the planet aged less than 30, 90% live in emerging and developing economies.

What happens when these young people reach working age?

According to Justin Yifu Lin, former Chief Economist of the World Bank, the bulge represents both a threat and an opportunity:

> If the increase in the number of working age individuals can be fully employed in productive activities, other things being equal, the level of average income per capita should increase as a result. The youth bulge will become a demographic dividend. However, if a large cohort of young people cannot find employment and earn satisfactory income, the youth bulge will become a demographic bomb, because a large mass of frustrated youth is likely to become a potential source of social and political instability.

A simple measure of a country's success in turning the youth bulge into a demographic dividend is therefore the youth employment rate.

In North Africa and the Middle East, with 67% of the population under 30 and a median age of just 21, the statistics are frightening. Across Egypt and Algeria, Jordan and Iran, 25% of young people aged 15 to 24 are unemployed. In the Occupied Palestinian Territory, the figure is 49%.

For Soraya Salti, Regional Director of INJAZ al-Arab, the choice is stark: "Either these youth become a burden on our economies or they become an engine for growth and prosperity".

In India, where 700 million people are under 30, and half of them, 30% of the total population, are aged less than 15, youth unemployment is a comparatively low 10%, but there are 10 million or more children living on the streets. Many more lack simple social and financial skills.

Jeroo Billimoria, Founder and Managing Director of Child and Youth Finance International, sees this as an opportunity: "Many of these street kids are smart, creative and entrepreneurial. If we are able to teach these children, they have the power and ability to be the agents of change".

JEROO BILLIMORIA

"What I like doing is starting organisations. I was 16 when I argued with my Mum and started my first organisation. It was basically to teach maths skills to students so that they would not fail in school". No doubt Mum, who was a social worker, and Dad, a former accountant who had been quietly helping less fortunate neighbours for years, were both secretly pleased. As Billimoria told Alexis Kalagas of *The Global Journal*: "If you're brought up in a family like mine, the first thing they teach you is duty, duty, duty".

But first, before signing up for serious duty, Billimoria did some serious training. She completed a Master of Arts in social work at the Tata Institute of Social Sciences (TISS) in Mumbai and a Master of Science in nonprofit management at the New School for Social Research, New York.

While there, she also became involved in the work of the Coalition for the Homeless, which had just completed a landmark campaign to guarantee emergency shelter to homeless individuals in New York City.

Returning to Mumbai in 1989 to take up a teaching position at TISS, she continued to be drawn toward social issues: "It started on the streets of Bombay, when I used to sit with kids on the street corners. They asked for only one thing: 'Can we have someone to talk to in the middle of the night when we are sick, when we are hungry, or when the police beat us up'?"

In a pattern that has continued throughout her life, Billimoria decided that she would be that someone. She gave her phone number to any child who asked for it, and was soon fielding calls at all hours of the night from sick or injured street children.

As it turned out, answering their calls was the easy part. Doing something about it was a different matter. Billimoria soon found that few of the organisations providing the services needed by street children worked cooperatively together, and it sometimes took days for her to find the right place for a suffering child. She asked herself, what if there was a phone service, a single phone service, with the capability of directing any needy child to the right place? And what if it served all the street kids in Mumbai, or even all the street kids in India? And what if it were free?

Who better to ask than the street kids? Working with her students at TISS, Billimoria recruited a group of street children to conduct a survey of their peers. How and how often would they use such a service?

The response of the street children was enthusiastic, that of the telecommunication authorities much less so: "They thought I was crazy. A phone service for street kids? Who will run it?"

"The kids will", said Billimoria, and proceeded to bombard government departments and charitable foundations with requests for support.

Finally, six years after her first encounters with the street children of Mumbai, Childline was formed, with an initial budget of $6,000 and

15 staff - many of them street kids. And it was the children who hit the streets, putting on plays and pantomimes and plastering public buildings with posters publicising Childline. By 1999, the Mumbai Childline had received 500,000 calls.

Bolstered by that success, Billimoria's lobbying for a nation-wide service also began to bear fruit. In 1999, the Indian government formally recognised Childline as a nationally integrated child protection system, with 10 9 8 as the national toll-free number, and Billimoria founded the Childline India Foundation as an umbrella organisation to establish independently managed Childline services in major cities across the nation.

By 2013, Childline India was operating as a network of 540 independent partnerships in 291 locations, and had fielded 26 million calls. It had also spawned an international counterpart, Child Helpline International, which now operates in 141 countries under the guidance of a supervisory board chaired by Billimoria.

And Billimoria herself had long since done what she does best: although still a governing board member of the Childline India Foundation, she had successfully converted the organisation from a one-woman band into a self-sustaining structure, freeing her to move on to the next challenge.

Like Childline, the next big thing came from the kids on the street. Asked what they needed to help them break out of the cycle of poverty, they told Billimoria: "Make us believe in ourselves. Teach us to save, teach us about money. And teach us about enterprise so that we can make our own livelihood".

Drawing on her successful work with MelJol, an NGO she had established in 1992, Billiomoria founded a new organisation, Aflatoun, to provide the street children with the social and financial education that they sought. Named after a Bollywood film character, the much-loved Aflatoun appears throughout the training program as an imaginary fireball from outer space, providing support and advice to children as they learn about their rights and responsibilities, how to manage money, and how to collaborate as a team to build social and financial microenterprises.

Not everyone agreed that children in Billimoria's target range of 6 to 14 years were old enough to learn about money. "When we started everyone said 'We're not funding this. How can young children handle money'?" Undeterred, she and her husband provided the initial seed funding themselves. Others soon followed.

In fact, most of the savings accumulated by the children were very small. By the end of 2010 Aflatoun had reached just over a million children, of whom almost half were actively saving. Between them, they had accumulated €1.5 million, just €3 each. But much more important is what they did with the money.

Some of them spent their money on school supplies, some on toys and treats. And some started businesses, often focused on food: potato patches, chicken runs, even school canteens. As Billimoria puts it: "When children save a single coin, it does not represent more than what they carry in their pockets, but once they save a few more, it begins to represent something very different, a choice".

By the end of 2010, the children of Aflatoun had established over 3,000 social and 5,000 financial microenterprises.

And once again, the time had come to pass the baton. Having transformed Aflatoun into a network of partnerships sharing curricula and other materials provided by the parent organisation, Billimoria handed the reins to a general board, chaired by Professor Jaap Doek, Chairperson of the UN Committee on the Rights of the Child, and a full-time secretariat.

And moved on to the next challenge: "We had a lot of kids saving in Aflatoun, so we were able to disprove the myth that poor kids don't save. But we couldn't take children to the next level, because there were no banks. It's like teaching a child or woman to cook, and not providing a stove".

In 2011, Jeroo Billimoria founded Child and Youth Finance International, whose mission is to provide financial inclusion and education to 100 million children and youth in 100 countries by 2015. In Billimoria's view, the key to achieving that goal is working with banks on child-friendly banking products, including enabling children to manage their savings through access to low-cost bank accounts.

It's not obvious that any of Billimoria's street kids will ever be "Slumdog Millionaires". But if they are not, it won't be for want of trying. As Billimoria says: "Every one of us can do something to change the world. Together we build a movement".

SORAYA SALTI

Unlike their counterparts in India, most of the young people hanging out on the streets of Arabian cities come from comfortable homes. Indeed, many have university degrees. Their problem is not a lack of education, but the fact that their education fails to match the needs of potential employers.

As Soraya Salti told Amanda Pike of *Frontline World*:

> Historically speaking, governments were the ones responsible for the employment of youth, and the education system catered to that assumption. So education systems are focused on rote memorisation, and students are completely isolated from the surroundings of what's happening today. They're completely isolated. It's all studying the past, taking exams and then expecting a government job. Well, the skills that they have are only good enough for a government job. So when government is not employing them, there is frustration and anger. And you see education attainment increasing across the region, but the more educated our youth have become, the more unemployable they have become, because the education system is not meeting the needs of the private sector.

The result, according to a 2003 World Bank report, is "the need to create close to 100 million new jobs by 2020, a doubling of the current level of employment" across the Middle East and North Africa, by transforming their public-sector-dominated economies into ones where the private sector plays the dominant role.

Salti breaks the problem down into two parts: first, the need to train employees with the skills to work in private enterprise; and, second, the need to establish private enterprises, particularly SMEs, to employ them.

And then she proposes a single elegant solution: training programs that give youth not only the skills required to work in innovative businesses, but also the ability to create them.

ଔଔଔ

As for Billimoria, the seeds of Salti's approach to life are evident in those of her parents. Her Palestinian-born father studied on a scholarship at Brigham-Young University in the United States before pursuing a successful career as a banker in Jordan, where he was actively involved in the development of the private sector, both in business and education. Her American mother, on the other hand, played an extensive role in Save the Children and other social ventures in Jordan.

"It would have been great", says Salti, tongue in cheek, "if she had spent more time saving us". But Salti doesn't seem to have suffered too badly. Nurtured within an inspired and privileged blend of Islam and high finance from her father and Christianity and social work from her mother, she split her time between Jordan and her grandmother's home in the United States, where she completed a BA in Utah and an executive MBA at Northwestern's Kellogg School before returning to Jordan in 2001.

And there, with just a tiny push from Mum, she jumped in at the deep end as head of INJAZ al-Arab in Amman, Jordan.

INJAZ al-Arab (literally, the Arab Achievement) is part of Junior Achievement Worldwide, an international network of volunteer businesspeople providing school programs in work readiness, entrepreneurship and financial literacy. Founded in the United States in 1916, it now reaches almost 10 million students in 124 countries. But its first venture into Arabia, begun in 1999 under the auspices of Save the Children, was struggling by the time Salti arrived in 2001. Government and businesses were disinterested, and many local communities, schools and religious groups were actively opposed to the idea of encouraging students to think, let alone speak, outside the box.

One of the hardest nuts to crack was Ma'an, a conservative Islamist town of 50,000 in southern Jordan, where the head of the school district, supported by the local imam, instructed schools not to cooperate with INJAZ in corrupting the minds of their youth. Salti needed a champion, and found one in Salfa abu Tayeh, principal of The Ma'an Secondary School for Girls and a powerful advocate for the rights of young women as equal partners in society.

Salfa abu Tayeh not only welcomed INJAZ into her school, but also offered Salti the opportunity to use it as a base to initiate programs elsewhere in the region. A year later, following a graduation ceremony at which INJAZ students from surrounding towns showcased the skills and confidence that they had gained from the program, Salfa abu Tayeh publicly thanked the head of the school district for his support. Unaware of the irony, the principals of all the other schools in the district rushed to join.

The concept of recruiting champions from within continued to be a key part of Salti's strategy as she spread out across Jordan and then, commencing in 2004, throughout Arabia. Starting with corporate volunteers intent on improving the productivity of their future employees, she soon mobilised armies of teachers and finally ministers of education. As Salti put it: "To every door there is a key". The question is "who holds it"?

But working from the bottom up didn't stop her from working top down. Two of her strongest supporters have been Jordan's Queen Rania, who is not only Junior Achievement's regional ambassador but has also taught courses as a volunteer, and the Minister for Higher Education, Dr Khaled Tuqan, who wrote personally to his counterparts throughout the Middle East and North Africa urging them to embrace the program. By 2008, leading Arabian businessmen and women were chairing the governing boards of INJAZ in Egypt and Omar, Kuwait and Qatar, Morocco and Bahrain. Its educational programs had reached more than 300,000 students and engaged almost 5,000 volunteers.

Although tailored to individual countries and cultures, the INJAZ program has a number of common elements, with staff from local businesses providing students aged 14 and upwards with 1 hour/week of practical classes on everything from personal finance to job hunting. In their final semester, each class establishes a functioning start-up venture, taking it all the way from business plan to liquidation in 15 weeks. And best of all, they get the opportunity to take their company to an international stage, competing for the title of Best Student Company of the Year.

In 2011, 162 student companies and 11,000 students from 12 countries participated in the Fifth Annual INJAZ al-Arab Young Entrepreneurs Competition. The winner was ESCO, the Electric Solutions Company, with a device that enabled individuals to manage electric power usage in their homes from remote locations. The directors and staff of the company were all 11th grade students of Kamal Jumblatt in the Palestinian city of Nablus, trained by enthusiasts at PalTel, the Palestinian telecommunications company. Even amid the volatility of the West Bank, INJAZ al-Arab is giving new meaning to young Arabian lives.

And Palestine's electronics whiz kids are only the start. As the youth-led Arab Spring began to surge across North Africa and the Middle East in late 2010 and 2011, once voiceless Arab youth employed Twitter to orchestrate street marches, posted YouTube videos of the outcomes, and shared their newfound social and political empowerment with their peers at home and abroad via Facebook.

Salti, intent on training 1 million students per annum by 2018, sees her next challenge as being to exploit Arab youths' familiarity with social

media to help drive new partnerships between them and the Injaz
network of CEOs and companies, and then to exploit those connections
to build new industries. And to help drive those connections, in 2013
she launched a new TV series, Generation Entrepreneur, to show young
people throughout the Arab world how "they, too, can add value to their
own communities".

MANAGING UPWARD AND DOWNWARD

Both Salti and Billimoria have used their cross-cultural networks to
become powerful and persuasive voices in the developed and developing
world, attracting the support of business and political leaders, as well as
royalty, to their cause.

Both of them instinctively recognised not only the capacity of youth to
change the world, but also the need to provide the financial and business
skills that will enable them to do so.

And both of them have built enterprises offering these skills to children,
on the streets and in schools, and scaled them successfully throughout
large parts of the developing world.

But why stop there?

In 2012, unemployment among 15 - 24 year-olds in the United States
and the United Kingdom was 16.3% and 20.5%, respectively. In Spain,
the unemployment rate among young people is over 50%. With aging
demographics, no nation on earth has that many young people to waste.

And what of financial literacy in the Western world? In the United
States, less than 20% of adults in the baby boomer generation are able
to calculate compound interest, and more than half of US credit card
holders claim to have learnt little or nothing about finance at school. Not
surprisingly, perhaps, many borrowers with subprime variable rate home
loans in the lead up to the Global Financial Crisis were unaware that their
monthly repayments would increase with increasing interest rates.

"My mistake", says Billimoria, "I never thought it would be needed in developed countries".

In 2012 Child and Youth Finance International launched Global Money Week, which has since reached a million children in over 80 countries. And in March 2013, Jeroo Billimoria accepted an invitation to celebrate its arrival in the world's largest economy, ringing the opening bell of the NASDAQ stock exchange.

KEY SOURCES

Justin Yifu Lin, " Youth bulge: a demographic dividend or a demographic bomb in developing countries?", *Let's Talk Development*, January 2012.

"Special Report: The world's youngest populations", *Euromonitor International*, February 13, 2012.

JEROO BILLIMORIA

Jeroo Billimoria, "ChildLine/ChildFinance", *TEDxHamburg*, July 1, 2010.

David Bornstein, *How to Change the World: Social Entrepreneurs and the Power of New Ideas*, Oxford University Press, 2007.

"Financial literacy: getting it right on the money", *The Economist*, April 3, 2008.

Indian Womenpreneurs, "Jeroo Billimoria", June 30, 2011.

Alexis Kalagas, "Banking on kids", *The Global Journal*, March 6, 2012.

Jerry Pinto, "Help's at hand", *LiveMint*, October 25, 2008

SORAYA SALTI

Amanda Pike, "Extended Interview: Soraya Salti", *Frontline World*, 2009.

David Rosenberg, "Education hinders Arab economies", *Morocco World News*, October 23, 2011.

Soraya Salti, "Students Incorporated: INJAZ on a mission to send Arab youth to Planet Free Enterprise", in *Garden in the Desert, Innovations*, MIT Press, 2008.

Soraya Salti, "Egypt: harness the youth to create a culture of social entrepreneurship", *AllAfrica*, December 19, 2012.

"Soraya Salti of INJAZ al-Arab", *Wamda TV*, January 6, 2011.

Schwab Foundation Team, (2011) "We discovered we can do anything", *WEF Blog*, July 5, 2011.

Stefan Theil, "Teaching entrepreneurship in the Arab world", *Newsweek International*, August 14, 2007.

An individual with an epic ambition to change the world, who ...	Jeroo Billimoria	Soraya Salti
	Born: 1969, Mumbai, India Education: MA, Tata Institute of Social Sciences; MSc, The New School for Social Research, New York Organisation: Child & Youth Finance International	Born: ca 1970, raised in Jordan Education: BA, University of Utah; MBA, Kellogg School, Northwestern University Organisation: INJAZ al-Arab
.. sees and seizes opportunities for change..		
Opportunistic: aggressively seeks and adopts new ideas	Working in New York City with the Coalition for the Homeless as a young postgraduate student, Billimoria gained "a close view of the problems of the homeless. It threw me into their painful lives. I saw the spirit of survival among them" ...	Offered the job as head of Injaz al-Arab in Jordan, Salti went to observe the work of one of the organisation's private-sector volunteers in a poor rural school: "The volunteer asked the class 'Why are you here?'. And one little nerd, the smallest one in the class, said 'Because I want to be confident' ...
& Visionary: intuitively grasps the big picture and how it might evolve	... and began to imagine what could be achieved by capturing the spirit and intelligence of the street children of India.	... and I realised that for me to lead that organisation I had to be the voice of that little nerd, to speak on his behalf, to find ways to enable every Arab youth to be confident".
.. senses the way forward..		
Innovative: thinks creatively, ignores boundaries, disrupts the status quo	She envisaged a 24-hour toll-free emergency help line, run for street kids by street kids, ...	Salti saw an opportunity to use corporate volunteers to teach kids not only the practical business skills to work in the private sector...
but Pragmatic: recognises constraints, devises practical solutions, creates value	... backed by a dedicated management team and personal commitments from senior police and health care officials.	... but also the entrepreneurial skills to create it.

.. attracts the necessary resources..

Persuasive: articulate and convincing communicator, consummate networker	"Anyone of you can have an idea, and then, if you just follow your heart and your dream ...	Faced with government and community scepticism, she argued: "All we ask for is a classroom full of students ...
& Empowering: attracts talent, inspires loyalty, rewards excellence	.... it's easy, just go ahead, and just do it".	... and for every one of them who makes it to go back and give to the next generation".

.. and pursues the dream...

Focussed: passionate and highly energetic perfectionist, totally committed to an overriding vision	"We work for the child. The child comes first".	"You know what? If you say no I'm going to find a way around you, ...
& Confident: driven by unconditional self-belief, assumes absolute authority and accountability	"Childline is not a charity service or a welfare service. It is a rights service".	... and eventually you are going to be coming back to me and saying 'How can I help you'".

.. regardless of the odds..

Resilient: flexible, thrives on change and uncertainty, learns from mistakes	"There are always daily challenges and mountains to climb. The important thing is to evolve as your organisations evolve and as the external environment evolves. So, stay flexible	"The more obstacles you find in your way, ...
& Courageous: bold, intelligent risk-taker, undaunted by criticism, determined to succeed	... and learn to let go. Everything will not be exactly the way you want it. You have to let people take charge".	... the more you can overcome, the more you are determined, the more you are resilient, and you make it".

Chapter 15

LIVING OFF THE LAND

AS THE WESTERN WORLD LETS its belt out yet another notch, close
to a billion of the world's population are chronically undernourished.
What chance of feeding another 2 billion by 2050?

The minimum amount of agricultural land necessary to feed people with
a typical Western diet, including meat, is 0.5 hectare per person. At the
other end of the consumption spectrum, the absolute minimum of arable
land required to support one person - assuming a largely vegetarian
diet - is 0.07 of a hectare.

Given the planet's total of 1.5 billion hectares of arable land, and a current
population of 7 billion, we have 0.21 hectares each. In 2050, with a
population of 9 billion, and assuming current rates of land degradation,
we will have about 0.12 hectares per person. In the absence of dramatic
breakthroughs in agricultural productivity, much more of our dwindling
natural habitat will have to be cleared and cultivated if mankind as a
whole is to enjoy anything approaching today's typical western diet.

In fact, many relatively wealthy countries are already at or below the
arable land "poverty line" (China 0.08 hectare/person, United Arab
Emirates 0.01), while others have much less than the areas required to
match the lifestyles to which they are accustomed or aspire (Saudi Arabia
0.12, India 0.12).

The staggering vulnerability of these nations to shortages of food and water has recently been driven home by dramatic increases in food prices. Powered by record energy costs, and exacerbated by associated demand for cereals for biofuel production, grain prices increased by more than 100% between 2006 and 2008. The resulting food riots led to many countries banning grain exports, leaving food importers to think long and hard about not just rising prices, but the frightening prospect of no food at all. Inevitably, a global market in arable land is rapidly developing between buyers who can afford to purchase future food security and sellers who simply can't afford to refuse.

ଝଝଝ

Enter the überpreneurs:

Twice nominated for a Nobel Peace Prize, Roy Prosterman is a US lawyer with a mission to help a billion tenant farmers own a patch of earth of their own.

Sheik Mohammed Hussein Ali Al-Amoudi is a self-made Ethiopian-born billionaire with a passion to develop Ethiopia as well as a mandate from King Abdullah bin Abdulaziz Al Saud to help feed the people of Saudi Arabia.

And Sai Ramakrishna Karuturi is an Indian engineer with a burning desire to feed the people of Africa, from Africa.

ROY PROSTERMAN

In 1970, at the height of the Vietnam War, the South Vietnamese government passed legislation enabling revolutionary land reforms known as the "land-to-the-tiller" program. Its aim was to increase rural prosperity and reduce recruitment of tenant farmers into the Viet Cong by granting them ownership of the land that they farmed. Remarkably, the man responsible for envisaging and drafting that legislation was an unassuming academic from the University of Washington.

Roy Prosterman, a Harvard-trained lawyer, had begun his career with
New York law firm Sullivan and Cromwell. He specialised in defending
the commercial interests of transnational corporations, but became
increasingly uncomfortable with focusing his time and energy on the
concerns of corporate giants while seeing little direct impact on the
abject poverty of the communities in which they often operated.
A three-month stint representing a client on a construction contract
in the West African nation of Liberia crystallised his unease, and in 1965
he accepted a position on the law faculty at the University of Washington
in Seattle, to teach property law and research ways to address global
poverty.

But the real impetus for what was to occupy the rest of Prosterman's
long career was the appearance in 1966 of a law review article proposing
that land ownership inequities in Latin America could be addressed
by confiscating land from wealthy property owners and giving it to
indigenous people. Right idea, wrong approach, thought Prosterman,
whose alternative solution, "Land reform in Latin America: how to have a
revolution without a revolution", soon captured the interest of officials at
the US Agency for International Development, who were actively seeking
nonmilitary solutions to the conflict in Vietnam.

Prosterman accepted their invitation to assist, and in September 1967
found himself in Vietnam, in the middle of a war, investigating the
relationship between land ownership, rural prosperity and social unrest.
What he found was an unsustainable feudal farming system in which
tenant farmers paid up to 50% of their profits to landowners, reducing
their ability to feed their families, and increasing the probability of their
joining the ranks of the Viet Cong.

Prosterman's conclusions were characteristically blunt. On the one hand,
political stability in the region would not occur unless peasant farmers
were provided with land to help them lift themselves out of poverty. On
the other hand, government would have to provide fair and reasonable
compensation to the land barons, who owned most of the fields, before
they could redistribute land to the peasants.

Ultimately, his argument prevailed. The Vietnamese government, with the support of the United States, passed the legislation, and over the course of the next three years the program delivered land rights to a million poor tenant farmers in the Mekong Delta region, increasing national rice production by almost a third and reducing Viet Cong recruitment rates by up to a staggering 80%.

And in a striking demonstration of the long-term value of his thinking, Prosterman was invited back to Vietnam 25 years later by the postwar communist government to witness the impact, including a doubling in national grain production, of a similar transition from collective to individual land holdings in northern Vietnam.

But not everyone was as happy as the Vietnamese with Prosterman's interventions. As debate raged over proposed land reforms in El Salvador in the early 1980s, the right-wing *El Diaro de Hoy* denounced Prosterman as an enemy of landowners, while back home in Seattle the left-wing student *Committee in Solidarity with the people of El Salvador* denounced him as an enemy of socialism. Prosterman, described by one journalist as looking like everyone's favourite uncle, was literally in everyone's sights.

Undaunted by these attacks, Prosterman continued to travel the globe promoting land reform in developing nations, often assisted by student volunteers from the University of Washington. In 1981, he formalised these activities with the establishment of the Rural Development Institute (RDI), operating out of a one-bedroom Seattle apartment, funded by grants from foundations and foreign aid agencies, and staffed by volunteers and students.

Over the course of the next 25 years, RDI worked with governments in China and the former Soviet Union to grant secure, marketable land rights to millions of peasant farmers. In each case, the basic premise was the same. Land ownership would encourage farmers to increase long-term investments, thus enhancing both productivity and income, increasing rural purchasing power and stabilising agricultural communities.

And it worked. In China, land management laws, introduced with the benefit of RDI's advice, have resulted in a threefold increase in long-term infrastructure investment among the 40% of China's farmers who have received documented 30-year land rights.

But Prosterman didn't stop there. In 1992, he founded the University of Washington Law School's graduate program in the law of sustainable international development, providing graduates not only with training in transnational and international law, but also with the broad knowledge of politics, economics, public health and social and environmental sciences needed to pursue his mission.

And in 1996, working with the support of the Gates Foundation, RDI pioneered the idea of empowering India's landless rural poor by granting them ownership of small homestead plots, averaging less than 0.04 hectare, but sufficient for a vegetable garden and a simple home. Reminiscent of Muhammad Yunus's micro-lending, the process Prosterman calls micro-owning has already benefited over 400,000 Indian families. As Roy Prosterman says "A little land goes a long way".

And 40 years on, Prosterman sees himself as having a long way to go. In 2005, he handed operational control of RDI, now renamed Landesa, to his long-term lieutenant, Tim Hanstad, but retained the position of Founder and Chairman Emeritus, with a brief to tackle thorny issues and mentor the next generation.

One of the thorniest issues will be Africa. On the one hand, 60% of the planet's cultivatable but as yet uncultivated land is to be found in Sub-Saharan Africa. It's soil and water will be the key to feeding future populations. On the other hand, 250 million Africans, many of them children of small farmers scratching a living from land that they do not own, are chronically undernourished due to lack of food.

Just the sort of problem that Prosterman thrives on, and he's already on the case.

In 2010, Landesa launched four new programs in Africa, including a collaborative project with the University of Washington to develop a

Land Tenure Institute at Ethiopia's Haramaya University. The purpose of the institute is to "engage students and faculty in research on land tenure issues in Ethiopia ... and build the capacity of local government officials to develop policy and law to address land administration and land dispute resolution".

There won't be any shortage of work!

SHEIKH MOHAMMED HUSSEIN ALI AL-AMOUDI

When Gambella National Park, in the swampy lowlands of far-west Ethiopia, was first planned in 1973, its purpose was to protect migrating herds of two endangered antelope species, the white-eared kob and the Nile lechwe. The region in and around the park was also a traditional source of food and shelter for Gambella's Anuak and Nuer tribes, and more recently for their ethnic cousins fleeing across the border from war-torn Sudan.

But Gambella is also rich in water and soil. Since 2008 the Ethiopian government, eager to attract sufficient infrastructure investment to reverse its dependence on international food aid, has delineated millions of hectares of "unutilised" land in this and other parts of the country for lease to foreign investors for large-scale commercial farming. There is no shortage of takers.

One of the first off the mark was Sheik Mohammed Hussein Ali Al-Amoudi, an Ethiopian-born Saudi billionaire who was already a significant investor in Ethiopia's hospitality, transport, gold and leather industries. Like Prosterman, Al-Amoudi is a man with a mission, albeit a somewhat different one: his stated goal is to help drive the economic development of Ethiopia while simultaneously contributing to the food security of the people of Saudi Arabia.

ଔଔଔ

One of eight children of a Yemeni father and Ethiopian mother, Mohammed Al-Amoudi grew up in the hillside market town of Weldiya,

Ethiopia, about 500 km north of Addis Ababa, in a home adjacent to his parents' clothing shop. According to childhood friends, he loved playing soccer and excelled at mental arithmetic: both signs of things to come!

In 1965, aged 19, Al-Amoudi emigrated to Saudi Arabia, where his initial involvement in supplying concrete and other building materials to the construction industry soon led to a lucrative and long-lasting relationship with the Saudi royal family, for whom he handled major construction contracts. It also led to his links to the Swedish construction firm, Armerad Betong Vägförbättringar, or ABV.

ABV was one of a consortium of Swedish excavation and construction companies involved in a 1987 bid to construct the Saudi Strategic Storage Program, a massive underground oil storage network designed to buffer the kingdom against military attacks or other disruptions to oil supply. The vehicle for their ultimately successful bid was the Saudi-based ABV Rock Group.

But the bid was still in progress when a bribery and corruption scandal erupted around another major Swedish defence contract: the sale of Bofors 155mm field howitzers to India. The Swedish consortium saw the writing on the wall, decided that they'd be safer in the back seat, and sold the bid vehicle to a group of Saudi businessmen, led by Al-Amoudi.

Bingo! Over the course of the next 22 years, Al-Amoudi's MIDROC Group and its affiliated companies constructed five huge underground caverns, with total capacity for 12 million barrels of oil, linked to each other and Red Sea port facilities by 700 km of pipeline. At its peak, the project employed 12,000 people, and cost almost $3 billion.

ꖢꖢꖢ

The contacts, experience and wealth created from the construction of the Saudi Strategic Storage Program provided the perfect launching pad for Al-Amoudi's next moves: on the one hand into oil; and on the other into Ethiopia.

During the 1990s, under the umbrella of Corral Petroleum Holdings, itself owned by his Cypriot holding company, Moroncho, Al-Amoudi acquired major oil refineries in Sweden and Morocco and associated oil exploration and production facilities off West Africa and around the North Sea. One of these businesses alone, Preem Petroleum, accounted for 80% of Swedish refinery capacity.

Ten years later, Al-Amoudi's two operating arms, MIDROC Group and Corral Group, were employing over 40,000 people in the Middle East, Europe and Africa, all built on investment decisions that Al-Amoudi describes as "based on calculated risks and benefits".

Of Ethiopia, on the other hand, he says: "Ethiopia means so much to me that even my friends wonder about my investment decisions in the country. When I invest in Ethiopia, my decisions to invest are based on what I feel in my heart for my motherland".

Beginning in the 1980s, he began to invest in Ethiopian health, education and tourism infrastructure, as well as acquiring major interests in gold mining and leather production. By 2009, he had invested around $2 billion in more than 30 Ethiopian companies, and was far and away the nation's largest foreign investor.

And even more importantly perhaps, given his childhood passion, there was his investment in soccer. By 2009, Al-Amoudi was patron of St George Football Club, for which he had paid 90% of the cost of a 60,000-seat stadium. He had also hired a French coach for the national team, sponsored the East and Central Africa Cup, and contributed to the construction of three more regional stadiums.

And then came food.

Saudi Arabia, like many Middle Eastern nations, is not just short of arable land. It also suffers from massive water shortages, depending on desalination plants for about half of the nation's drinking water. In 2008, the Saudi government announced its intention to conserve water by reducing domestic cereal production by 12% per year. And to back

up that intention it offered low-interest loans totalling $5 billion to
Saudi companies willing to invest in grain production in countries with
untapped land and water resources.

Al-Amoudi moved fast, gaining the support of Saudi King Abdullah bin
Abdul Aziz after presenting His Majesty with samples of his succulent
Ethiopian rice, and that of Ethiopian Prime Minister Meles Zenawi with
his plans to help create more jobs and infrastructure. His track record
as a philanthropist sponsoring hospitals, sports facilities and overseas
scholarships for Ethiopian students no doubt also helped to convince the
Ethiopian Prime Minister.

Al-Amoudi's company, Saudi Star Agricultural Development Plc, began
its agricultural activities in 2010 with a 60-year lease over 10,000 hectares
in Gambella, and within 2 years had invested a massive $200 million
in equipment, construction and landclearing. The company intends to
expand its rice-farming operation to 300,000 hectares, investing $2.5
billion, employing 250,000 people, and producing 1.5 million tonnes of
rice per annum by 2020.

SAI RAMAKRISHNA KURUTURI

But if Al-Amoudi was fast off the mark, the next arrival was even faster.
Sight unseen, Sai Ramakrishna Karuturi signed up for a 50-year lease over
300,000 hectares - about the size of Luxembourg - in Gambella.

ಜಜಜ

Ram Karuturi's first job when he returned to Bangalore in 1990, after
completing an MBA at Case Western Reserve University in the United
States, was as technical director of the electrical contracting business
founded by his father and mentor, a former farmer. It was a time of rapid
growth in the Indian economy, and the demand for power infrastructure
was escalating. But Karuturi was keen to do his own thing, and still
hankered after his childhood days on the farm.

With these memories in mind, Karuturi visited Israel, intent on the prospect of employing his mechanical engineering skills to set up a business manufacturing greenhouses. But, to his surprise, he found the contents of the greenhouses much more exciting than their construction. And so it was that, in 1995, Karuturi and his wife, Anitha, founded Karuturi Floritech, and set out to capitalise on Bangalore's tropical savannah climate with four hectares of long-stemmed roses destined for the under-serviced European market.

It was a tough business, plagued by logistic difficulties in getting roses from greenhouse to airport, and airport to distant markets, but Karuturi thrived on the challenge. Working with the state government, he established a rose trading exchange based on the Dutch auction model, and followed up with an Internet portal that enabled him to cut costs by streamlining the supply chain from greenhouse to customer. And, in a coup that clearly still delights him, he made his first million when, after a cancelled flight to Europe left his local competitors desperate to get rid of their stock, he bought the lot and drove 350 km to dispatch it from another airport.

By 2003, Karuturi was the biggest rose producer in India, and wondering what to do next, when he learned - over coffee with an ex-employee - of the huge agricultural potential of Africa. Within three weeks, attracted by the concept of cheap land and lower freight costs, combined with duty-free access to European markets, Karuturi was in Ethiopia, and two weeks after that he had established his first African company, Ethiopian Meadows plc.

And it worked. Despite limiting his initial investment to a 10-hectare farm, the popularity of the resulting long-stem hybrid tea roses in the European market soon led to rapid expansion. Just three years later, in 2007, Karuturi placed his biggest and riskiest bet yet, buying a 200-hectare Kenyan rose farm - complete with township and football team - from his largest competitor, the private Dutch company Sher Agencies, for $67 million.

In one sense, his timing could not have been worse: the outbreak of ethnic violence following the contested 2007 Kenyan election threatened the company's ability to reach export markets, forcing Karuturi to hire armed guards to protect both the farm complex and the convoys of trucks transporting roses to the airport in the quiet hours between midnight and dawn each morning, and to provide both emergency food and housing for those of his workers and their families who were not already living on the site.

In another sense, his timing couldn't have been better. As he told *Bloomberg* reporters Mehul Srivastava and Subramaniam Sharma: "I got in on the ground floor, others got in on the second floor, but there's a lot of floors left to go in Africa's economic cycle. Africa offered us a scale we could never reach in India". With 4,000 workers cutting over a million stems per day, Karuturi had just become the world's biggest rose producer.

So, where next? Should he extend his horticulture business to encircle the globe, acquiring additional farms in tropical regions of Asia and South America, or would it be smarter to take advantage of his African foothold to expand his activities into food?

It was as he considered that question, in 2008, that the Ethiopian government approached him with an offer of 300,000 hectares of uncultivated - but cultivatable - land in Gambella. The answer was a matter of simple arithmetic.

First, the $13 billion cut rose industry, of which he had now acquired a substantial slice, was insignificant in comparison to the $6 trillion global food industry - he had to get into food.

Second, the combination of burgeoning population, faster than average GDP growth and increased urbanisation of African nations would further exacerbate the continent's existing 25% shortfall in food supplies - more food had to be grown in Africa.

Third, the projected cost of $350 million over 3 - 5 years to clear the land, cultivate crops and build infrastructure, including roads, dams and towns complete with education, sports and health care facilities, could be met, at least in part, from the cash flows of the cut rose business.

Karuturi did the deal.

After a trial planting in 2009, Karuturi had over 30,000 hectares under cultivation just one year later: 5,000 hectares of palm oil, 15,000 hectares of sorghum and maize, and the rest rice. In 2011, with 100,000 hectares, including 10,000 hectares of sugar, under cultivation, the project was temporarily set back by flooding, which wiped out 12,000 hectares of maize. Undeterred, Karuturi built levees and replanted. By 2014, he anticipates having 300,000 hectares tended by up to 60,000 workers.

And he has no qualms whatsoever about the move to Africa. As he explained to *Bloomberg*: "In Ethiopia, I am the largest investor, the second largest employer after the government. In India, I am not even a fly on the wall".

A QUESTION OF SCALE

Prosterman, Al-Amoudi and Karuturi come from very different backgrounds, and certainly from different philosophical positions, but they have all achieved their remarkable success in very similar ways.

Each of them built their enterprise step by step, working closely with national governments to consolidate each stage before using it as a platform to move onto the next.

Each of them operates instinctively on a truly global scale:

Prosterman has enabled millions of poor tenant farmers to feed their families, gaining them rights to almost 100 million acres of land in 40 developing nations. All up, he has improved the lives of 400 million people in his quest to promote peace, freedom and justice through schemes of land tenure in the third world. His fundamental credos - poverty reduction results in peace enhancement - has been proven time and time again.

Al-Amoudi, whose agreement with the Ethiopian government requires 40% of the product to be available domestically, will use the remainder to provide sustenance to millions of Saudi Arabians. Perhaps anticipating that, he is building port facilities in Djibouti, Ethiopia's neighbour and access point to the Red Sea, and in February 2012 he announced a further investment in Ethiopia of $3.4 billion, including a World Bank-backed cement company that will no doubt supply the concrete to build the port through which Saudi Star will ship the grain.

And, for his part, Karuturi wants to become the largest food producer in the world. His goal is to acquire and cultivate 3 million hectares - roughly the size of Belgium - of commercial farmland. Most of it will be in Africa, and that's where he expects that most of his product will be consumed: "We are a clear proponent of food security in Africa, not from Africa". Already, he has a $400 million contract with the Djibouti government to supply 40,000 tonnes of rice per year for the next 20 years, and expects even larger contracts with other African nations seeking to replace imports from Asia.

And, ultimately, each of them is focused on the same thing: feeding people in an increasingly hungry world.

So, who's right? Which is the best approach? There are strong arguments, and advocates, on all sides.

On the one hand, much is made of the fact that Ethiopia is leasing land to foreign investors at peppercorn rentals while remaining one of the world's largest recipients of food aid.

The former head of the UN Food and Agriculture Organisation, Jacques Diouf, for example, although initially in favour of joint venture agreements between countries with financial resources and those with land, water and labour, has since warned that the rise in land deals could create a form of neocolonialism, with poor states producing food for the rich at the expense of their own hungry people.

The Barcelona-based advocacy group, GRAIN, has a similar view, claiming that domestic farmers are being dispossessed by Ethiopia's policy of renting land cheaply to foreign investors, who are using it to grow cash crops. In Gambella, the Anuak and Nuer tribesmen who once earned their livelihood farming and fishing in the national park, which they assumed was theirs by right, are now humble employees working for foreign investors on the same land.

Others counter that investments in commercial agriculture are the nation's only hope of weaning more than 10% of Ethiopia's 80 million people off donor-funded food programs.

"African dependence on Western aid must stop", proclaimed the late Ethiopian Prime Minister and former revolutionary, Meles Zenawi, who staked his nation's future on the belief that the new farms will bring foreign exchange and technology as well as creating thousands of jobs. For Zenawi, foreign investment in large-scale commercial agriculture, alongside the commercialisation of smallholder agriculture, was an essential component of the nation's "Agricultural Development-Led Industrialization" strategy.

Youba Sokona, of the UN Economic Commission for Africa, agrees: "Africa is importing a lot of food despite availability of fertile land and water. What we need is know-how and investment. This is coming largely from India and China, whose technologies and know-how can be comfortably implemented in African countries".

Or, as Karuturi puts it:

> Why do they need to import food? It's a shame, I sometimes feel like it's a conspiracy - that people want Africa to remain with a begging bowl. Here we are creating employment, food, wealth - isn't that what Adam Smith spoke about - isn't that the reason the West is self-sufficient?

In an interview with *AllAfrica*'s Tami Hultman, Bill Gates, co-chair of the Gates Foundation, summed it up like this:

> Many of those land deals are beneficial, and it would be too bad if some were held back because of Western groups' ways of looking at things. Whenever somebody invests in Africa and actually builds infrastructure in Africa, they're the ones who are at risk. You can't take the infrastructure home!

KEY SOURCES

FEEDING THE WORLD

"How to feed the world in 2050", Background Paper for High-Level Experts Forum, FAO, Rome, October 12 - 13, 2009.

Norman Myers, "The next green revolution: Its environmental underpinnings", Interdisciplinary Dialogue on Malthus and Mendel: Population, Science and Sustainable Security, Chennai, January 28, 1998.

"The 9 billion people question. A special report on feeding the world", *The Economist*, February 26, 2011.

World Bank, "World Development Indicators. Arable Land (hectares per person). Data. Table, Arable land (hectares per person)", 2009.

AFRICA

Peter Gill, "Ethiopia: defining its own path", *Making It Magazine: Industry for Development*, June 22, 2011.

Tami Hultman, "Africa: 'best chance' to end polio - Bill Gates promotes vaccines and food programs to attack poverty", *allAfrica*, February 9, 2011.

Gyanendra Kumar Keshri, " African farmland to Indian firms no cause for worry: UN official", *sify.com Finance*, February 13, 2011.

Jonathan Rugman, "Africa succumbs to colonial-style land grab", Britain's Channel 4 News, January 7, 2012.

ROY PROSTERMAN

Lily Eng, "Call Roy Prosterman another Indiana Jones", *Seattle Times*, June 7, 1993.

Landesa *Annual Report*, 2010.

Peter Monaghan, "A gentle but tough-minded visionary", *The Chronicle of Higher Education*, June 16, 1995.

Alissa Sandford, "Salt of the earth", *Claremont McKenna College Magazine*, Fall, 2006.

Shivani Vora, "A conversation with: Landesa founder Roy Prosterman", *The New York Times*, September 25, 2012.

SHEIKH MOHAMMED HUSSEIN ALI AL-AMOUDI

William Davison, "Saudi billionaire's company will invest $2.5 billion in Ethiopia rice farm", *Bloomberg*, March 23, 2011.

Georgis Kefale, "Sheik Mohammed Al Amoudi, Ethiopia's eternal love", *Washera Ethiopian Politics*, Sunday, March 9, 2008.

K S Ramkumar, "Saudis invest heavily in Ethiopian farm sector", *Arab News*, May 29, 2010.

Desalegn Sisay, "Silence over Ethiopian land grab broken", *AFRIK News*, February 17, 2011.

SAI RAMAKRISHNA KARUTURI

Anoop Babani, "Blooming in Africa", *Business India*, November 15 - 28, 2010.

Anirvan Ghosh, "Ramakrishna Karuturi, world's largest producer of rose buds", *The Economic Times*, August 25, 2008.

Peter Heinlein, "Foreign agro firms scoop up Ethiopian farmland", *Negaritethiopia blogspot*, 22 February 2010.

Ramakrishna Karuturi, "My story", *Slideshare*, December 26, 2011.

Ram Karuturi, "Founder and Managing Director", *Karuturi Global Columbia Business School Videos*, October 19, 2010.

Anuradha Raghunathan, "Coming up roses", *Forbes Magazine*, April 27, 2009.

Mehul Srivastava and Subramaniam Sharma, "India billionaires go on buying spree in 'last frontier' Africa", *Bloomberg*, October 25, 2010.

MK Venu, "Karuturi and the conquest of the African mind space", *The Financial Express*, May 24, 2011.

John Vidal, "Ethiopia at centre of global farmland rush", *The Guardian*, March 21, 2011.

An individual with an epic ambition to change the world, who ...	Roy Prosterman	Sheikh Mohammed Hussein Ali Al-Amoudi	Sai Ramakrishna Karuturi
	Born: 1935, Chicago, Illinois, USA Education: BA, Chicago; JD, Harvard Organisation: Landesa	Born: 1946, Dessie, Ethiopia Education: Weizero Siheen Secondary School Organisation: MIDROC	Born: 1965, India Education: Mech Eng, Bangalore; MBA, Case Western Reserve University Organisation: Karuturi Global
... sees and seizes opportunities for change.			
Opportunistic: aggressively seeks and adopts new ideas	Reacting to a law review article that promoted land confiscation as an acceptable tool for land reform in Latin America ...	In 1985, when his partners suggested investing in Paris, Al-Amoudi responded: "Paris is far away. I would like to start in Africa".	Karuturi recognised that land and water shortages in many developed nations offered unprecedented opportunities to ...
& Visionary: intuitively grasps the big picture and how it might evolve	... Prosterman urged negotiated change rather than revolutionary violence. He called it "a revolution without a revolution".	"I want to be there first".	... arbitrage developing world assets (land, labour and climate) into first world products.
... senses the way forward..			
Innovative: thinks creatively, ignores boundaries, disrupts the status quo	Working with national governments to create new laws, ...	He saw the potential to leverage transcontinental public-private partnerships ...	Given the choice between further dominance of the world's flower markets or expanding his African operations into food, Karuturi chose food ...
but Pragmatic: recognises constraints, devises practical solutions, creates value	... he helped developing nations solve land conflicts and improve agricultural production, nutrition and regional security.	... and build value chains from oil well to gas pump, from farm land to food security.	... partly, perhaps, because he still gets "nightmares about the Chinese producing a plastic rose that lasts forever, smells better, and then the Indians putting in a software program to make it smile".

.. attracts the necessary resources..			
Persuasive: articulate and convincing communicator, consummate networker	"A person of gentle manner and gentle voice who has, with the use of powerful ideas and energy, ..."	He brings on board princes and prime ministers ...	"Companies are investing in India for services and they are flocking to China for manufacturing. But if you want to grow food you have to be in Africa".
& Empowering: attracts talent, inspires loyalty, rewards excellence	... been able to lift the lives and hopes of tens of millions" - Nobel Peace Prize nomination, 1993.	... but delights in transforming the lives of his employees and his countrymen.	"What Karuturi Global is doing is what Africa needs, wants and deserves. What we put in is our money", including investments in housing, schools, hospitals and sporting facilities for his employees and their families.
.. and pursues the dream...			
Focussed: passionate and highly energetic perfectionist, totally committed to an overriding vision	A workaholic and a perfectionist, who doesn't like "typos in my memos".	In Ethiopia, he has invested billions of dollars in more than 30 companies ...	"I want to be among the top four or five integrated agri-product companies in the world".
& Confident: driven by unconditional self-belief, assumes absolute authority and accountability	"Land reform neither creates nor destroys land. It simply puts a given population - present or future - into a relationship with that land base that is most productive and equitable".	... that "will benefit the country in terms of foreign currency, job creation and increased domestic food production".	"And I will implement this vision out of Africa".
.. regardless of the odds..			
Resilient: flexible, thrives on change and uncertainty, learns from mistakes	Following the assassination of three of his friends and colleagues in El Salvador, he and Tim Hanstad resorted to bullet-proof vests as they worked on facilitating the introduction of land ownership for tens of thousands of tenant farmers and landless labourers ...	"When other investors come, they open the door and they see there".	As riots and strikes closed businesses throughout Kenya in January 2008, Karuturi provided free food, accommodation and protection for all his workers as well as their families, and continued to export roses daily to European markets.
& Courageous: bold, intelligent risk-taker, undaunted by criticism, determined to succeed	... before returning to the United States to face student activists with "Wanted" posters displaying a target superimposed on a photograph of his head. He was not deterred.	"Either they join me or they fight me".	"We have built the world's largest floriculture business. Now for agriculture".

Part V

THE ORIGIN OF THE SPECIES

FOR MANY PEOPLE, THE UNITED STATES is the prototypical home of entrepreneurship. The nation was founded by risk-takers and innovators, and generations of new immigrants from around the globe have maintained their spirit and their vision. The result? More than two-thirds of all net new jobs in the USA and almost one-third of all export value are created by small businesses. When it comes to sheer numbers of entrepreneurs, at least with a small "e", the USA is undoubtedly where they come from.

But what of the überpreneurs, the ones who are seriously changing your world? Are they, too, predominantly from the United States? There's no simple measure, but a proxy indicator, at least in the field of big business, is provided by the Forbes annual rich list. Of the 1,226 billionaires on Forbes 2012 list, just over a third dwell in the United States. And that proportion has scarcely changed since the publication of the original Forbes list in 1987, when US citizens accounted for 31% of the world's 140 billionaires.

Life hasn't been quite so straightforward in other nations. Japan, ranked immediately below the United States in 1987, plummeted from 17% to 2% in 2012, and Germany fell from 9% to 4%. Meanwhile, the billionaire oligarchs of Russia, revelling in the chaotic aftermath of the collapse of the Soviet Union, increased their numbers from zero to close to 100, as did China's billionaires following the reforms of Deng Xiaoping. Together with Brazil and India, they (the BRIC nations) account for 23% of the world's billionaires in 2012, and the growth markets of Mexico, Indonesia, South Korea and Turkey (the MIST nations) add 7% more. Africa, with no billionaires on the list in 1987, now has 16, or a little more than 1% of the total.

Clearly, at least if measured by the proxy of extreme wealth, überpreneurs come from all over our planet.

ଧ୍ୟଧ୍ୟଧ୍ୟ

And many of our 36 überpreneurs are indeed seriously rich. More than half of them are billionaires, and another quarter are multi-millionaires. Like the Forbes billionaires, they come from all over the planet: 11 are from the USA, 6 from Europe, 6 are from the Middle-East and North Africa, 8 from the BRIC nations, predominantly India and China, and 5 from elsewhere in Asia, including one from Australia.

But our choice was not guided by their wealth, and nor were we driven by any need to balance the representation of countries or regions around the globe. Our selection was directed solely by the desire to identify individuals who have comprehensively transformed our world, not just economically, but also socially and environmentally, and the hope that in so doing we might identify some of the factors that underpinned their extraordinary achievements.

In the next chapter we revisit their stories in this light, seeking to explore which of their shared characteristics may best explain their überpreneurial success; to understand the extent to which their presence among us is determined by nature or driven by nurture; and to learn from them how we can play our part in ensuring that they survive, prosper and continue to transform our world.

KEY SOURCES

Sean Kilachand, "Forbes history: the original 1987 list of international billionaires", *Forbes Magazine*, March 21, 2012.

The Economist, "Special Report: Entrepreneurship: The United States of Entrepreneurs", March 12, 2009.

Chapter 16

THE NATURE OF ÜBERPRENEURS

THE MASSIVE CHANGES DESCRIBED IN this book have all been achieved by individuals.

Nine of them, Joseph Schumpeter's high-level entrepreneurs, have driven economic transformations that span the planet, and beyond.

Nine more, Francis Bacon's "merchants of light", have sourced and implemented technologies that pervade all aspects of life in the 21st century.

Another nine, Émile Durkheim's social network builders, have enriched the lives of billions of individuals suffering the anonymity of modern urban environments.

And the last nine, Bill Drayton's change-makers, have successfully embarked on the massive task of restoring the balance between the haves and have-nots of our world.

ରୟରୟ

So, what are their key characteristics? Why can they do things that the rest of us can't? Can we produce more of them? And, if not, how should we make better use of the ones we've got?

WHAT MAKES THEM TICK?

In the opening pages of this book we offered the following definition of a typical überpreneur:

An individual with an epic ambition to change the world, who sees and seizes opportunities for change, senses the way forward, attracts the necessary resources and pursues the dream, regardless of the odds.

How well do the elements of this definition stack up against the real-life attributes of our überpreneurs?

SEES AND SEIZES OPPORTUNITIES …

Few, if any, of our 36 überpreneurs were the first to think of the ideas that they have so successfully exploited. Like Francis Bacon's merchants of light, all of them are *opportunists*, constantly alert, ceaselessly looking for new ideas. When opportunity strikes, they seize it.

George Rathmann, citing genetic engineering as "the most important thing I had ever seen", didn't hesitate to leave his career in big pharma to pioneer the nascent biotechnology industry. For Barry Marshall, Robin Warren's microscope slides of previously undescribed bacteria living in the hostile, acid-filled environment of the stomach were not a microbiological impossibility but a medical opportunity. And Craig Venter, learning of the invention of an automated gene-sequencing machine, purchased the very first one built, describing its arrival in his laboratory as "my future in a crate".

"Luck", as the Roman philosopher and politician Seneca the Younger is reputed to have said, "is what happens when preparation meets opportunity". And men like Richard Branson, Jeff Bezos and Elon Musk certainly made their own luck when they saw and seized their opportunities to steal a march on the complacent incumbents of the airline, bookselling and automobile industries.

But ultimately, of course, their successes have little or nothing to do with luck, and everything to do with vision. All of them are *visionaries*, people, as Anita Roddick described them, "who imagine things as they might be, not as they are, and have the drive to change the world around them".

A glance at Bill Gross's sponsored search model was sufficient for Larry Page to visualise the future multibillion-dollar advertising strategy of Google, just as Niklas Zennström recognised peer-to-peer communication as the obvious basis for "letting the whole world talk for free". And Bill Gates certainly didn't need a second look at the graphical user interface being developed for the Apple MacIntosh by Steve Jobs - who himself had acquired the idea with equal alacrity from Xerox - to know that it was the way of Microsoft's future: Windows.

None of them have ever found any need to refer, or defer, to others in reaching their decisions. Like grandmasters glancing at a chessboard, they instantly and instinctively grasp the big picture, visualise its potential evolution, and go for it.

... SENSES THE WAY FORWARD ...

Equally importantly, all of them are *innovators*, who pinpoint the missing links - be they products, processes, sources of supply, organisational structures or markets - between where things are and where they might be. And all of them are *pragmatists*, who find practical ways to forge the links that make those transitions happen.

Mark Zuckerberg saw the power of the Internet to collect and harness information through networks of computers, and asked himself why it wasn't being used to link networks of people. Pony Ma took the next step, extending those social networks to the hundreds of millions of young Chinese who access the Internet using mobile phones. And Gilad Japhet, observing the soaring popularity of Facebook and LinkedIn among networks of friends and professionals, asked himself why no one was doing the same thing for family.

And speaking of family, Nayana Patel and Doron Mamet both saw firsthand the difficulties faced by infertile and gay couples seeking the joys of parenthood, and found win-win ways to make it easier for them. At Nayana Patel's fertility clinic in Anand, newly empowered surrogates earn enough to build a family home and educate their children, while their delighted customers go home with a child of their own. And Doron Mamet's inspired approach to gay fatherhood uses FedEx and liquid nitrogen tanks to unite Israeli sperm with eggs from the United States and surrogate mothers in India.

And in Brazil and Indonesia, the innovative genius of Luiz Seabra and Martha Tilaar extends all the way from the sustainable harvesting of endemic flora through to modern R&D laboratories creating natural cosmetics that are delivered through networks of salons and beauty consultants to women of all ages, races and creeds.

All of them have created new products, structures and processes, and used them to build spectacular new markets. Like structural engineers creating orbital space stations, they circumvent every obstacle in their paths as they devise smart and effective solutions to realising their dreams.

... ATTRACTS THE NECESSARY RESOURCES ...

All of them are both *persuasive* and *empowering*.

Despite building their organisations into the world's largest furniture, fashion and liquor retailers, Ingvar Kamprad, Amancio Ortega and Chuck Feeney have always been accessible, working on the shop floor with their staff. Whether as father figures, as cult leaders, or simply as human beings, their care and concern for their employees inspired both corporate excellence and remarkable personal loyalty. When the Swedish press unearthed details of Ingvar Kamprad's youthful flirtation with far-right political ideology, the IKEA family responded with "Ingvar, we are here whenever you need us". And when a competitor won the bid for the Honolulu duty-free concession in 1981, Japanese tour guides simply continued bringing their charges to Chuck Feeney.

One might have hoped that the facts alone would have been enough to allow Mechai Viravaidya and Mitch Besser to attract support for the prevention of AIDS, or to enable Jeroo Billimoria and Soraya Salti to gather the resources needed to train the street kids of Calcutta and the unemployed youth of the Middle East. But ultimately it was not the facts that brought prime ministers and presidents, princesses and police commissioners to their doors.

It was Mitch Besser's extraordinary charisma that not only attracted the sponsorship and support needed to run his organisation, but also inspired thousands of young HIV-positive women to work with him, mentoring and counselling other young mothers-to-be diagnosed with the disease.

Mechai Viravaidya's unflagging good humour won him the support of the public and politicians alike, and enabled him to recruit farmers and schoolteachers, sex workers and policemen to help him dispense condoms and advice to those at risk of AIDS.

Jeroo Billimoria's tireless enthusiasm brought together hospital administrators, police chiefs and community leaders, and empowered street children to establish and staff toll-free emergency call centres for children throughout India.

And Soraya Salti's self-deprecating determination overcame the resistance of sceptical public servants and fundamentalist imams, enabling thousands of Arab youth to establish and run their own entrepreneurial enterprises.

All of them have built their organisations using their own powers of *persuasion*, attracting and *empowering* thousands of others to work with them to change the world. Like conductors exhorting their orchestras, theirs are the batons harmonising everyone from the tin trumpets to the double bassoons.

… AND PURSUES THE DREAM …

All of them *focus* single-mindedly on their goals, and are so *confident* of achieving them that they do not hesitate to take absolute control, and to accept absolute responsibility.

Listen to Olivia Lum, Shai Agassi and Zhengrong Shi as they talk of their clean technology companies and their opportunities in China:

Lum: "Opportunities don't wait for you: you have to seize them".

Agassi: "When someone tells you something won't work, but they don't have a good reason, ignore them".

Zhengrong Shi: "I realised if I come back to China, I can really do something because I have so much more advanced experience and knowledge than people here do. So I think my country needs me".

And Muhammad Yunus and Claus-Peter Zeitinger on their plans for expanding their micro-banking operations globally:

Yunus: "We got rid of colonialism, we got rid of slavery, and we got rid of apartheid - everyone thought each one of them was impossible. Let's take the next impossible, ... and create a world free from poverty. Let us create the world of our choice".

Zeitinger: "We are not polite, we know what we want, we have it our way".

Like big game hunters stalking their prey, their eyes never stray from the target, their minds never doubt the result.

... REGARDLESS OF THE ODDS

All of them are both *resilient* and *courageous*, thriving on change and uncertainty, always ready to tackle the next challenge.

Following the assassination of three of his colleagues in El Salvador, Roy Prosterman continued his campaign for land reform wearing a bulletproof vest; Sheikh Al-Amoudi stared down the competition for agricultural land in Ethiopia, warning, "When other investors come, they open the door and they see me there. Either they join me or they fight me"; and Ram Karuturi came anyway, proclaiming, "We have built the world's largest floriculture business. Now for agriculture".

Pilloried by the tabloid press, Jamie Oliver nevertheless prevailed on the British government to improve the nutritional standards of school lunches, and then moved on to the fast-food capital of the world, the United States, in a brave bid to tackle its national overdose of salt, sugar and fat. And Oprah Winfrey, more bravely still, perhaps, risked losing a substantial chunk of her immense television audience as she pressed home the distinction between the fanaticism of Al-Qaeda and the power of Islam as a religion of peace.

Bemoaning the state of affairs in Africa, Mo Ibrahim did not hesitate to tell it as it is - "After fifty years of independence, we have a catastrophic failure of leadership and governance: too many dictators, too many megalomaniacs, too many thieves" - and proceeded to develop an annual ranking of the performance of 53 African nations and their leaders. In China, Liu Yonghao faced public criticism in the aftermath of Tiananmen Square - "Some people advised us to quit, saying we had to choose between the capitalist and socialist paths" - but nevertheless went on to build an even bigger, and more plainly capitalist, empire. And Kiran Mazumdar-Shaw, who once said "I have only one child - it is Biocon", responded to rabid unionists burning her effigy by giving them severance pay and automating their jobs.

Like mothers protecting their children, they will not be moved.

ଈଈଈ

So, are they born or made? What accident of birth or education might give rise to individuals who combine the intuition of chess grandmasters, the ingenuity of structural engineers, the passion of philharmonic conductors, the focus of big game hunters and the courage of mothers protecting their young?

MADE OR BORN?

Two recent studies of identical and non-identical twins suggest that it is nature rather than nurture that plays the key role.

Corina Greven and her colleagues at King's College London studied 3,700 pairs of twins aged between 7 and 10, concluding that self-confidence is much more heavily influenced by genetic factors than by shared environments. And, in a survey of personality traits in 800 twin pairs, Timothy Bates and his colleagues at the University of Edinburgh found that genetic factors also played the major role in persistence and self-control.

But for every expert study that demonstrates that a key characteristic is genetically determined, there are a thousand gurus ready to say: "I can change that".

And there are plenty of big guns on their side. Soraya Salti, reviewing the impact of business training on the outcomes of INJAZ al-Arab's competition for the best student company of the year, has no doubt: "Made they are indeed!" And Ernst and Young, reporting the results of a survey of 685 entrepreneurial business leaders from around the world, are equally insistent: "Entrepreneurial leaders are made, not born".

The World Economic Forum, likewise, in a comprehensive report providing extensive examples of good practice for entrepreneurship education programs, concludes that entrepreneurship can be taught and that "there is a positive relationship between entrepreneurship education and the generation of growth enterprises".

On balance, it seems, entrepreneurs can be made. But what of überpreneurs?

In our view, there is little to suggest that the key characteristics of our überpreneurs - an extraordinary blend of opportunism and vision, innovation and pragmatism, persuasion and empowerment, focus and confidence, resilience and courage - can be traced to anything in their business experience or education.

But that's not to say that they haven't been influenced, sometimes profoundly, by the circumstances that they have encountered along the way.

In the following sections, we will use their experiences, and their achievements, to consider how the key players in their environment - governments, educators, investors, businesses, philanthropists, friends and families - influenced their development as überpreneurs, and how we might learn from their successes, and their failures.

GOVERNMENT

While few, if any, of our überpreneurs have benefited from the recent surge in government-led training programs for innovators and entrepreneurs, at least half of them have interacted with government in other ways, and their experiences provide some salutary lessons on the role of government in promoting überpreneurship:

Grasp The Big Picture,

Too many 21st-century political leaders lack the technological know-how required to make balanced judgments on the merits or otherwise of current debates on subjects such as climate change, genetically modified crops or even vaccination against childhood disease. Like those whose ignorance fuelled the catastrophic AIDS epidemics in South Africa and Thailand prior to the arrival of Mitch Besser and Mechai Viravaidya, they are increasingly swayed not so much by the quality of the debate as by the volume at which it is conducted.

This situation is exacerbated by the prevalence of three- and four-year fixed-term elections, often denying any party the opportunity to develop and pursue policies that might progress the 30- and 40-year agendas typical of many of our überpreneurs. As Jamie Oliver, whose "Feed me Better" campaign was a casualty of the 2010 change of government in the United Kingdom, puts it: "One of the downfalls of democracy is that by nature politicians are transient. Many only think about the next three to four years, not the next 20 to 50".

... Tilt The Playing Field,

Government programs that offer positive incentives to individuals
or companies seeking innovative solutions to major economic,
environmental and social challenges have often proved very effective.

The massive farms of Ram Karuturi and Mohammed Al-Amoudi in the
Gambella region of Ethiopia, for example, would never have been there
without the late Prime Minister Zenawi's "Agricultural Development-
Led Industrialization" strategy, just as the millions of small land-owners
now prospering in Vietnam would never have done so if the Vietnamese
government had not adopted the land reform programs proposed by Roy
Prosterman.

And the impact of negative government policies is equally substantial.

Although released from the post-revolutionary constraints of Nehru, Mao
and Nasser, Kiran Mazumdar-Shaw, Liu Yonghao and Mo Ibrahim had
to employ every ounce of their innovative ability to deal with the red tape
in which their enterprises were swathed by bureaucratic governments,
and are still fighting to achieve the social outcomes that they seek for
their nations. Similar regulatory obstacles created by slow-moving and
inconsistent legislation continue to handicap the businesses of Nayana
Patel, Luiz Seabra and Doron Mamet.

Tax is also a factor. Although few, if any, of our überpreneurs are
interested in wealth for its own sake, taxation levels that work against
effective reinvestment of capital clearly dampen überpreneurial ardour.
Chuck Feeney, for example, has spent much of his working life figuring
out how to avoid paying taxes, only to give it all away through his
charitable foundation. He has no doubt that individuals can do more with
money than governments.

And when red tape and high taxes are combined with the profound
social stigma of failure, as in Japan, or its serious legal repercussions, as
in many European countries, the cost of negative government policies
may well extend beyond a simple reduction in wealth, as seen in the

Forbes billionaires list, to an equivalent reduction in the population of überpreneurs.

… And Stand Back.

In some cases governments have much to gain from simply handing responsibility for complex problems over to überpreneurial individuals. The success of Elon Musk in restoring Western supply chains to the International Space Station, and the corresponding work of Richard Branson and Jeff Bezos in implementing suborbital space travel, are good examples.

Similarly in the social arena. The huge success of Muhammad Yunus and Claus-Peter Zeitinger in using their very different models to address the issues around banking for the poor has shown clearly the advantage of private organisations over governments in addressing complex social issues, as has that of Luiz Seabra and Martha Tilaar in developing enterprises with win-win-win outcomes for urban populations, biodiverse environments and indigenous cultures.

EDUCATION

Not everyone sees education as the future of mankind.

According to American business commentator Michael Ellsberg: "If I were betting on the engines of future job creation, I wouldn't put my money on college students cramming for tests and writing papers. I'd put my money on the kids who are dropping out of college to start new businesses".

And PayPal co-founder Peter Thiel has gone one step further, creating a foundation that provides fellowships of $100,000 over two years, along with mentorship from a network of entrepreneurs and innovators, to people under the age of 20 who drop out of college (or high school) to focus full-time on building a business. On May 25, 2011, the Thiel Foundation announced its first 24 fellowships with the statement: "We're excited to be working with them, and we hope they will help young people everywhere realise that you don't need credentials to launch a company that disrupts the status quo".

Certainly, and consistently with Thiel's view, our überpreneurs started young. Around half were under 25 when they started the enterprise described here, and all bar two were under 40. Some on our list, like Sheikh Al-Amoudi, Luiz Seabra and Amancio Ortega, never had the opportunity to finish high school. Others, like Richard Branson and Ingvar Kamprad, both of whom suffer from dyslexia, couldn't wait to leave school and set up their lemonade stands.

And it's true that three of our biggest names - Larry Page, Bill Gates and Mark Zuckerberg - dropped out of college to launch their companies. But was it dropping out that led to their success, or pursuit of success that led to them dropping out? Clearly, for Gates, Zuckerberg and Page, it was the latter. They imagined the future before any of their college professors. They saw vast opportunities, and realised that they had to move hard and fast to win. No one paid them to drop out. They had no choice. They simply didn't have time to keep studying.

So, is Peter Thiel on a winner with his fellowships encouraging kids to drop out of college and start a business? Probably not. He'd be better off backing the ones who have the belief, and the courage, to drop out of their own accord.

ଛଛଛ

So, what can schools and universities do for those who stay? The stories of our überpreneurs suggest that education has two roles: first, providing them with the core skills of their trade; and, second, providing the key resources to progress it:

Teach Them The Facts,

Counter to the arguments advanced by Ellsberg and Thiel, 29 of our group completed university degrees, and 5 of them have PhDs. In most cases their degrees are in specialist areas related to their work: Craig Venter, Barry Marshall, Roy Prosterman and Nayana Patel, for example, could not do the things they do without specialist training. Interestingly, only two of them, Soraya Salti and Ram Karuturi, have MBAs.

Equally importantly, however, while many see their university education as vital to their achievements, others see benefit in the school of hard knocks. Two-thirds of our überpreneurs had some sort of work experience before starting their own ventures, and a handful of them - Shai Agassi, Niklas Zennström, Gilad Japhet, Doron Mamet and George Rathmann - clearly benefited from working in very innovative business environments.

… And What To Do With Them.

As noted by Gilad Japhet, explaining the extraordinarily high levels of entrepreneurship in Israel: "Israelis are incredibly good at problem solving. They are trained to never accept barriers and always try and solve an issue - no matter how difficult it is. This makes Israel very strong in technology".

Of course, not every 18-year-old has the benefit of Israel's compulsory military service, and not every middle school student has the single-minded self-confidence to build an ink-jet printer out of Lego blocks, like Larry Page; conjure a solar cooker from an umbrella and tin foil, like Jeff Bezos; design an instant messaging system, like Mark Zuckerberg; or earn sufficient money to feed a family from part-time jobs while still in primary school, like Olivia Lum.

But many believe real-world problem solving can and should be taught. When asked what use he had for his studies, Niklas Zennström replied: "I learnt that no problem is too big to solve if you have the right methods".

Help Build Their Networks,

Mark Zuckerberg, Larry Page and Chuck Feeney all met their first business partners while studying at university, and Olivia Lum and Zhengrong Shi based their businesses on the research expertise of their teachers at the University of Singapore and the University of New South Wales.

But it's the wider networks that are really important. Entrées to venture capital and technological networks, like those accessed by Larry Page and Sergey Brin at Stanford University, are increasingly being offered by commercially savvy universities. Stanford's Graduate School of Business, for example, offers programs in innovation and entrepreneurship that bring together doctoral and nonbusiness graduate students with Silicon Valley innovators, investors, scientists and engineers to gain greater understanding of how to formulate, develop and commercialise their ideas.

... And Supply Them With Talent.

According to the US National Academy of Sciences, "virtually all quality jobs in the knowledge economy will require certain scientific and mathematical skills". And yet, the quality and the proportions of students graduating in science, technology, engineering and mathematics (STEM) in the Western world are in free fall, while the corresponding numbers in China and India are climbing equally dramatically. But whereas STEM students and graduates from Asia once came to the West to work, there are now many more opportunities in the world's developing economies. More than half of Pony Ma's 20,000 employees work in R&D, as do most of the 5000 graduates employed by Kiran Muzumdar-Shaw.

Facebook, Microsoft, Amazon and Google, already known for poaching each other's staff, may soon have little other choice.

INVESTORS

Of our 36 überpreneurs, approximately one-third have funded the growth of their organisations from internal cash flow, and another third have attracted private capital from venture capitalists or other sources, often followed by a public listing. Most of the remaining third have been funded initially by governments or nongovernment organisations, subsequently supplemented by income generated within their organisations.

But most important, perhaps, from the viewpoint of would-be investors, are the lessons to be learnt from the history of their endeavours:

Back People With Passion,

Happily for the losers, some venture capitalists actually prefer those that have tried and failed to those that have not had that unfortunate experience.

But our überpreneurs have scarcely a failure to their names, and not one of them would so much as contemplate changing horses in midstream: they are all in for the long haul.

For the majority of our cast, the enterprise that we describe is their first, and often only, venture. Martha Tilaar and Luiz Seabra, for example, have devoted their lives to physically pampering and economically liberating the women of Brazil and Indonesia, just as Claus-Peter Zeitinger and Muhammad Yunus have never ceased to focus on delivering financial services to poor people in poor countries. Which is not to suggest that their enterprises are stagnant: on the contrary, each of them regularly creates new products and services, and enters new markets, as they constantly expand their businesses. But their core businesses remain the same.

The remainder are serial business-builders, but the businesses that they have built are all focused on a single business model that has remained virtually unchanged throughout their careers. Richard Branson and Jeroo Billimoria, for example, have expanded their empires organically through the creation of structurally distinct but philosophically related businesses, such as Virgin Air and Virgin Rail, or Childline and Aflatoun, with each stage being built on the success of the last.

… And Let Them Get On With It,

The history of technology companies is replete with tales of battles between investors and founders over who should be in charge. But the successes of the nine individuals in the technology section of this book send a clear message: the stellar performances of companies like Microsoft and Facebook, Amgen and Hyflux, could never have occurred without the extraordinary passion, stubborn perseverance, and technological insight possessed by their founders and CEOs: Bill Gates, Mark Zuckerberg, George Rathmann and Olivia Lum. Until 2012, when Shai Agassi and Zhengrong Shi both stepped down as CEOs of their enterprises, only one - Larry Page - had ever ceded control of his company, and even that was temporary.

In the words of space invader Elon Musk: "Great things will never happen with VCs or professional managers. They have high drive but they don't have the creativity or the insight".

Or, as fellow space invader Jeff Bezos puts it: "One of the dangers of bringing in professional managers is that the first thing they want to do is alter the vision. Founders are more stubborn about the vision and keep working on the details".

… Wherever They May Be.

When it comes to high technology, Silicon Valley has always been the place to be, and there's no doubt that venture capital investors there have been integral to helping the likes of Larry Page and George Rathmann build their businesses.

But Silicon Valley is becoming far from unique in providing access to these resources. Mo Ibrahim and Zhengrong Shi kicked off their ventures in Africa and China with private equity capital raisings that would be the envy of many Silicon Valley companies, and Gilad Japhet and Shai Agassi were equally successful in attracting venture capital in Israel.

As Sarah Lacy notes in her revealing exploration of entrepreneurship in the developing world, *Brilliant, Crazy, Cocky*, even the venture capitalists of Sand Hill Road, once famed for never investing in anything further than an hour from their offices, are now touring the globe seeking new opportunities.

Few know the strengths of those opportunities better than the shareholders of Naspers, the South African media company whose $34 million investment in a tiny Chinese company with the inauspicious name of Tencent was turned into $3 billion by an inauspicious Chinaman named "Pony" Ma. In the words of Niklas Zennström: "Think globally. If you don't think big, it's unlikely you'll become big".

BUSINESS

Back in 1968, the American economist William J Baumol lamented the absence of enterprise and initiative in prevailing economic models:

> The theoretical firm is entrepreneurless - the Prince of Denmark has been expunged from the discussion of Hamlet. The management group becomes a passive calculator that reacts mechanically to changes imposed on it by fortuitous external developments over which it does not exert, and does not even attempt to exert, any influence. One hears of no clever ruses, ingenious schemes, brilliant innovations, of no charisma or of any of the other stuff of which outstanding entrepreneurship is made; one does not hear of them because there is no way in which they can fit into the model.

Too few businesses heeded Baumol's warning. As a delighted Steve Jobs observed when senior management at Xerox gave him free access to their groundbreaking research into graphic user interfaces, many major corporations are still operating as if oblivious to the innovations occurring around them, or even in their own firms.

Again, our überpreneurs have some simple lessons:

Innovate,

As George Rathmann learnt at 3M, and as he, Larry Page, Jeff Bezos and Amancio Ortega later demonstrated at Amgen, Google, Amazon and Zara, the best way to stay ahead of the latest technological wave is to encourage employees to do their own thing, to take risks exploring new ideas, and, if necessary, to fail. Ingvar Kamprad, whose company and fortune are based on the introduction of flat-pack furniture by one of his employees, sums it up with: "innovation demands risk, risk-takers make mistakes".

... Implement,

George Rathmann and Zhengrong Shi both told their employers of the immense business opportunities that they saw in emerging technologies. Mo Ibrahim, Jeff Bezos, Shai Agassi and Olivia Lum were all equally visionary, and their employers equally vision-free. Ultimately, all six quit their highly paid jobs and seized their opportunities to change the world.

Chuck Feeney, Ingvar Kamprad and Amancio Ortega picked up and ran with opportunities to compete with furniture, fashion and luxury goods businesses that were complacently focused on the wealthy, ignoring the vast potential of increasingly well-off middle classes. And Richard Branson, Jeff Bezos and Elon Musk are busily making hay at the expense of declining airline, bookselling and automobile industries.

The solution? Even the largest and most successful companies cannot afford to rest on their laurels, ignoring the emergence of new technologies, new products and new markets. They cannot afford to retain boards stocked with aging lawyers and once-successful businessmen. They need to move outside their comfort zones, recruiting board members and senior management who are not only familiar with the technological opportunities of our times, but also ready, willing and able to act upon them.

... Invest In The Best People,

Elon Musk and Jeff Bezos personally interview candidates for positions throughout their empires, offering talented individuals the opportunity to "do something bold and new", "have fun" and "make history", while Richard Branson relies on the absolute loyalty of a corps of trusted lieutenants to drive each new branch of his business.

Some, like Bill Gates and Larry Page, have recruited their best people, and many of their best ideas, from rival companies, while Niklas Zennström scours the globe for the untapped talent in the high technology world's most neglected nations. And in the United States, Mark Zuckerberg has formed an organisation of entrepreneurial technology leaders seeking to boost the nation's knowledge economy through immigration reforms aimed at attracting "the most talented and hard-working people, no matter where they were born".

... And Don't Forget The Triple Bottom Line.

Martha Tilaar and Luiz Seabra have both built businesses that are not only commercial enterprises but also instruments of social change: both have worked with botanists and ecologists to develop sustainable processes for harvesting their nations' biodiversity, thus helping to preserve both the lifestyle and the environment of the peoples who dwell in their rain forests; both have created employment in the beauty industry for hundreds of thousands of previously unemployed women from harsh urban environments; and both have made massive fortunes in the process.

Likewise, Jamie Oliver and Oprah Winfrey. Both are hard-headed business people who maintain absolute control over their vast empires, but both are also soft-hearted evangelists, who spend their days seeking to improve the lives of their millions of fans. And neither hesitates for a moment to attack governments and businesses whose social policies or environmental actions they believe to be wrong.

And what of Ram Karuturi and Sheikh Al-Amoudi? Karuturi describes his goal in Africa as to be "a good stranger", changing the environment around him in a positive way. And, even more poignantly perhaps, Al-Amoudi says: "Ethiopia means so much to me that even my friends wonder about my investment decisions in the country. When I invest in Ethiopia, my decisions to invest are based on what I feel in my heart for my motherland. All my other investment decisions in the rest of the world are based on calculated risks and benefits".

PHILANTHROPY

The challenge of the Millennium Development Goals has inspired thousands of individuals and small organisations around the globe. Many are supported by philanthropic organisations, including *Ashoka: Innovators for the Public* and the foundations established by Jeff Skoll and Klaus and Hilde Schwab, which aim to drive large-scale change by building stronger networks among these individuals and linking them with leaders from the public and private sectors.

All of them are seeking answers to the same questions. How can interventions that have proved successful at a local level be scaled up to meet the needs of billions of people around the world? And even if they can, where will we find the money? Not surprisingly, expert opinions vary.

Small Is Beautiful,

Some, like Bill Drayton, founder and CEO of *Ashoka* and the man commonly credited with coining the term social entrepreneurship, argue that the pathway to scale will require a quasi-infectious process whereby leading social entrepreneurs encourage others to follow in their footsteps, and are themselves in turn encouraged by the followers' recognition of their endeavours. In Drayton's words: "This virtuous cycle catalyzed by leading social entrepreneurs and local changemakers is the chief engine now moving the world toward an 'everyone a changemaker' future".

And some of our überpreneurs offer support for Drayton's view. The success of the organisations founded by Jeroo Billimoria, an Ashoka Fellow, in delivering social, financial and entrepreneurial skills to homeless youth has been due in large measure to her ability to attract influential supporters, build partnerships, delegate to others, and ultimately spin out self-propagating structures under new leaders. In similar vein, the spread of microcredit from Bangladesh into communities around the globe is generally attributed to the evangelical enthusiasm of the prototypical social entrepreneur, and Ashoka Global Academy Member, Muhammad Yunus.

… But Big May Be Better,

Others, like philanthrocapitalist Pierre Omidyar, founder of eBay, say Yunus' approach is too small and too slow to drive microcredit to its full global potential. He argues that the capital required to make a real difference will never be sourced solely from donors: ultimately it will require commercial investors. With that in mind, Omidyar rejected an opportunity to pledge Omidyar Network funds to Yunus' Grameen Foundation. Rather, he and his wife decided to give $100 million to Tufts University to endow the Omidyar-Tufts Microfinance Fund, which subsequently became a major investor in Claus-Peter Zeitinger's much more commercially oriented ProCredit Holding.

… Especially When Leveraged!

A third viewpoint, shared by Chuck Feeney and Bill Gates, is that the massive contributions made by their foundations should be used to leverage equally substantial donations from governments, businesses and other philanthropic organisations. Gates calls his model "catalytic philanthropy", and has attracted tens of billions of dollars from Warren Buffet and other philanthropists. And, on an almost equivalent scale, the billions of dollars donated to medical research by Chuck Feeney's Atlantic Philanthropies have been used to leverage up to three times as much from government and other sources.

And finally, there are those who believe in leverage of another kind: the lure of a prize! As Peter Diamandis, chairman and CEO of the X Prize Foundation puts it: "I think innovation fundamentally comes from the hearts and minds of individuals … and we can focus that by identifying clear, inspirational objectives and providing people with incentives to go and try and solve those problems". And, by way of example, he points to the massive boost in space exploration stimulated, at least in part, by the $10 million Ansari X Prize. No doubt Mo Ibrahim, with his multimillion-dollar Prize for Achievement in African Leadership, is hoping for a similar outcome.

FRIENDS AND FAMILY

It's said that friends, family and fools are the classic, and essential, early-stage investors in most start-up companies, but surprisingly few of our überpreneurs have availed themselves of that opportunity. Apart from Richard Branson, whose mother bailed him out of jail, Jeff Bezos and Martha Tilaar were the only ones to seek significant investments from their families, and they both returned them in spades. And Olivia Lum did the same for the group of friends and colleagues who put up $1.2 million to back a 30-year-old's brave venture into China.

But cash isn't the whole story. Kiran Mazumdar-Shaw describes her husband as the rock upon which she built Biocon, and Niklas Zennström relied on his wife for sustenance as he and Janus Friis plotted the future course of KaZaA and Skype. Soraya Salti and Mechai Viravaidya benefited from parental networks that ranged all the way from social workers and business leaders to royalty. And where would Liu Yonghao have been, traversing the shifting sands of China's post-Mao economy, without the strength and solidarity of his brothers?

Clearly, when it comes to building a business, families and friends make a difference.

But what about earlier in life? What role for mums and dads? Our überpreneurs have three special lessons:

Let Them Take Risks,

Where did Barry Marshall and Craig Venter acquire the grit to back their own judgement in the face of the universal and damning criticism of the medical research establishment, or George Rathmann the bravado to leave the security of the pharmaceutical industry for the uncertainty of biotechnology? Perhaps there was a hint of it in their childhood games.

According to Rathmann: "When you learn about chemistry, the first thing you want to do is practice it. And one of the ways to do that is to get your hands on nitrates and potassium and sodium and things that blow up". Marshall recalls: "We used to buy chemicals and make gunpowder and explosives and fireworks. All kinds of interesting boy-type of projects. I could have grown up to be a Unabomber, I know". And Venter foreshadowed his future military career: "There was a big annual trip up to Chinatown in San Francisco where one could buy all kinds of explosive devices, from fire crackers to cherry bombs. We'd build these elaborate, miniature forts with little plastic army men and blow them up with all these fireworks".

Venter's advice to parents is clear: "I think they should *make* kids play with firecrackers". And Elon Musk takes an even tougher view: "I had a terrible upbringing. I had a lot of adversity growing up. One thing I worry about with my kids is they don't face enough adversity".

... Do Their Own Thing,

Nearly half of our überpreneurs established businesses while they were still at school. Musk, Gates and Zuckerberg all wrote and sold software; Bezos was running science camps, Billimoria mathematics classes. What's more, two-thirds of them really did start their enterprises in garages: Ingvar Kamprad, the founder of IKEA, began his career peddling matches and other small household items from the back of his bicycle.

In short, they did their own thing. As Mark Zuckerberg's father puts it: "If you were going to say no to him, you had better be prepared with a strong argument backed by facts, experiences, logic, reasons".

... With The Benefit Of Impeccable Examples!

How do you prepare a child for the responsibility of wielding power like that possessed by Mark Zuckerberg, whose personal decisions direct the flow of private information between a billion Facebook users around the globe? What social perspective shepherded Pony Ma as he created Weixin, the mobile phone service used by hundreds of millions of young Chinese to chat up, share photographs, and link up with any other user within a 1-km radius?

Who taught them their ethics?

About a quarter of our überpreneurs came from poor backgrounds, and as many again were clearly privileged. A handful, including Richard Branson and Bill Gates, were raised in loving but intensely competitive environments. Others, like Jeroo Billimoria and Soraya Salti, followed in the footsteps of parents who were actively involved in caring for the less well-off members of their communities. And just as Jamie Oliver no doubt learnt many of the skills of his trade in the kitchen of his parents' country pub, Oprah's Book Club may never have happened without her uncle's insistence that she read, and review, a book each week.

Who knows? Perhaps the remarkable dedication of Mitch Besser and Mechai Viravaidya to reversing the AIDS epidemics in Africa and Thailand can ultimately be traced to the formidable example of Besser's dad, who spent his summer vacations relieving public health physicians on Indian reservations in Arizona or Dakota, or the prescient remarks of Mechai's mum: "If people like you, with an education, don't work for the poor, who will"?

BOTTOM LINE

So, are they made or born?

In one sense, all 36 of our überpreneurs are clearly born. Despite the genuinely positive influences of upbringing, education and experience on their lives, there is little evidence to suggest that any or all of these might be the causal factors underpinning their überpreneurial careers.

And in another sense they are made, self-made to be precise: all of them have made themselves from the raw materials and talents with which they were born.

Überpreneurs. Overtakers!

KEY SOURCES

As listed in Chapters 1 - 15, plus:

Despina Archontaki, Gary J. Lewis and Timothy C. Bates, "Genetic influences on psychological well-being: a nationally representative twin study", *Journal of Personality*, February 5, 2013.

William J Baumol, "Entrepreneurship in economic theory", *The American Economic Review*, Vol. 58, No. 2, Papers and Proceedings of the Eightieth Annual Meeting of the American Economic Association, May, 1968.

Michael Ellsberg, "Will dropouts save America?", *The New York Times*, October 22, 2011.

Ernst and Young, "Nature or nurture: decoding the DNA of the entrepreneur", *EYGM Limited*, 2011.

Corina U. Greven, Nicole Harlaar, Yulia Kovas, Tomas Chamorro-Premuzic and Robert Plomin, "More than just IQ", *Psychological Science*, June, 2009.

"Rising above the gathering storm: energizing and employing America for a bright economic future", Committee on Prospering in the Global Economy in the 21st Century, National Academies Press, 2007.

Jennifer Wang, "Nobel laureates and space entrepreneurs talk shop", *Entrepreneur*, April 28, 2009.

World Economic Forum, "Educating the next wave of entrepreneurs", *World Economic Forum Global Education Initiative*, 2009.

Mark Zuckerberg, "Immigration and the knowledge economy", *The Washington Post*, April 10, 2013.

INDEX

Printed and bound by CPI Group (UK) Ltd, Croydon, CR0 4YY